General Knowledge 2024

Manohar Pandey

ARIHANT PUBLICATIONS (INDIA) LTD.

arihant

Arihant Publications (India) Ltd.

Administrative & Production Offices

Regd. Office
'Ramchhaya' 4577/15, Agarwal Road, Darya Ganj, New Delhi -110002
Tele: 011- 47630600, 43518550; Fax: 011- 23280316

Head Office
Kalindi, TP Nagar, Meerut (UP) - 250002
Tel: 0121-7156203, 7156204

Sales & Support Offices
Agra, Ahmedabad, Bengaluru, Bareilly, Chennai, Delhi, Guwahati, Hyderabad, Jaipur, Jhansi, Kolkata, Lucknow, Nagpur & Pune.

ISBN : 978-93-57013-78-9

PO No : TXT-XX-XXXXXXX-X-XX

Published by Arihant Publications (India) Ltd.

For further information about the books published by Arihant
log on to www.arihantbooks.com or email to info@arihantbooks.com

Follow us on

CONTENTS

Current Affairs

NATIONAL

UNION BUDGET 2023-24

Finance Minister Nirmala Sitharaman presented Union Budget 2023-24 on February 1, 2023.

7 Priorities of Budget

1. Inclusive Development
2. Reaching the Last Mile
3. Intrastructure & Investment
4. Unleashing the Potential
5. Financial Sector
6. Green Growth
7. Youth Power

Highlights

- The capital expenditure is almost 3 times of the capital expenditure in FY 2019-20.
- Fiscal Deficit estimated to be 5.9% of GDP in BE 2023-24.
- Tax exemption up to ₹ 7 lakh/year is under new tax regime.
- Agriculture Credit Target to be increased to ₹ 20 lakh crore.
- **PM Vishwa Karma Kaushal Samman** : For the first time package of assistance for traditional artisans and craftspeople has been conceptualised.
- **New sub scheme of PM Matsya Sampada Yojana**, with targeted investment of ₹ 6000 crore, to further enable activities of fishermen, fish vendors and micro and small entrepreneurs, improve value chain efficiencies and expand the market.
- A capital outlay of ₹ 2.40 lakh crore has been provided for the **Railways**.
- This highest ever outlay is about 9 times the outlay made in 2013- 14.
- Finance Minister Nirmala Sitharaman increased allocation to **Defence Budget** to ₹ 593537.64 crore for 2023-24 from last year's allocation of ₹ 5.25 lakh crore.
- For 2022-23, the budgetary allocation for capital outlay was ₹ 1.52 lakh crore but the revised estimate showed the expenditure at ₹ 1.50 lakh crore.
- A separate amount of ₹ 138205 crore has been allocated for **defence pensions**.
- A one-time new small savings scheme, **Mahila Samman Savings Certificate**, will be made available for a two-year period up to March 2025.
- This will offer deposit facility upto ₹ 2 lakh in the name of women or girls for a tenor of 2 years at fixed interest rate of 7.5% with a partial withdrawal option.
- 157 new nursing colleges to be established in colocation with existing 157 medical colleges set-up since 2014.
- **National Digital Library for Children and Adolescents** to be set up for facilitating availability of quality books across languages, geographies and genres.
- For business establishments required to have Permanent Account Number, the PAN will be used as a common identifier for all Digital Systems of specified government agencies.

- **Aspirational Blocks programme** covering 500 blocks has been launched for saturation of government programmes; **PM Primitive Vulnerable Tribal Groups Development Mission** is being launched to improve conditions of vulnerable tribal groups.
- Outlay for **PM Awas Yojana** is being enhanced by 66% to over ₹ 79000 crore.
- 100 labs for developing applications using 5G services to be set-up in engineering institutions, to realise new range of opportunities, business models and employment potential.
- **National Green Hydrogen Mission** with outlay of ₹ 19700 crore will facilitate transition to economy to low carbon intensity, our target is to reach annual production of 5 MMT by 2030.
- **Phase 3 of e-courts project** to be launched with outlay of ₹ 7000 crore, for efficient administration of justice.
- Government to provide higher limit of ₹ 2 lakh per member for cash deposit and loans by **Primary Agricultural Credit Societies**.

Some Notable Achievements

- 11.7 crore household toilets under Swachh Bharat Mission
- 9.6 crore LPG connections under Ujjawala
- 220 crore Covid vaccination of 102 crore persons
- 47.8 crore PM Jan Dhan bank accounts
- Insurance cover for 44.6 crore persons under PM Suraksha Bima and PM Jeevan Jyoti Yojana
- Cash transfer of ₹ 2.2 lakh crore to over 11.4 crore farmers under PM Kisan Samman Nidhi

ECONOMIC SURVEY 2022-23

The Economic Survey 2022-23 was tabled by Finance Minister Nirmala Sitharaman in Parliament on January 31, 2023.

Key Features

- India's GDP growth is expected to remain robust in FY23 at 7% (in real terms).
- The GDP forecast for FY24 to be in the range of 6-6.8%.
- The Gross Tax Revenue registered a Year-on-Year (YoY) growth of 15.5% from April to November 2022.
- Central & State Government's budgeted expenditure on health sector touched 2.2% of GDP in FY22 (RE).
- Social sector expenditure increases to ₹ 21.3 lakh crore in FY23 (BE) from ₹ 9.1 lakh crore in FY16.
- India declared the **Net Zero Pledge** to achieve net zero emissions goal by 2070.
- India achieved its target of **40% installed electric capacity** from non-fossil fuels ahead of 2030.
- **National Green Hydrogen Mission** to enable India to be energy independent by 2047.
- Private investment in agriculture increases to 9.3% in 2020-21.
- **Institutional Credit to the Agricultural Sector** continued to grow to 18.6 lakh crore in 2021-22.
- Overall Gross Value Added (GVA) by the Industrial Sector (for the first half of FY 22-23) rose 3.7%.
- The services sector is expected to grow at 9.1% in FY23, as against 8.4% (YoY) in FY22.
- India's share in world commercial services exports increasing from 3% in 2015 to 4% in 2021.
- India is the **largest recipient of remittances** in the world receiving $ 100 bn in 2022.

74th Republic Day 2023 Celebrated

India celebrated its 74th Republic Day on 26 January, 2023. This year's parade was special with many events taking place for the first time.

It was the first time that the President of the Arab Republic of Egypt, Abdel Fattah el-Sisi, had been invited as the chief guest on the Republic Day.

For the first time, 12 women riders were part of the Border Security Force's (BSF) camel contingent and 16 march contingents of the armed forces. The formations like 'Bheem' and 'Vajrang' showcased over the Kartavya Path for the first time.

During the Beating Retreat Ceremony 2023, 3D anamorphic projection was held for the first time on the facade of North and South Block.

World's First Intranasal COVID19 Vaccine Unveiled

Union Health Minister Dr. Mansukh Mandaviya unveiled world's first intranasal COVID-19 vaccine, iNNCOVACC in New Delhi on January 26, 2023.

It is developed by Bharat Biotech International Limited (BBIL) in collaboration with Biotechnology Industry Research Assistance (BIRAC).

iNCOVACC has been priced at ₹ 325 per dose. Bharat Biotech's intranasal COVID-19 vaccine is a recombinant replicating adenovirus vectored vaccine.

Government Launched U-WIN

After the success of the Co-WIN platform, the government has now replicated it to set-up an electronic registry for routine vaccinations U-WIN on January 25, 2023.

Named U-WIN has been launched in a pilot mode in two districts of each state and Union Territory. It is the programme to digitise India's Universal Immunisation Programme (UIP).

Moidams' Nominated for UNESCO World Heritage Site

PM Narendra Modi has selected the 'Pyramids of Assam' as the country's sole nomination for the UNESCO World Heritage Site out of 52 heritage sites on January 24, 2023.

The Ahom-era 'Moidams' (cemetery of the royal family) in Assam's Charaideo district will be India's only nomination for recognition as a UNESCO World Heritage Site.

21 Andaman Islands Named after Param Vir Chakra Awardees

Prime Minister Narendra Modi on January 23, 2003 named the 21 largest unnamed islands of the Andaman & Nicobar Islands after 21 Param Vir Chakra awardees.

The 21 Param Vir Chakra winners named after these islands are : Major Somnath Sharma, Subedar and Honorary Captain (then Lance Naik) Karam Singh, MM, Second Lieutenant Ram Raghoba Rane, Naik Jadunath Singh, Company Havildar Major Piru Singh, Capt GS Salaria etc.

Brand Guardianship Index 2023 Released

Billionaire Mukesh Ambani ranked No.1 among Indians and second globally on the Brand Guardianship Index 2023, published on January 20, 2023.

He has overtaken the likes of Satya Nadella of Microsoft and Google's Sundar Pichai to be ranked No.1 among Indians and 2nd globally in this Index.

Nvidia CEO Jensen Huang and Reliance Industries Ltd's Mukesh Ambani are ranked first and second respectively in the Index (BGI).

Indian Scientists made First of its Kind Discovery on Mars

The first instance of solo electromagnetic waves has been discovered by Indian researchers on January 16, 2023.

The results were established using information from the Mars Atmosphere and Volatile Evolution (MAVEN) mission of the National Aeronautics and Space Administration.

Using high-resolution electric field data from MAVEN's captured by Langmuir Probe and Waves sensors, scientists have detected the lone waves in the Martian magnetosphere.

112-ft Tall Adiyogi Shiva Statue Unveiled

The 112-ft face of Adiyogi, the source of Yoga, was unveiled at the Sadhguru Sannidhi in Chikkaballapura near Bengaluru on January 15, 2023.

Statue unveiled by Karnataka Chief Minister Basavaraj Bommai in the presence of Sadhguru, founder of Isha Foundation. Adiyogi Divya Darshanam, a unique 14-minute video imaging show mapped on the 112-foot Adiyogi, followed the unveiling.

'Aarogya Maitri' Project Announced

Prime Minister Narendra Modi has announced a new 'Aarogya Maitri' project on January 14, 2023.

Under this project India will provide essential medical supplies to developing countries affected by natural disasters or humanitarian crises.

PM proposed to set-up a 'centre of excellence' to facilitate development solutions to these countries.

PM announced this at the Concluding Session of the two-day virtual 'Voice of Global South Summit'.

World's Longest River Cruise – MV Ganga Vilas Launched

Prime Minister Narendra Modi flagged-off the world's longest river cruise, MV Ganga Vilas, and inaugurated the Tent City in Varanasi *via* video conference on January 13, 2023.

MV Ganga Vilas has three decks with all luxury amenities, 18 suites with a capacity of 36 tourists. MV Ganga Vilas travel about 3200 km in 51 days to reach Dibrugarh in Assam via Bangladesh, crossing 27 river systems in India and Bangladesh.

National Youth Festival-2023 Held

Prime Minister Narendra Modi inaugurated the National Youth Festival-2023 on January 12, 2023 on the Birth Anniversary of Swami Vivekananda.

It was organised in the twin cities of Hubballi – Dharwad in Karnataka from January 12 to 16, 2023. Theme of this year's Youth Festival was 'Vikasit Yuva, Vikasit Bharat'.

Successful Test Launch of Prithvi II

DRDO successfully carried out a training launch of a Short-Range Ballistic Missile, Prithvi-II on January 11, 2023.

It is launched from Integrated Test Range, Chandipur off the Odisha coast.

The user training launch successfully validated all operational and technical parameters of the Prithvi-II missile, which has a range of around 350 km.

Joshimath Declared as 'Landslide-Subsidence Zone'

Joshimath (a city in Chamoli district in Uttarakhand) has been declared a landslide-subsidence zone by respective authorities on January 9, 2023. Joshimath is the gateway to Hemkund Sahib and Badrinath. Big cracks are being seen between people's houses and roads.

17th Pravasi Bharatiya Divas Convention Held

Prime Minister Narendra Modi inaugurated the 17th Pravasi Bharatiya Divas Convention in Indore, Madhya Pradesh on January 8, 2023.

The 17th PBDC organised from January 8-10, 2023 in collaboration with the Government of Madhya Pradesh. The theme of the conference was "Diaspora : Reliable Partners for India's Progress in Amrit Kaal".

India Surpassed Japan to become 3rd Largest Auto Market Globally

India has surpassed Japan on January 8, 2023 in terms of auto sales in 2022 to become the 3rd-largest auto market globally for the first time. India's new vehicle sales were at least 4.25 million units, ahead of the 4.2 million sold in Japan, based on preliminary results.

DRDO Developed Unmanned Vehicle

The Defence Research & Development Organisation (DRDO) has developed an unmanned aerial vehicle on January 7, 2023 with the aim of targeting logistics operations on the Himalayan border.

This aircraft has been displayed by DRDO at the 108th Indian Science Congress held in Nagpur, Maharashtra. This UAV can fly with a load of 5 to 25 kg. and is also capable of dropping bombs in enemy territory.

National Green Hydrogen Mission Approved

The Union Government has approved the National Green Hydrogen Mission, with an initial outlay of ₹ 19744 crore on January 4, 2023. The Mission aims to make India a Global Hub for the production, utilisation, and export of Green Hydrogen.

The targets by 2030 are likely to bring in over ₹ 8 lakh crore investments and create over six lakh jobs.

India took over Leadership of the Asian Pacific Postal Union

India has taken over the leadership of the Asia Pacific Postal Union (APPU) on January 3, 2023.

Dr. Vinaya Prakash Singh will take over the charge of Secretary General of the Union for a tenure of 4 years. This is the result of the elections during the 13th APPU Congress held in August-September 2022.

India's Largest Single Unit of Women Peacekeepers

It is mentioned on January 6, 2023 that India will deploy a platoon of women peacekeepers to UN Mission in Sudan.

This will be India's largest single unit of women Peacekeepers in a UN Mission since it deployed the first-ever all-women contingent in Liberia in 2007.

The deployment in Abyei (Sudan) will also herald India's intent of increasing significantly the number of Indian women in Peacekeeping contingents.

3 More Sites Added to UNESCO's Tentative List

Three more sites in India have made it to the tentative list of UNESCO's world heritage sites on December 21, 2022.

Sun Temple at Modhera, historic Vadnagar town in Gujarat, and rock-cut relief sculptures of Unakoti in Tripura, have been added to the tentative list of UNESCO world heritage sites.

The Sun Temple in Modhera, Gujarat, is dedicated to Surya Dev and is situated on the left bank of the Pushpavati River, a tributary of the River Rupan.

Social Progress Index Released

The SPI for States and Districts of India as mandated by the EAC-PM was released on December 20, 2022. It was released by the Economic Advisory Council to Prime Minister (EAC-PM) along with Institute for Competitiveness and Social Progress Imperative. The top three performing districts are Shimla in Himachal Pradesh, Solan in Himachal Pradesh, and Aizawl in Mizoram.

Millet Food Festival Held

Prime Minister Narendra Modi has called upon the Members of the Parliament to make the International Year of Millets 2023, a mass movement.

Mr. Modi informed this while addressing the BJP parliamentary party meeting in Parliament House Complex on December 20, 2022.

PM Modi along with other attended a lunch in Parliament where millet dishes were served as India prepares to mark 2023 as the International Year of Millets.

New National Food Processing Policy

The Centre has completed the consultation process on the new National Food Processing Policy on December 20, 2022. MoS for Food Processing Industries Prahlad Singh Patel said that the Ministry has approved 41 Mega Food Park, MFP, projects for assistance under Pradhan Mantri Kisan SAMPADA Yojana, PMKSY.

Gaya and Nalanda Selected for Swadesh Darshan 2.0 Scheme

Central government informed on December 19, 2022 that Gaya and Nalanda in Bihar has been included by the Government of India under the Swadesh Darshan 2.0 scheme.

Punaura Dham in Sitamarhi District of Bihar has been selected for development under the PRASHAD Scheme of the Government of India.

INS Mormugao Commissioned by Defence Minister in Mumbai

INS Mormugao commissioned by Union Defence Minister Rajnath Singh on the eve of the Goa Liberation Day 2022 on December 19, 2022.

INS Mormugao is the second ship of the Visakhapatnam-class stealth guided missile destroyers of the Indian Navy.

Named after the port city in Goa, this stealth destroyer is 163 metres long and 17 metres wide, with a displacement of 7.400 tonnes .

India Successfully Tested Nuclear-Capable 'Agni-5' Missile

India successfully carried out the night trials of the Agni-5 nuclear-capable ballistic missile on December 15, 2022. Agni-5 is developed by the DRDO.

Agni 5 missile capable of striking targets at ranges up to 7000 kilometres with a very high degree of accuracy.

Indian Navy Gets 5th Scorpene Class Submarine INS Vagir

The fifth Scorpène submarine, Vagir of Project– 75 Kalvari Class submarines has been delivered to the Indian Navy by Mazagon Dock Shipbuilders Limited (MDL) Mumbai.

INS Vagir can undertake anti-surface, anti-submarine, intelligence gathering, mine laying, area surveillance missions.

Central Bank Digital Currency Launched

The RBI has launched the pilot for a central-bank-backed digital rupee for the wholesale segment.

RBI announced this in a statement on 'Operationalisation of Central Bank Digital Currency-Wholesale (e ₹-W) Pilot'. The 9 banks selected for the pilot are State Bank of India, Bank of Baroda, Union Bank of India, HDFC Bank, ICICI Bank, Kotak Mahindra Bank, Yes Bank, IDFC First Bank and HSBC.

Prime Minister Modi flagged off 6th Vande Bharat train

PM Narendra Modi, inaugurated 6th Vande Bharat Express train on December 11, 2022. This Vande Bharat Express will run on Bilaspur (Chhattisgarh)-Nagpur (Maharashtra) route. Government proposes to run 75 Vande Bharat express trains in the country by 15 August 2023, which will give a big boost for the Country's Transportation Network.

India Assumed G20 Presidency

As India assumed G20 Presidency on December 1, 2022, 100 centrally-protected monuments, including UNESCO world heritage sites spread across the country were lit up bearing the G20 logo.

The monuments that were lit up included Red Fort (Delhi), Royal Palace (Mandu MP), Sanchi Stupa (MP), Kumbhalgarh Fort (Rajasthan), Shankracharya Temple (Srinagar), and Five Rathas (Mahabalipuram, Tamil Nadu).

India Assumed Presidency of the UNSC

India has assumed the Presidency of the UNSC on December 1, 2022 for the month of December 2022. India will be the President of the UNSC for one month as the 2 year term of India as a non-permanent member of the UNSC ends on December 31, 2022.

India's First Private Space Vehicle Inaugurated

Agnikul Cosmos launched India's first private launchpad and mission control centre at the Satish Dhawan Space Centre (SDSC) in Sriharikota on November 28, 2022.

Agnikul Cosmos is Chennai-based space tech startup company. The facility was inaugurated by ISRO Chairman S. Somanath.

Yak Approved as 'Food Animal'

The Food Safety and Standard Authority of India (FSSAI) has approved the Himalayan Yak as a 'Food Animal' on November 26, 2022. The move is expected to help check decline in the population of the high-altitude bovine animal by making it a part of the conventional milk and meat industry.

Indo-Pacific Regional Dialogue 2022 Held

The Indo-Pacific Regional Dialogue 2022 (IPRD-2022) the annual apex-level regional strategic dialogue of the Indian Navy in New Delhi from 23 November, 2022 to 25 November, 2022.

India took over Chair of Global Partnership on AI

India has taken over the chair of Global Partnership on Artificial Intelligence (GPAI) from France on November 21, 2022. The Minister of State for Electronics and Information Technology Rajeev Chandrasekhar will represent the country at the GPAI meeting in Tokyo.

India Ranked 61st on Network Readiness

India has been ranked 61st in the Network Readiness Index 2022 released on November 19, 2022. The index was prepared by a US-based Portulans

Institute, an independent non-profit research and educational institute. India's overall score improved from 49.74 in 2021 to 51.19 in 2022.

Kashi Tamil Sangamam Held

The PM Narendra Modi inaugurated 'Kashi Tamil Sangamam' – a month-long programme organised in Varanasi (UP) on November 19, 2022.

The objective of the programme is to celebrate, reaffirm and rediscover the age-old links between Tamil Nadu and Kashi– two of the country's most important and ancient seats of learning.

Power System Operation Corporation Limited Renamed

India's national grid operator 'Power System Operation Corporation Ltd. (POSOCO)' has announced that it has changed its name to 'Grid Controller of India Ltd.' on November 18, 2022.

The name has been changed to reflect the critical role of grid operators in ensuring integrity, reliability, economy, resilience and sustainable operation of the Indian electricity grid.

4th Phase of Digital Shakti Campaign Launched

The National Commission for Women launched the 4th phase Digital Shakti 4.0 on November 16, 2022. It is a pan-India project on digitally empowering and skilling women and girls in cyberspace.

India's First Private Rocket 'Vikram-S' Launched

India's first privately developed rocket Vikram-S launched on November 15, 2022 from the ISRO at the Sriharikota launchpad. The launch of Vikram-S Rocket by ISRO is a historic moment. The launch of India's first privately developed rocket was a technology demonstration flight to showcase the capabilities of the company. The rocket will help validate the technologies that will be used in the subsequent Vikram-1 orbital vehicle of Skyroot.

President Attended Janjatiya Gaurav Diwas Programme

President Droupadi Murmu attended the state-level program of Madhya Pradesh on the occasion of Janjatiya Gaurav Diwas on November 15, 2022 at Shehdol. This day is celebrated nationwide to mark the birth anniversary of Adivasi icon Birsa Munda.

SC Announced Forced Conversion as a Very Serious Issue

The Supreme Court on November 15, 2022 described forced conversion as a very serious issue that affects the security of the nation. The observation was made by a bench of Justices MR Shah and Hima Kohli.

The SC has directed the center to take a stand on the matter and file a response in a week about steps being taken to prevent it.

2022 Declared as ASEAN-India Friendship Year

The year 2022 has been declared as the ASEAN-India Friendship year, as ASEAN and India commemorate 30 years of partnership on November 11, 2022. A series of events has been planned to celebrate the occasion throughout the year.

19th ASEAN-India Summit Held in Cambodia

The Vice-President of India led the Indian delegation at the 19th ASEAN-India Summit in Phnom Penh, Cambodia on November 12, 2022. The Vice-President hailed the deep cultural, economic and civilisational ties that have existed between India and South-East Asia from time immemorial.

India and ASEAN adopted a joint statement announcing the evaluation of the existing Strategic Partnership to Comprehensive Strategic Partnership.

Logo, Theme and Website of India's G20 Presidency Unveiled

Prime Minister Narendra Modi unveiled logo, theme and website of India's G20 presidency on November 8, 2022.

The logo and theme of G20 reflects India's message and overarching priorities to the world. The G20 logo is created with four colours of India's national flag and represents sitting atop lotus.

SC Upholds 10% Quota for EWS

The Supreme Court (SC) upheld the 10% reservation on November 7, 2022 for the Economically Weaker Section (EWS) among forward castes in government jobs and colleges. A Bench comprising CJI UU Lalit and Justices Dinesh Maheshwari, S. Ravindra Bhat, Bela M. Trivedi, and JB Pardiwala delivered the judgment.

UDISE+ Report Released

The number of children entering pre-primary classes in 2021-22 has declined by 30% as per UDISE+ report released on November 3, 2022.

A total of 94.95 lakh students entered preprimary school in 2021-22, registering a drop of 10%, as compared to 1.06 crore in the previous years. Enrolment in primary school, classes 1 to 5, saw a drop from 12.20 lakh in 2020-21 to 12.18 lakh in 2021-22.

Centre to Grant Citizenship to Minorities of Gujarat

The Union government has decided on November 1, 2022 to grant Indian citizenship to Minorities from Afghanistan, Bangladesh and Pakistan.

Centre to grant citizenship to Hindus, Sikhs, Buddhists, Jains, Parsis and Christians and currently living in two districts of Gujarat.

PM Attended 'Mangarh Dham ki Gaurav Gatha'

The PM Narendra Modi attended a public programme 'Mangarh Dham ki Gaurav Gatha' on November 1, 2022.

He paid homage to the sacrifices of unsung tribal heroes and martyrs of the freedom struggle. As part of Azadi ka Amrit Mahotsav, the government has initiated several steps to celebrate unsung tribal heroes of the freedom struggle.

INTERNATIONAL

International Day of Education 2023 Dedicated to Afghan Girls

The UNESCO has decided to dedicate the International Day of Education to be celebrated on January 24, 2023, to Afghan girls and women.

Currently around 80% of Afghan girls and young women of school-age are out of school under Taliban rule, as they are denied access to secondary schools and universities.

World Economic Forum Meet 2023

The annual meeting of World Economic Forum (WEF) 2023 held in Davos, Switzerland, from January 16 to 20, 2023. The theme for this year's meeting was 'Cooperation in a Fragmented World'.

The goal of the WEF was to promote innovative solutions and encourage cooperation between governments and the business sectors.

Chris Hipkins Sworn-in as New Zealand Prime Minister

Labour leader Chris Hipkins was sworn-in as New Zealand's Prime Minister in a formal ceremony on January 20, 2023.

Hipkins was Minister for police, education and public service, as well as leader of the House. Chris replaced Jacinda Ardern.

UNICEF Report on Child Mortality Rate

'Levels and Trends in Child Mortality' report was published by United Nations (UN) on January 14, 2023.

Another global reports on stillbirths (Never Forgotten) was also released by UN Inter-agency Group for Child Mortality Estimation (UN IGME).

As per the report released, an estimated 5 million children died before their 5th birthday and another 2.1 million children and youth aged between 5-24 years lost their lives in 2021.

UN Report on Ozone Hole

According to a UN-backed report created by an international body of experts on January 9, 2023, the Earth's ozone layer is on track to completely recover within 4 decades.

Ozone is a special form of oxygen with the chemical formula O_3. The oxygen we breathe and that is so vital to life on earth is O_2. Ozone layer depletion leads to an uptick in the incidence of skin cancer and cataracts in humans.

Pushpa Kamal Dahal 'Prachanda' Appointed as the PM of Nepal

President Bidya Devi Bhandari of Nepal has appointed Pushpa Kamal Dahal 'Prachanda' as the new prime minister of Nepal on December 25, 2022. Prachand will become the prime minister for the third time. In the recently held parliamentary election no party got any clear majority.

Sitiveni Rabuka became the PM of Fiji

Sitiveni Rabuka became Fiji's Prime Minister on December 24, 2022 after a coalition of parties voted narrowly to install him as leader of the country.

It also signals the end of the former Prime Minister Frank Bainimarama's 16 years in power. In the 55 member Parliament of Fiji, Sitiveni Rabuka secured 28 votes against Bainimarama's 27 votes.

Taliban Banned University Education for Afghan Girls

The Taliban government has passed an order to suspend university education for all female students in Afghanistan on December 20, 2022.

The education ministry under Taliban Regime said that the decision was made in a cabinet meeting and the order will go into effect immediately.

Resolution on 'Education for Democracy' Adopted

The United Nations General Assembly (UNGA) adopted a resolution titled 'Education for Democracy' that reaffirms the right of everyone to education on January 18, 2023.

The resolution, which was co-sponsored by India, recognises that 'education for all' contributes to the strengthening of democracy. The resolution encourages member states to integrate education for democracy into their education standards.

Leo Varadkar Elected as the PM of Ireland

Indian origin Leo Varadkar was elected as the Prime Minister of the Republic of

Ireland for the second time on December 17, 2022. He took over from Michael Martin under an arrangement struck between their two parties under a 2020 coalition pact. Leo Varadkar was earlier Prime Minister of Ireland from 2017 to 2020.

US President Joe Biden Signed Gay Marriage Legislation

United States (US) President Joe Biden signed gay marriage law on December 14, 2022. On the occasion, the President said that "the law that protects love strikes a chord against hate in all its forms".

This law establishes statutory authority for same-sex and interracial marriages. The House of Representatives passed the law on December 8 by a vote of 258-169-1.

US Prints First Banknotes with Women's Signatures

The US the Treasury (United States of America's Finance Ministry) has printed the first US banknotes (currency notes) with two women's signatures on December 11, 2022.

The new currency notes of $1 and $5 value carry the signature of the Secretary of Treasury (American Finance Minister) Janet Yellen and Lynn Malerba.

Indonesia's Parliament Passed Law Criminalising Adultery

Indonesia's parliament passed a long-awaited and controversial revision of its penal code on December 6, 2022 that criminalises extramaritial affairs.

The new criminal code must be signed by the President, according to Deputy Minister of Law and Human Rights Edward Hiariej. Indonesia's amended criminal code includes articls that make sex outside marriage punishible by a year in jail and cohabitation by 6 months.

'Goblin Mode' is the Word of the Year 2022 of Oxford Dictionary

Oxford dictionary chosen 'Goblin Mode' as word of the year 2022 on December 6, 2022. It is a "slang term" means "a type of behaviour which is unapologetically self-indulgent, lazy, slovenly, or greedy, typically in a way that rejects social norms or expectations".

Forbes the World's 100 Most Powerful Women

The 2022 list of the **World's 100 Most Powerful Women** was released on December 6, 2022. European Commission President Ursula von der Leyen is ranked at the top, while Iran's Mahsa Amini is ranked at 100.

Ranked at number 36, Nirmala Sitharaman has made it to the list for the fourth time in a row.

The other Indians to feature on the list are

- HCL Tech Chairperson Roshni Nadar Malhotra (rank : 53),
- SEBI Chairperson Madhabi Puri Buch (rank: 54) and
- Steel Authority of India Chairperson Soma Mondal (rank : 67).

'Gaslighting' is Merriam-Webster Word of the Year 2022

- When British playwright Patrick Hamilton wrote Gas Light in 1938, little did he know how often the word would be used in the 21st Century. Merriam-Webster, America's oldest dictionary publisher, has just chosen 'gaslighting' as its Word of the Year.

EIU's Worldwide Cost of Living 2022

London-based Economist Intelligence Unit (EIU) released the Worldwide Cost of Living 2022 report on Dec. 6, 2022.

The report compares the prices of more than 200 goods and services in 172 countries. Moscow and St. Petersburg witnessed a drastic increase in the rank. Moscow has been ranked 37th in 2022 as compared to 72nd in 2021.

Voting Age of 18 Changed in New Zealand

New Zealand's Supreme Court ruled that the country's current voting age of 18 is discriminatory on November 30, 2022. New Zealand's minimum voting age of 18 was inconsistent with the country's Bill of Rights, mentioned the court.

Great Barrier Reef to be Listed as a World Heritage Site

UN panel has recommended on November 28, 2022 that Australia's Great Barrier Reef should be listed as a World Heritage site that is in danger.

The UN also informed that the world's biggest coral reef ecosystem was significantly impacted by climate change and the warming of oceans.

Powerful Earthquake on Java Killed at Least 162

A powerful earthquake struck Indonesia's main island of Java on November 21, 2022. 162 people lost their lives and hundreds more were injured when a building collapsed in the capital Jakarta.

The earthquake of magnitude 5.6 struck Cianjur town in West Java, at a shallow depth of 10 km according to the US Geological Survey data.

World's Most Popular Leaders

PM Narendra Modi remains the world's most popular leader with an approval rating of 77% on November 25, 2022. This was revealed in a Global Leader Approval Ratings released by a US-based consulting firm Morning Consult. The Indian PM is followed by Mexican President Andrés Manuel López Obrador at 69% and Australian PM Anthony Albanese at 56%, on the second and third spots, respectively.

Russian Parliament Passed Law Banning 'LGBT Propaganda'

The Russian Parliament approved a Bill to prohibit 'LGBT Propaganda' on November 24, 2022.

The Bill widens a prohibition of 'LGBT Propaganda' and restricts the 'demonstration' of LGBT behaviour, making any expression of an LGBT lifestyle almost impossible.

Anwar Ibrahim Sworn-in as the Prime Minister of Malaysia

Malaysia's opposition leader Anwar Ibrahim was sworn-in as the country's tenth Prime Minister on November 24, 2022. The new leader was appointed by King Al-Sultan Abdullah.

With this, the political uncertainty that continued for several days after the general elections with a fractured mandate in Malaysia has come to an end.

New York Became First US State to Restrict Cryptocurrency Mining

New York is the first nation to sign legislation to resist the spread of cryptocurrency mining on November 23, 2022. This new development happened in the light of the collapse of the FTX exchange. The legislation which was passed in June is concerned more with the environmental aspect of crypto.

Australian Parliament Approved Free Trade Agreement with India

The Australian Parliament approved a free trade agreement with India on

November 22, 2022. The India-Australia Economic Cooperation and Trade Agreement (AI-ECTA) had to be ratified by the Australian Parliament. The agreement was signed between the two countries in April this year.

Cambridge Dictionary Revealed Word of the Year 2022

The Cambridge Dictionary has revealed Homer as the word of the year 2022 on November 18, 2022. It was inspired by the global word game sensation, Wordle. The word was searched for about 75000 times in the first week of May 2022.

COP27 Summit 2022 Held

The United Nations Climate Change Conference 2022 or Conference of the Parties of the UNFCCC, more commonly referred to as COP27 was held from November November 6-18, 2022 in Sharm El Sheikh (Egypt). COP 27 took place under the Presidency of Egyptian Minister of Foreign Affairs Sameh Shoukry. It was the first climate summit held in Africa since 2016.

UNFCCC COP 27 Climate Summit 2022 was attended by 197 countries, 45000 people and 120 world leaders.

First Global Media Congress Held

The three day first World Media Congress opened on November 15, 2022 at Abu Dhabi (United Arab Emirates). The conference-cum- exhibition Congress is organised by ADNEC Group in partnership with Emirates News Agency (WAM). The theme of the World Media Congress was Shaping the Future of the Media Industry.

Climate Change Performance Index 2023 Released

The Climate change performance Index 2023 was published by the New Climate Institute and the Climate Action Network on November 15, 2022.

It was published in 2005 and aims to promote transparency in international climate politics. The CCPI considers 4 categories : GHG Emissions, Renewable Energy, Energy Use and Climate Policy.

Bali G20 Summit 2022

The 2022 G20 summit was held on November 15 and 16, 2022 in Bali (Indonesia). It was the 17th meeting of G20 Summit.

The theme of G20 Summit 2022 was Recover Together, Recover Stronger. Prime Minister Narendra Modi along with other G20 Leaders visited and planted Mangroves at the 'Taman Hutan Raya Ngurah Rai' Mangrove forests on the sidelines of G20 Summit in Bali.

World's Population Reached 8 Billion

According to World Population Prospects 2022, released on World Population Day, the global population is projected to reach 8 billion on November 15, 2022.

The UN's latest projections suggest that by 2030, the global population could grow by half a billion to reach 8.5 billion. According to UNFPA projections, India will continue to have one of the youngest populations in the world till 2030.

Natasa Pirc Musar Elected Slovenia's First Female President

Natasa Pirc Musar, won the second round of Slovenia's Presidential elections on November 14, 2022. Natasa Pirc Musar becomes the first female President of the country.

She won 58.86% of votes in the runoff, while the opposition right-wing politician and the former Foreign Minister Andze Logar won 46.14% of votes.

UNESCO World Heritage Glaciers Set to Disappear by 2050

The UNESCO on November 10, 2020 said that World Heritage Glaciers would disappear by 2050. Yellowstone and Kilimanjaro National Park will likely vanish by 2050. The warning followed a study of 18000 glaciers at 50 World Heritage Sites.

'November 18' Designated as World Day for Prevention of Child Sexual Abuse

The United Nations General Assembly (UNGA) has adopted a resolution for child sexual exploitation, abuse and violence on November 8, 2022.

The UNGA has declared November 18 as the World Day for the Prevention of and Healing from Child Sexual Exploitation, Abuse, and Violence.

UNEP Adaptation Gap Report 2022 Released

The report titled "The Adaptation Gap Report 2022 : Too Little, Too Slow – Climate Adaptation Failure puts World at Risk" was released by the UNEP on November 2, 2022. The Adaptation Gap Report (AGR) has been published each year since 2014 by the UNEP.

'Permacrisis' is Collins Dictionary's Word of the Year 2022

Collins Dictionary has announced Permacrisis as the Word of the Year on November 2, 2022. Permacrisis is a word describing the feeling of living through a period of war, inflation, and political instability. It was first noted as a word in academic contexts in the 1970s.

SPORTS AND GAMES

ATHLETICS

Mumbai Marathon 2023

Over 55000 people participated in the iconic Tata Mumbai Marathon 2023, held on January 15, 2023.

India's international runner Thonakal Gopi as he finished first in the Indian category of the Tata Mumbai Marathon.

Ethiopia's Hayle Lemi (Time – 2:07:32) and Anchalem Haymanot (2:24:15) won the elite foreign men's and women's race in a course record.

BADMINTON

India Open 2023

Shuttler Kunlavut Vitidsarn from Thailand won the India Open Badminton Championship 2023 on January 22, 2023.

Earlier, Korean sensation An Seyoung won the Women's Singles final.

The Championship, officially named 'Yonex-Sunrise India Open 2023' was held at KD Jadhav Indoor Stadium in New Delhi, India from January 17 to 22, 2023.

Hylo Open 2022

The Hylo Open 2022 was a badminton tournament held at the Saarlandhalle in Saarbrücken (Germany) from November 1 to 6, 2022.

Winners List

Category	Winner
Men's Singles	Anthony Sinisuka Ginting (Indonesia)
Women's Singles	Han Yue (China)

34th National U-13 Tournament 2022

Telangana's Nishanth Bhukya and Odisha's Tanvi Patri won in the boys and girls singles, respectively at the 34th Under-13 National Badminton titles on November 23,

2022. Bhukya came from behind to beat Andhra Pradesh's Akhil Reddy Boba in 44 minutes.

CRICKET

ICC Under-19 Women's T20 World Cup 2023

South Africa hosted the ICC Under-19 Women's T20 World Cup 2023 from January 14-29, 2023. This was the inaugural edition of this competition. India won the title after defeating England in the final.

England's Grace Scrivens named as 'Player of the Series'. India's Shweta Sehrawat scored most runs (297), while Australian Maggie Clark took most wickets (12) during the competition.

India-New Zealand ODI Series 2023

India climbed to the top of the ICC Men's ODI rankings after winning the series 3-0 against New Zealand at the Holkar Stadium in Indore on January 25, 2023.

Shardul Thakur was awarded the Player of the Match in the third ODI. Shubman Gill won the Player of the Series award.

India-Sri Lanka ODI Series 2023

India scripted history by defeating Sri Lanka by the largest ever margin of 317 runs in the third and final ODI in Thiruvananthpuram (Kerala) on January 15, 2023. With this, India also clean sweeped the series by 3-0. Player of the series won by Virat Kohli (India).

India-Sri Lanka T20 Series 2023

India defeated Sri Lanka by 91 runs In the third and final T20 International cricket in Rajkot on January 8, 2023.

With this victory, India clinched the three-match series 2-1.

Suryakumar Yadav was declared Man of the Match and Axar Patel Player of the Series.

India -Bangladesh Series 2022

The Indian cricket team led by K L Rahul won the cricket test series against the Shakib Al Hassan led Bangladesh team 2-0 to win the 2 match test series in Bangladesh on December 25,2022.

Man of the match of second match was Ravichandran Ashwin. Man of the Series award won by Cheteshwar Pujara.

India lost the ODI series against Bangladesh by 2-1.

Ishan Kishan made a world record by scoring fastest double century in ODI. He made his double century against Bangladesh in just 126 balls.

Blind T20 Cricket World Cup 2022

India defeated Bangladesh by 120 runs in the final to win the 3rd T20 World Cup for Blind on December 17, 2022. Final played at the M. Chinnaswamy Stadium in Bengaluru, Karnataka.

It was the third title for India having won it in 2012and 2017. All the three T20 World Cup for Blind has been hosted by India. Batting first India made 277 runs for the loss of 2 wickets in 20 allotted overs.

Vijay Hazare Trophy 2022-23

Saurashtra beat Maharashtra by 5 wickets in the final to win the Vijay Hazare Trophy at the Narendra Modi Stadium in Ahmedabad on December 2, 2022. Batting first, Maharashtra scored 248 runs for the loss of 9 wickets in 50 overs.

India-NZ ODI Series 2022

The final One Day international match of the series was held on November 30, 2022. It was held at the Hagley Oval in Christchurch. New Zealand won the opening ODI at Eden Park, in Auckland by seven wickets.

ICC Men's T20 World Cup 2022

The England men's cricket team won its second ICC T20 men's cricket world cup by defeating Pakistan in the finals, at the Melbourne cricket stadium (Australia) on November 13, 2022.

It was the 8th edition of the tournament and in the first round, Sri Lanka played against Namibia. Originally, it was to be held in 2020 but was postponed to 2022 due to covid.

Syed Mushtaq Ali Trophy 2022-23

Mumbai won the Syed Mushtaq Ali Trophy 2022-23 on November 5, 2022 after defeating Himachal Pradesh by 3 runs in the final played at Eden Gardens (Kolkata). It was the 15th edition of domestic T20 Cricket tournament in India, which was played from October 11 to November 5, 2022.

HOCKEY

FIH Hockey Men's World Cup 2023

The FIH Hockey Men's World Cup 2023 was held in Bhubaneswar and Rourkela cities of Odisha from January 13-29, 2023. Germany won the title by defeating Belgium 5-4 in penalty shoot out in the final.

This is Germany's third men's hockey world cup title. Earlier, Germany won this title in the year 2002 and 2006. India finished ninth in this competition. Major award winners are as follows :

- *Top Scorer* Jeremy Hayward (Australia)
- *Best Player* Niklas Wellen (Germany)
- *Best Young Player* Mustapha Cassiem (South Africa)
- *Best Goalkeeper* Vincent Vanasch (Belgium)
- *Fair Play Award* Belgium

Women's FIH Nations Cup 2022

The Indian women Hockey team led by Captain Savita Punia beat Spain 1-0 in the final to win the inaugural FIH Nations Cup played at Valencia (Spain) on December 17, 2022.

The winning goal was scored by Gurjit Kaur of India. The inaugural FIH Nations cup was held in Valencia (Spain) from 11-17 December 2022.

TENNIS

Australian Open 2023

The first tennis Grand Slam tournament of the year 'Australian Open 2023' was held in Melbourne (Australia) from January 16-29, 2023. The winners and runner-ups in the major categories are as follows

Category	Winner	Runner-up
Men's Singles	Novak Djokovic (Serbia)	Stefanos Tsitsipas (Greece)
Women's Singles	Aryna Sabalenka (Belarus)	Elena Rybakina (Kazakhstan)

Tata Open Maharashtra 2023

Tata Open Maharashtra 2023 was a professional men's tennis tournament played in Pune from January 2 to 7, 2023.

Winners List

Category	Winner	Runner-up
Men's Singles	Tallon Griekspoor (Netherlands)	Benjamin Bonzi (France)
Men's Doubles	Sander Gillé / Joran Vliegen (Belgium)	Sriram Balaji / Jeevan Nedunchezhiyan (India)

Adelaide International-1 2023

Adelaide International-1 2023 was held at the Memorial Drive Tennis Centre from January 1 to 8, 2023. Ace Tennis player Novak Djokovic defeated America's

Sebastian Korda in the final to win the Adelaide International men's singles title. The 21-time Grand Slam winner also equalled Rafael Nadal's tally of 92 ATP singles titles in the Open Era.

Davis Cup 2022

Canada won their first Davis Cup title after Felix Auger-Aliassime beat Australia's Alex de Minaur by 6-3, 6-4 in the second match of the finals on November 28, 2022. Felix Auger-Aliassime had to guard against three break points in the first set but also found his rhythm in the eighth game.

ATP Finals 2022

Novak Djokovic defeated Norway's Casper Ruud to collect 6th ATP Finals title in Turin (Italy) on November 20, 2022. This victory brings Djokovic at par with Federer's record. This was Djokovic's first title at the event since 2015 and the one that matches Roger Federer's record.

Billie Jean King Cup 2022

Switzerland won their first Billie Jean King Cup title on November 13, 2022 after Belinda Bencic saw off Australia's Ajla Tomljanovic in the second match of the finals with a lead of 2-0.

Seven-time winners Australia had beaten hosts Britain in the semi-final and were seeking their first title since 1974.

Next Gen ATP Finals 2022

American Brandon Nakashima won the Next Gen ATP Finals tennis trophy in Milan on November 13, 2022. He was ranked 49 while his opponent Lehecka was ranked 74th in the tournament which featured 8 best players aged 21-years and under.

Paris Masters 2022

19-year-old Holger Rune won his maiden Masters 1000 title when he beat Novak Djokovic in the final on Nov. 7, 2022. Rune defeated Novak Djokovic in 3 sets in the Paris Masters final.

ITF Men's Tournament 2022

Digvijay Pratap Singh earns the maiden title in the $ 15000 ITF men's tennis tournament at the DLTA Complex on November 6, 2022.

Digvijay Pratap Singh won his first ITF Title at the RK Khanna Tennis Stadium, New Delhi on November 6, 2022.

SHOOTING

Asian Airgun Championship 2022

The 15th Asian Airgun Championship 2022 concluded at Daegu International Shooting Range, Daegu (Republic of Korea) on November 19, 2022.

The Asian Airgun Championship was held from November 9 to 19, 2022.

FOOTBALL

Spanish Super Cup

Barcelona beat Real Madrid 3-1 in Riyadh to win their 14th Spanish Super Cup title on January 15, 2023.

Gavi (33rd minute), Robert Lewandowski (45th minute) and Padry (69th minute) scored for Barcelona in the final match played at the King Fahd Stadium in Riyadh, Saudi Arabia.

FIFA World Cup 2022

Lionel Messi's Argentina won the Golden Ball FIFA World Cup 2022 for his outstanding performance on December 18, 2022.

Argentina won the final, defeating defending champions France 4–2 on penalties following a 3–3 draw after extra time. French player Kylian Mbappé won the Golden Boot as he scored the most goals (eight) during the tournament.

He became the first player to score a hat-trick in a World Cup final since Geoff Hurst in the 1966 final.

Argentine captain Lionel Messi was voted the tournament's best player, winning the Golden Ball. Emiliano Martínez, also from Argentina, won the Golden Glove, awarded to the tournament's best goalkeeper. FIFA World 2022 took place in Qatar from November 20 to December 18, 2022.

KABADDI

9th Pro Kabaddi League

Jaipur Pink Panthers won the Pro Kabaddi League Season 9 Final against a hard-fighting Puneri Paltan by a score of 33-29 to win their second PKL championship on December 17, 2022.

After Patna, Jaipur Pink Panthers, the league's first-ever winners, are currently only the second team to win multiple titles. The tournament was played across Bengaluru, Pune, and Hyderabad while the playoffs were played in Mumbai.

AWARDS & HONOURS

NATIONAL

Padma Awards 2023

The Centre has announced the Padma Awards on the eve of Republic Day January 25, 2023. Of the total 106 Padma Awards announced, 6 are Padma Vibhushan, 9 are Padma Bhushan and 91 are Padma Shri.

The list of awardees includes 19 women and 2 persons from the category of Foreigners/NRI/PIO/OC and 7 posthumous awardees.

Gallantry Awards

President Droupadi Murmu approved 412 Gallantry awards, including 6 Kirti Chakras and 15 Shaurya Chakras for Armed Forces personnel and others on January 25, 2023.

These include 6 Kirti Chakras, including 4 posthumous, and 15 Shaurya Chakras including 2 posthumous.

ICC Awards 2022

The International Cricket Council (ICC) announced the winners of ICC Awards 2022 on January 25-26, 2023.

Major award winners are listed below

Award/Category	Winner
Sir Garfield Sobers Trophy	Babar Azam (Pakistan)
Rachael Heyhoe Flint Trophy	Nat Sciver (England)
Men's Test Cricketer of the Year	Ben Stokes (England)
Men's ODI Cricketer of the Year	Babar Azam (Pakistan)
Women's ODI Cricketer of the Year	Nat Sciver (England)
Men's T20 International Cricketer of the Year	Suryakumar Yadav (India)
Women's T20 International Cricketer of the Year	Tahlia McGrath (Australia)
Men's Emerging Cricketer of the Year	Marco Jansen (South Africa)
Women's Emerging Cricketer of the Year	Renuka Singh (India)

Pradhan Mantri Rashtriya Bal Puraskar

President Droupadi Murmu has conferred upon Pradhan Mantri Rashtriya Bal Puraskar at a ceremony in New Delhi.

This year, 11 children have been selected for the Pradhan Mantri Rashtriya Bal Puraskar from which,

- 4 are from Art and Culture field
- 1 for Bravery
- 2 for Innovation
- 1 for Social Service
- 3 for Sports

Subhash Chandra Bose Aapda Prabandhan Puraskar-2023

Odisha State Disaster Management Authority and Lunglei Fire Station, Mizoram, selected in the Institutional Category for Subhash Chandra Bose Aapda Prabandhan Puraskar-2023.

The award is announced every year on January 23, the birth anniversary of Netaji Subhash Chandra Bose.

Miss Universe 2022

The 71st Miss Universe pageant was held in the city of New Orleans in the US state of Louisiana on January 15, 2023.

America's R'Bonnie Gabriel won the Miss Universe 2022 title at the 71st Miss Universe pageant.

Amanda Dudamel of Venezuela was declared the first runner up while Anderina Martinez of Dominican Republic became the second runner-up.

UN Medal

Indian peacekeepers serving in the United Nations Mission in South Sudan (UNMISS) were awarded the prestigious UN Medal on January 12, 2023.

At a special award ceremony in Upper Nile, 1171 peacekeepers from India deployed with the UNMISS were awarded the UN Medal for their exemplary service.

Golden Globe Awards 2023

The Golden Globe Awards 2023 ceremony was held on January 10, 2023 to recognise excellence in film, both American and international, and American television. This was the 80th edition of the annual event by the Hollywood Foreign Press Association.

One of the films in contention at the Golden Globe awards was Telugu title RRR, directed by SS Rajamouli. The film ultimately won the award for Best Original Song for 'Naatu Naatu' out of the two categories it was nominated for. 'Naatu Naatu' became the first Asian song to win the coveted award.

Sahitya Akademi Awards 2022

The central government has announced the Sahitya Akademi Award for literature on December 22, 2022.

Writer M. Rajendran from Tamil Nadu has received this award for his novel 'Kala Pani'.

The awardee will be presented with a cash prize of ₹ 1 one lakh and a copper Shield. This 'Kala Pani' novel is a historical novel based on the war of Kalayarkovil or Kalayarkool.

A total of 17 books were selected for the Sahitya Akademi Prize for Translation 2022.

National Award for Empowerment of Persons with Disabilities 2021-22

President Droupadi Murmu was Chief Guest at a ceremony to celebrate the 'International Day of Persons with Disabilities' in Delhi on December 3, 2022. The event organised by the Ministry of Social Justice and Empowerment.

National Sports Awards 2022

President Droupadi Murmu given away the National Sports Awards on November 30, 2022.

List of Winners

Major Dhyan Chand Khel Ratna Award 2022 Achanta Sharath Kamal (Table Tennis)

Dhyan Chand Award for Lifetime Achievement in Sports and Games 2022 Ashwini Akkunji C. (Athletics), Dharamvir Singh (Hockey), BC Suresh (Kabaddi), Nir Bahadur Gurung (Para Athletics)

Rashtriya Khel Protsahan Puruskar 2022 TransStadia Enterprises Private Limited, Kalinga Institute of Industrial Technology, Ladakh Ski & Snowboard Association

Maulana Abul Kalam Azad (MAKA) Trophy 2022 Guru Nanak Dev University, Amritsar

'Para Sportsperson of Year' Award

Paralympic medallist Avani Lekhara received the 'Para Sports Person of Year' award at the Turf 2022 and India Sports Awards of FICCI on November 28, 2022. Former Ranji cricketer Sarkar Talwar was honoured with the Lifetime Achievement of the Year award.

53rd IFFI Award

The 53rd IFFI, held in Panaji (Goa) from November 20 to 28, 2022, was organised by National Film Development Corporation and Entertainment Society of Goa.

Award Winners

Award	Winner
Satyajit Ray Lifetime Achievement Award	Carlos Saura (Spain)
IFFI Indian Film Personality of the Year	Chiranjeevi
Golden Peacock for the Best Film	Tengo sueños eléctricos/ I Have Electric Dreams
Silver Peacock for Best Director	Nader Saeivar
Silver Peacock for Best Actor (Male)	Vahid Mobasseri
Silver Peacock for Best Actor (Female)	Daniela Marín Navarro (I Have Electric Dreams)
Special Jury Award	Lav Diaz (Philippines)
Best Debut Feature Film of a Director	Asimina Proedrou (Greece)
Special Mention by Jury Award	Praveen Kandregula

Gandhi Mandela Award

The 14th Dalai Lama was presented with the Gandhi Mandela Award 2022 on November 19, 2022. The award was conferred at Thekchen Choeling in Dharamshala's McleodGanj by Himachal Pradesh governor Rajendra Vishwanath Arlekar.

31st & 32nd Bihari Puraskar

Writer Madhu Kankariya and Madhav Hada were awarded the Bihari Puraskar on November 10, 2022. Madhu Kankariya and Dr. Madhav Hada were awarded the 31st and 32nd Bihari Puraskar, respectively.

INTERNATIONAL

Mrs World 2022

Sargam Kaushal has won the title of Mrs. World 2022 on December 18, 2022, becoming the winner among contestants from 63 countries. This title has returned to India after 21 years. Mrs. Polynesia was named the first runner-up, followed by Mrs. Canada as the second runner-up.

PETA's Person of the Year 2022

Bollywood actress, Sonakshi Sinha has been named PETA India's 2022 Person of the Year on December 15, 2022.

Sonakshi's actions helped save the lives of many animals killed for fashion, but her strong advocacy of dog and cat rights earned her the title. She is actively involved in animal welfare activities and regularly voices the need for stronger animal protection laws.

'World Athlete of the Year' Awards 2022

The World Athelete of the Year Awards 2022 were presented to McLaughlin-Levrone and on December 6, 2022. Sydney McLaughlin-Levrone is a world champion American hurdler and Mondo Duplantis is a Swedish pole vaulter. McLaughlin-Levrone broke the world women's 400m hurdles record twice while Duplantis set three new world highs this year.

UNESCO Award for Cultural Heritage Conservation 2022

Chhatrapati Shivaji Maharaj Vastu Sangrahalaya (CSMVS). Mumbai was conferred with the 'Award of Excellence' of UNESCO on November 26, 2022.

This award given at the UNESCO Asia-Pacific Awards for Cultural Heritage Conservation 2022.

Indira Gandhi Prize 2021

Pratham, an NGO functioning in the field of education was awarded Indira Gandhi Prize 2021. The award was presented for peace, disarmament and development.

The award is in recognition of Pralnam's work in ensuring quality education for children of country.

'Champions of the Earth' Award 2022

Assam's wildlife biologist Purnima Devi Barman has been awarded the United Nation's highest environmental honour, 'Champions of the Earth' for 2022 on November 23, 2022. Barman has been given this honour for his transformative action to prevent degradation of ecosystems.

UN's Highest Environmental Award

India's Purnima Devi Barman was honoured with UN's highest environmental award on Nov. 22, 2022.

Purnima Devi is Assam's wildlife biologist working to protect the stork, and the founder of the Hargila Army.

JCB Prize for Literature 2022

Khalid Jawed's 'The Paradise of Food' won the JCB Prize for Literature 2022 on November 20, 2022. Khalid Jawed's 'The Paradise of Food' was translated by Baran Farooqi from Urdu.

UNESCO-Madanjeet Singh Prize 2022

Franca Ma-ih Sulem Yong won the 2022 edition of the UNESCO-Madanjeet Singh Prize for the Fromotion of Tolerance and Non-Violence on November 18, 2022.

The UNESCO-Madanjeet Singh Prize for the Promotion of Tolerance and Non-Violence is conferred every two years by the UNESCO.

PERSONS IN NEWS

Aruna Miller

Aruna Miller has scripted history by becoming the first Indian-American politician to be sworn-in as the Lieutenant Governor of Maryland (US) on January 19, 2023. Aruna, 58, a former delegate to the Maryland House, made history when the Democrat became the 10th Lieutenant Governor of the state.

Nilamani Phukan

Renowned Assamese poet and recipient of Jnapith Award, Nilamani Phookan has passed away on January 19, 2023. He was 89. Phookan was one of the most celebrated poets of Assam and has been awarded the country's highest literary award, the 56th Jnanpith for the year 2021.

Jacinda Ardern

The Prime Minister of New Zealand 'Jacinda Ardern' has announced her resignation from her post at the annual meeting of her party on January 18, 2023. PM Jacinda Ardern will hold the post of Prime Minister till February 7, 2023 and will resign after that.

Lucile Randon

World's oldest person, Lucile Randon, died on January 17, 2023 at the age of 118. In the year 2022, the world's oldest person Ken Tanaka of Japan died. He was 119 years old.

After Tanaka's death, 118-year-old Sister Lucille Randon became the oldest person in the world.

Nguyen Xuan Phuc

Vietnam's President Nguyen Xuan Phuc has submitted his resignation on January 17, 2023.

The ruling Communist Party found him responsible for corruption, scandals and wrongdoings. The resignation of the President requires approval from the National Assembly.

Janani Ramachandran

Janani Ramachandran has emerged as the youngest and the first queer woman of colour to take oath as the Oakland City Council member in the California (US) on January 17, 2023.

She took the ceremonial oath wearing a saree as the Oakland City Council member for District 4 in an inauguration ceremony.

Sharad Yadav

The 75-year-old veteran politician, Former Union Minister and RJD leader Sharad Yadav passed away on January 12, 2023. He was probably the first politician in India to be elected as a member of the Lok Sabha from three states (Madhya Pradesh, Uttar Pradesh, and Bihar).

Constantine II

Constantine II, the former and the last king of Greece, has died at the age of 82 in Athens on January 11, 2023. Constantine II acceded to the throne at the age of 23 in 1964. The dictatorship abolished the monarchy, in 1973, while a referendum after democracy was restored, in 1974, dashed any hopes that Constantine had of ever reigning again.

Manpreet Monica

Indian-origin Sikh woman, Manpreet Monica Singh became the first ever female Sikh judge on January 9, 2023 in the US after she was sworn in as a Harris county judge.

In her career expanding over two decades, the newly appointed judge has been involved in numerous civil rights organisations at the local, state, and national levels.

Keshari Nath Tripathi

Senior leader of the Bharatiya Janata Party (BJP) and former West Bengal governor, Keshari Nath Tripathi passed away at 88 on January 7, 2023.

He was a member of the Uttar Pradesh legislative assembly six times. He was Cabinet Minister of institutional finance and sales tax in UP during the Janata Party regime from 1977 to 1979.

Kaikala Satyanarayana

Veteran Telugu actor, producer and director Kaikala Satyanarayana died on December 23, 2022 in Hyderabad due to age related ailments.

He, also known as Navarasa Natana Sarvabhouma, was 87 years old.

He acted in around 750 movies and was known for 'Kurukshetramu' (1977), 'Daana Veera Soora Karna' (1977) and 'Sri Krishnarjuna Yudham' (1963).

Elon Musk

Elon Musk has announced on December 21, 2022 that he will resign as the CEO of Twitter, but that might take some time.

This comes after Musk ran a poll on the platform, asking users whether he should step down as the CEO of Twitter.

Mohit Seth

Major General Mohit Seth took over as the General Officer Commanding (GOC) of the Counter Insurgency Force Kilo on December 20, 2022. The General Officer was commissioned into 3 MADRAS Regiment in Dec 1991. An alumnus of National Defence Academy, the General Officer has attended the prestigious NDC at New Delhi.

Bhairon Singh Rathore

Bhairo Singh Rathore, the hero of the 1971 war, has passed away in AIIMS Jodhpur on December 19, 2022 .

He was admitted to the hospital after battling health issues. Bhairon Singh retired from BSF in 1987. He received the Sena Medal in 1972 for his gallant action.

Meghna Ahlawat

Meghna Ahlawat was elected the first-ever woman president of the Table Tennis Federation of India (TTFI) on December 8, 2022. Former veteran Kamlesh Mehta was also elected as the general secretary. Patel Nagendra Reddy was elected as the treasurer.

KV Shaji

KV Shaji has been named Chairman of the National Bank for Agriculture and Rural Development (NABARD) on December 7, 2022.

He formerly served as NABARD's Deputy Managing Director (DMD) till May 21, 2020. Before joining NABARD, he worked in Canara Bank in various capacities for 26 years.

Ravish Kumar

Senior journalist and Ramon Magsaysay awardee Ravish Kumar resigned from NDTV on November 30, 2022.

This comes just a day after the channel's founders and promoters Prannoy Roy and Radhika Roy resigned from their positions as directors on the board of RRPR Holding Private Limited (RRPRH).

Vikram Kirloskar

Toyota Kirloskar Motor Vice-Chairperson passed away at the age of 64 on November 30, 2022. He is India's automotive industry stalwart and Toyota Kirloskar Motor Vice-Chairperson.

Asim Munir

Former Inter-Services Intelligence (ISI) Chief Lt. Gen. Asim Munir has been appointed as the new Chief of the Pakistan Army on November 29, 2022. He is appointed by Prime Minister Shehbaz Sharif.

Prasanth Kumar

Prasanth Kumar has been elected as the President of the Advertising Agencies Association of India (AAAI) for fiscal 2022-23 at its annual general body meeting on November 29, 2022. Prasant Kumar is presently CEO, South Asia of GroupM Media (India) Pvt Ltd.

Ruturaj Gaikwad

Ruturaj Gaikwad, playing for Maharashtra, became the first batsman in List-A cricket to hit 7 sixes in an over in the quarter-finals of the Vijay Hazare Trophy on November 28, 2022. Gaikwad made this record against Uttar Pradesh in Ahmedabad. He remained unbeaten after scoring 220 runs off 159 balls.

Abdel Fattah el-Sisi

The Indian government has invited Egyptian President Abdel Fattah el-Sisi on November 27, 2022 as the Chief guest for the Republic day parade 2023. He will be the first Egyptian leader to be hosted by India for the Republic Day celebrations.

Vikram Gokhale

Veteran actor Vikram Gokhale, who worked in Hindi and Marathi cinema as well as numerous plays, passed away on November 26, 2022. His latest release was the Marathi film 'Godavari'.

Deepa Malik

Union Health Ministry appoints Deepa Malik as Nikshay Mitra ambassador on November 24, 2022 in New Delhi.

Nikshay Mitra is an initiative under Pradhan Mantri TB Mukt Bharat Abhiyaan.

Manju

Lance Naik Manju became the first woman skydiver of the Indian Army on November 16, 2022. Maju jumped off from the Advanced Light Helicopter (ALH) Dhruv chopper from a height of 10000 ft.

Vivek Joshi

The Indian government has nominated Department of Financial Services Secretary Vivek Joshi on November 15, 2022 as a director on the Reserve Bank of India's central board. Vivek Joshi will hold the position of Director at the central bank.

Greg Barclay

Greg Barclay has been re-elected unopposed as the chairman of the ICC on November 12, 2022. At an ICC Board meeting in Melbourne, Barclay's opponent Dr. Tavengwa Mukuhlani, the chairman of Zimbabwe Cricket withdrew from the contest.

Maura Healey

Maura Healey makes history as first openly lesbian US Governor and first woman elected Governor of Massachusetts on November 9, 2022.

Healey was the first openly gay Attorney General elected in the country in 2014 and was previously a civil rights lawyer. She led the first state challenge to the Defense of Marriage Act, which banned same-sex marriage.

Wes Moore

Wes Moore has been elected as the First Black Governor of the US State of Maryland on November 8, 2022.

Wes Moore is a celebrity author and former non-profit executive. He defeated the far-right Republican, Dan Cox backed by former Donald J. Trump.

Mohamed Irfaan Ali

The Government of India decided on November 5, 2022 that President of Guyana Dr. Mohamed Irfaan Ali will be the chief guest at the 17th Pravasi Bharatiya Divas Convention. It will be held from January 8 to 10, 2023 in Indore, Madhya Pradesh.

Benjamin Netanyahu

Former Israeli PM Benjamin Netanyahu has made a stunning come back to power as his Likud party and its far-right and religious allies emerged victorious in the November 3, 2022 elections.

According to final results released yesterday, the coalition has won 64 of 120 Parliament seats in the country's fifth election in less than four years.

Ela Bhatt

Ela Bhatt, Gandhian, SEWA founder, and women's empowerment activist, died at the age of 89 on November 2, 2022. She was globally recognised as a women leader and was awarded Padma Bhushan.

WHO'S WHO

President	Draupadi Murmu
Vice-President	Jagdeep Dhankar
Prime Minister	Narendra Modi

Cabinet Ministers

Minister	Portfolio
Raj Nath Singh	Defence
Amit Shah	Home Affairs; Cooperation
Nitin Jairam Gadkari	Road Transport and Highways
Nirmala Sitharaman	Finance; Corporate Affairs
Narendra Singh Tomar	Agriculture and Farmers Welfare
S. Jaishankar	External Affairs
Arjun Munda	Tribal Affairs
Smriti Zubin Irani	Women and Child Development; Minority Affairs
Piyush Goyal	Commerce and Industry; Consumer Affairs, Food and Public Distribution; Textiles
Dharmendra Pradhan	Education; Skill Development and Entrepreneurship
Pralhad Joshi	Parliamentary Affairs; Coal; Mines
Narayan Tatu Rane	Micro, Small and Medium Enterprises
Sarbananda Sonowal	Ports, Shipping and Waterways; AYUSH
Virendra Kumar	Social Justice and Empowerment
Giriraj Singh	Rural Development; Panchayati Raj
Jyotiraditya M. Scindia	Civil Aviation; Steel
Pashu Pati Kumar Paras	Food Processing Industries
Kiren Rijiju	Law and Justice
Gajendra Singh Shekhawat	Jal Shakti
Ashwini Vaishnaw	Railways; Communications; Electronics and Information Technology
Raj Kumar Singh	Power; New & Renewable Energy
Hardeep Singh Puri	Petroleum and Natural Gas; Housing and Urban Affairs
Mansukh Mandaviya	Health and Family Welfare; Chemicals and Fertilizers
Mahendra Nath Pandey	Heavy Industries
Bhupender Yadav	Environment, Forest and Climate Change; Labour and Employment
Parshottam Rupala	Fisheries, Animal Husbandry and Dairying
G. Kishan Reddy	Culture; Tourism; Development of North Eastern Region
Anurag Singh Thakur	Information and Broadcasting; Youth Affairs and Sports

Ministers of State (Independent Charge)

Minister	Portfolio
Rao Inderjit Singh	Statistics and Programme Implementation (I/C); Planning (I/C)); and Corporate Affairs
Jitendra Singh	Science and Technology (I/C); Earth Sciences (I/C); Prime Minister's Office; Personnel, Public Grievances and Pensions; Department of Atomic Energy; Department of Space

Ministers of State

Minister	Portfolio
Shripad Yesso Naik	Ports, Shipping and Waterways; Tourism
Faggansingh Kulaste	Steel; Rural Development
Prahalad Singh Patel	Jal Shakti; Food Processing Industries
Ashwini Kumar Choubey	Consumer Affairs, Food and Public Distribution; Environment, Forest and Climate Change
Arjun Ram Meghwal	Parliamentary Affairs; Culture
VK Singh	Road Transport and Highways; Civil Aviation
Krishan Pal	Power; Heavy Industries
Danve Raosaheb Dadarao	Railways; Coal; Mines
Ramdas Athawale	Social Justice and Empowerment
Sadhvi Niranjan Jyoti	Consumer Affairs, Food and Public Distribution; Rural Development
Sanjeev Kumar Balyan	Fisheries, Animal Husbandry and Dairying
Nityanand Rai	Home Affairs
Pankaj Chowdhary	Finance
Anupriya Singh Patel	Commerce and Industry
SP Singh Baghel	Law and Justice
V. Muraleedharan	External Affairs; Parliamentary Affairs
Rajeev Chandrasekhar	Skill Development and Entrepreneurship; Electronics and Information Technology
Shobha Karandlaje	Agriculture and Farmers Welfare
Bhanu Pratap Singh Verma	Micro, Small and Medium Enterprises

Minister	Portfolio
Darshana Vikram Jardosh	Textiles; Railways
Meenakashi Lekhi	External Affairs; Culture
Som Parkash	Commerce and Industry
Renuka Singh Saruta	Tribal Affairs
Rameswar Teli	Labour and Employment; Petroleum and Natural Gas
Kailash Choudhary	Agriculture and Farmers Welfare
Annapurna Devi	Education
A. Narayanaswamy	Social Justice and Empowerment
Kaushal Kishore	Housing and Urban Affairs
Ajay Bhatt	Defence; Tourism
BL Verma	Development of North Eastern Region; Cooperation
Ajay Kumar	Home Affairs
Devusinh Chauhan	Communications
Bhagwanth Khuba	New and Renewable Energy; Chemicals and Fertilizers
Kapil Moreshwar Patil	Panchayati Raj
Sushri Pratima Bhoumik	Social Justice and Empowerment
Subhas Sarkar	Education
Bhagwat Kishanrao Karad	Finance
Rajkumar Ranjan Singh	External Affairs; Education
Bharati Pravin Pawar	Health and Family Welfare
Bishweswar Tudu	Tribal Affairs; Jal Shakti
Shantanu Thakur	Ports, Shipping and Waterways
Munjapara Mahendrabhai	Women and Child Development; AYUSH
John Barla	Minority Affairs

Minister	Portfolio
L. Murugan	Fisheries, Animal Husbandry and Dairying; Information and Broadcasting
Nisith Pramanik	Home Affairs; Youth Affairs and Sports

Governors and Chief Ministers

State	Governor	Chief Minister
Andhra Pradesh	*Biswa Bhusan Harichandan*	YS Jagan Mohan Reddy
Arunachal Pradesh	*BD Mishra*	Pema Khandu
Assam	*Jagdish Mukhi*	Himanta Biswa Sarma
Bihar	*Phagu Chauhan*	Nitish Kumar
Chhattisgarh	*Anusuiya Uikey*	Bhupesh Baghel
Goa	*PS Sreedharan Pillai*	Pramod Sawant
Gujarat	*Acharya Dev Vrat*	Bhupendra Patel
Haryana	*Bandaru Dattatraya*	Manohar Lal Khattar
Jharkhand	*Ramesh Bais*	Hemant Soren
Karnataka	*Thaawarchand Gehlot*	Basavaraj S. Bommai
Himachal Pradesh	*Rajendra Vishwanath Arlekar*	Sukhvinder Singh Sukhu
Kerala	*Arif Mohammad Khan*	P. Vijayan
Madhya Pradesh	*Mangubhai Chhaganbhai Patel*	Shivraj Singh Chauhan
Maharashtra	*Bhagat Singh Koshyari*	Eknath Shinde
Manipur	*La. Ganesan*	N. Biren Singh
Meghalaya	*BD Mishra (Add. Charge)*	Conrad Sangma
Mizoram	*Hari Babu Kambhampati*	Pu. Zoramthanga
Odisha	*Ganeshi Lal*	Naveen Patnaik
Nagaland	*Jagdish Mukhi*	Nephiu Rio
Punjab	*Banwarilal Purohit*	Bhagwant Singh Mann
Rajasthan	*Kalraj Mishra*	Ashok Gehlot
Sikkim	*Ganga Prasad*	Prem Singh Tamang
Tamil Nadu	*RN Ravi*	MK Stalin
Tripura	*Satyadeo Narain Arya*	Manik Saha
Telangana	*Tamilisai Soundararajan*	K. Chandras-hekhar Rao
Uttar Pradesh	*Anandiben Patel*	Yogi Adityanath
Uttarakhand	*Gurmit Singh*	Pushkar Singh Dhami
West Bengal	*CV Ananda Bose*	Mamata Banerjee

Administration of Union Territories

Union Territory	Lt. Governor/ Administrator	Chief Minister
Andaman and Nicobar Islands	DK Joshi	—
Chandigarh	Banwarilal Purohit (Administrator)	—
Dadra & Nagar Haveli and Daman & Diu	Praful Patel (Administrator)	—
Delhi	Vinai Kumar Saxena	Arvind Kejriwal
Jammu-Kashmir	Manoj Sinha	—
Ladakh	Radha Krishna Mathur (Administrator)	—
Lakshadweep	Praful Patel	—
Puducherry	Tamilisai Soundararajan (Add. Charge)	N. Ranga-swamy

Chiefs of Armed Forces/ Intelligence Agencies

Force/Agency	Chief
Chief of Defence Staff (CDS)	Anil Chauhan
Air Force	VR Chaudhari
Army	Manoj Pande
Navy	R. Hari Kumar
CBI	Subodh Kumar Jaiswal
Integrated Defence Staff	Balabhadra Radha Krishna
IB	Tapan Kumar Deka
R&AW	Samant Kumar Goel

Important National Officials

Designation	Dignitary
Chief Justice of India	*DY Chandrachud*
Chairperson, NHRC	*AK Mishra*
Chairperson, University Grants Commission	*M. Jagadesh Kumar*
Chairman, ISRO	*S. Somanath*
Chairman, Atomic Energy Commission	*Kamlesh Vyas*
Chairperson, 15th Finance Commission	*NK Singh*
Chairperson,CBFC	*Prasoon Joshi*
Chairperson, CBSE	*Nidhi Chhibber*
Chief Election Commissioner	*Rajiv Kumar*
Chief Information Commissioner	*Yashvardhan Sinha*
Attorney General	*R. Venkataramani*
Solicitor General	*Tushar Mehta*
Chairman, UPSC	*Manoj Soni*
Governor, RBI	*Shaktikanta Das*
President, BCCI	*Roger Binny*
President, Indian Olympic Association	*PT Usha*

Heads of Nationalised Banks

Bank	Chairman/MD & CEO
State Bank of India	Dinesh Kumar Khara
Bank of Baroda	Sanjeev Chaddha
Bank of India	Atanu Kumar Das
Canara Bank	Lingam Venkata Prabhakar
Bank of Maharashtra	AS Rajeev
Central Bank of India	Matam Venkata Rao
Indian Bank	Shanti Lal Jain
Indian Overseas Bank	Ajay Kumar Srivastava
Punjab National Bank	Atul Kumar Goel
Punjab & Sind Bank	Swarup Kumar Saha
Union Bank of India	A. Manimekhalai
UCO Bank	Soma Sankara Prasad
IDBI Bank	Rakesh Sharma

Important International Officials

Designation	Dignitary
Secretary General, UNO	*Antonio Guterres*
President, World Bank	*David Malpass*
Managing Director, IMF	*Kristalina Georgieva*
Director General, ILO	*Gilbert Houngbo*
President, UNGA	*Csaba Korosi*
Director General, WTO	*Ngozi Okonjo Iweala*
Director General, UNESCO	*Audrey Azoulay*
Director General, WHO	*Tedros Adhanom Ghebreyesus*
Secretary General, UNCTAD	*Rebeca Grynspan*
Director General, IAEA	*Rafael Grossi*
Executive Director, UNICEF	*Catherine Russell*
Secretary General, SAARC	*Esala Weerakoon*
Secretary General, Amnesty International	*Agnes Callamard*
President, IOC	*Thomas Bach*
President, FIFA	*Gianni Infantino*
Chairman, ICC	*Greg Barclay*
CEO, ICC	*Geoff Allardice*

INDIAN HISTORY

ANCIENT INDIA

PRE-HISTORIC PERIOD

Palaeolithic Period

- **Homo sapiens** first appeared towards the end of this phase.
- In this period, man barely managed to gather his food and subsisted on **hunting.**
- Distinguished by the development of the first stone tools made up of **Quartzite**.
- Palaeolithic period is divided into **three phases**. *They are*
  1. Lower Palaeolithic
  2. Middle Palaeolithic
  3. Upper Palaeolithic

Mesolithic Period

- Domestication of animals (particularly, dogs) began and characteristic tools were used, called as **microliths**.
- **Bhimbetka** in Madhya Pradesh, is known for ancient caves depicting pictures of birds, animals and humans.

Neolithic Period

- Neolithic people knew about **fire** and **wheel**.
- An important site of this age is **Burzahom**, which means 'the place of birch'.

Chalcolithic Period

- Use of Copper and Stone made tools.
- They practised agriculture, venerated Mother Goddess and worshipped the bull.

INDUS VALLEY CIVILISATION

- Indus Valley Civilisation is one of the four earliest civilisations of the world.
- According to radiocarbon dating, initiation of Indus Valley Civilisation can be dated around 2500-1750 BC.
- **Systematic town planning** was based on grid system; burnt bricks were used to construct houses; well-managed drainage system; fortified Citadel; highly urbanised; absence of iron implements.
- The **Great Bath** (Mohenjodaro) was used for religious bathing. There were changing rooms alongside.
- Six **granaries** in a row were found in the Citadel at Harappa.
- The towns were divided into 2 parts: the Upper Part or **Citadel** and the **Lower Part**. Harappans were ruled by a class of merchants, as no evidence of weapons are found there.
- Indus people sowed seeds in November and reaped their harvest in April, because of the danger of flood.
- Produced wheat, barley, *rai*, peas, seasum, rice and mustard.
- Indus people were the first to produce cotton, which the Greeks termed as *Sindon* (derived from Sindh).
- **Animals** known were oxen, sheep, buffaloes, goats, pigs, elephants, dogs, cats, asses and camels.

- Well-knit external and internal trade. **Barter** system was prevalent.
- A very interesting feature of this civilisation was that iron was not known to the people.
- The Indus people used weights and measures in the multiples of 16.
- Harappans looked on Earth as fertility Goddess and phallic (*lingam*) and *yoni* worship was prevalent.
- **Unicorn** was the most worshipped animal. Many trees (pipal), animals (bull), birds (dove, pigeon) and stones too were worshipped though no evidence of temple has been found.
- **Dead bodies** were placed in North-South orientation.
- The Seal of **Pashupati** depicts elephant, tiger, rhinoceros and buffalo. Two deers appear at the feet of Pashupati.
- The Indus people believed in ghosts and evil forces evident by their use of amulets for protection against them. **Fire altars** are found at Lothal and Kalibangan.
- The greatest artistic creation of the Harappan culture were the seals, made of steatite. **Harappan script** is pictographic and hasn't been deciphered yet.
- The script was written from right to left in the first line and left to right in the second line. This style is called **Boustrophedon**.
- **Occupations** practiced were spinning, weaving, boat-making, goldsmiths, making pottery and seal-making.
- The possible causes of the decline of the civilisation may be invasion of the Aryans, recurrent floods, social break-up of Harappans and earthquakes, etc.
- **Boundaries** North-Mandu (J&K); South-Daimabad (Maharashtra); East- Alamgirpur; West-Sutkagendor.

Indus Valley Sites

Site	*Discovery/Finding(s)*
Harappa	Situated on river **Ravi** in Montgomery district of Punjab (Pakistan). It was excavated by **Daya Ram Sahni** in 1921-23. The Indus Civilisation is named after it as the Harappan Civilisation. Stone dancing Natraja and Cemetry-37 have been found here.
Mohenjodaro (*Mound of Dead*)	Situated on river **Indus** in Larkana district of Sind (Pak). It was excavated by **RD Bannerji** in 1922. The main building includes the Great Bath, the Great Granary, the Collegiate Building and the Assembly Hall. The dancing girl made of bronze has been found here. Pashupati Mahadeva/proto Shiva seal; fragment of woven cotton, etc are other findings .
Chanhudaro (*Sindh, Pakistan*)	On river Indus; discovered by **NG Majumdar** (1931); only Indus site without citadel; bronze figurines of bullock cart and *ekkas*; a small pot suggesting a an ink pot.
Lothal (*Gujarat*)	Discovered by **SR Rao** (1954); situated on river Bhogava. A part of the town was divided into citadel and the lower town and dockyard. Evidence of rice has been found here.
Kalibangan (meaning, *Black Bangles*) (*Rajasthan*)	Discovered by **BB Lal** (1961); situated on Ghaggar river, a ploughed field; a wooden furrow; seven fire-altars; bones of camel; and evidence of two types of burials namely—circular grave and rectangular grave.
Dholavira	It was found on river Luni of Kachchh district in Gujarat discovered by **JP Joshi** (1967-68). It has a *unique water management system*; only site to be divided into 3 parts; largest Harappan inscription and a stadium.
Surkotada (*Gujarat*)	Discovered by **JP Joshi** in 1972; evidence of horse found; oval grave; pit burials and seemingly a port city.
Banawali (*Haryana*)	On river Saraswati; discovered by **RS Bisht** (1973); evidence of both pre-Harappan and Harappan culture; lacked systematic drainage system; evidence of good quality barley.
Rakhigarhi (*Haryana*)	Largest Indus valley site.

VEDIC PERIOD

Rig Vedic Period (1500-1000 BC)

- Vedic civilisation started with the migration of Aryan people in North-Western part of India.
- The Aryans were semi-nomadic pastoral people and originally believed to have lived somewhere in the **Steppes,** stretching from Southern Russia to Central Asia.
- The whole region in which the Aryans were first settled in India was called **the Land of 7 Rivers** or **Sapta Sindhawa**. (the Indus and its five tributaries and the Saraswati).
- **The Dasrajan War** Battle of 10 kings against Sudas (Bharata king of Tritsus) on the bank of river Parushni. Sudas emerged victorious.

Political Organisation

- It was mainly a tribal system of government in which the military element was strong.
- Tribe was known as **Jana** and its king as **Rajan**.
- Although king's post was hereditary, we have also some traces of election by the tribal assembly called **Samitis**.
- Other tribal assemblies that were mentioned in Rigveda were **Sabha**, **Vidatha** and **Gana**.
- Villages were headed by **Gramani**.
- In day-to-day administration, the King was assisted by the **Purohita** (most important), a **Senani** and **Gramani**.

Society

People were loyal to the tribe, called **Jana** (mentioned 275 times in the Rigveda) as kingdom/territory was not yet established. Women enjoyed freedom and respect.

Religion

- Worshipped Nature, Indra (also called Purandara-breaker of forts) was the most important divinity.
- **Soma** was considered to be the God of plants.
- People worshipped the divinities mainly for **Praja** (children), **Pashu** (cattle), food, health and wealth. No temple or idol worship was noted.

Economy

No regular revenue system, kingdom maintained by voluntary tribute called **bali** and booty won in battles.

- Aryan's main occupation was mainly pastoral. Agriculture was a secondary occupation.
- Cow was a standard unit of exchange. Gold coins-*Nishka, Krishnal* and *Satmana*.
- The staple crop was **Yava** (barley).

Rigvedic Terms

Term	*Meaning*
Dasyus	Original inhabitant of India
Ayas	Copper/bronze
Vajrapati/ Kalapas	Officer enjoying authority over large tract of land
Gramini	Head of the village
Gavisthi	Fighting hordes, Search for cows/war for cows

Rigvedic Rivers

River	*Name in Rigveda*
Indus	Sindhu
Kurram	Krumu
Jhelum	Vitasta
Chenab	Asikni
Ravi	Parushini
Beas	Vipas
Sutlej	Sutudri
Gomati	Gomal
Saraswati	Sarasvati
Ghaggar	Drishadavati

Later Vedic Period (1000-500 BC)

- In this period, Aryans expanded from Punjab over the whole of Western Uttar Pradesh covered by the Ganga-Yamuna Doab.

Political Organisation

- King (*Samrat*) became more powerful and tribal authority tended to become territorial.
- King's position strengthened by rituals like **Ashwamedha** and **Vajapeya Yajnas**.

Society

- Society was clearly divided into four varnas—Brahmana, Kshatriya, Vaishya and Shudra. Position of women deteriorated. The institution of Gotra (descent from common ancestors) appeared for the first time.

Economy

- Beginning of town and settled life.
- Agriculture was the main livelihood.
- Wheat and rice (called **vrihi** in later Vedic texts) became the staple crop.
- New occupation like those of ironsmith, coppersmith and jewel work emerged. Weaving were reserved for women.

Religion

- **Prajapati** became the supreme God, followed by **Rudra** (animal God) and **Lord Vishnu** (preserver and protector of people).
- Idolatry began in this period.
- Pushana, who looked after the cattles was 'God of Shudras'.
- Sacrifices, rather than prayers, became more important.

Vedic Literature

The Vedas

- **Rigveda** The oldest Indo-European language text is a collection of hymns. Contains 1028 hymns divided into 10 mandalas. The 10th Mandala contains **Purushasukta hymn** that explain about four varnas, whereas 3rd Mandala contains Gayatri mantra, which was compiled in the praise of Sun God.
- **Samaveda** Collection of melodies, contains Dhrupad raga. It is a book of chants.
- **Yajurveda** Contains hymns and rituals/ sacrifices.
- **Atharvaveda** Charms and spells to ward-off evils and diseases.

The Brahmanas

- They explain the hymns of Vedas. Contains ritualistic formulae and explains the social and religious meaning of rituals. Each veda has several Brahmanas attached to it.

Rigveda :	*Kaushitaki* and *Aitareya*
Yajurveda :	*Taittiriya* and *Satapatha*
Samaveda :	*Panchvish* and *Jemineya*
Atharvaveda :	*Gopatha*

The Aranyakas

The word *Aranya* means the forest. These texts were called Aranyakas, because they were written mainly for the hermits and students living in the jungle.

The Upanishadas

- Philosophical texts emphasising value of right belief and knowledge; criticising rituals/sacrifices; and 108 in number. **Brihadaranyaka** is the oldest upanishada.
- Also known as 'Vedanta'.

Smritis

Explains rules and regulations in Vedic life. These are Manusmriti (the first law book); Naradasmriti, Yajnavalkya-smriti and Parasharasmriti.

Vedangas

These are Limbs of Vedas and are six in number.

- Shiksha (Pronunciation)
- Kalpa (Rituals)
- Vyakaran (Grammar)
- Nikrukta (Etymology)
- Chhanda (Metrics)
- Jyotish (Astrology)

Puranas

Deals with world creation, the geneologies of Gods and Rishis and the Royal dynasties. There are 18 famous 'Puranas'. The 'Matsya Purana' is the oldest puranic text.

Darshana

There are six schools of Indian philosophy, called Shada-darshana.

These are

Nyaya Darshana	*Gautam*
Vaishesika Darshana	*Kanada Rishi*
Sankhya Darshana	*Kapila*
Yoga Darshana	Patanjali
Purva Mimansa	*Jaimini*
Uttara Mimansa	*Badrayna or Vyasa*

Upavedas

There are four Upavedas

Upaveda	*Deals with*	*Upaveda of*
Dhanurveda	Art of warfare	Yajurveda
Gandharva-veda	Art and music	Samaveda
Shilpaveda	Architecture	Atharvaveda
Ayurveda	Medicine	Rigveda

Epics

Mahabharata by Vyasa, also called Jaya Samhita and Satasahasri Samhita has 100000 verses and are older than Ramayana, written by **Valmiki**, and has 29000 verses.

The Mahajanapadas

Mahajanapada (Locations)	*Capital (s)*
Gandhara (Between Kabul and Rawalpindi)	Taxila
Anga (Bhagalpur and Mungher in Bihar)	Champa
Magadha (Patna and Gaya district, Bihar)	Girivraj, Rajagriha (Bimbisara); Patliputra (Udayin); Vaishali (Shishunaga); Patliputra (Ashoka)
Kashi (Varanasi district, UP)	Varanasi
Vajji (Vaishali district, UP)	Vaishali
Malla (South of Vaishali district, UP)	Kusinagara and Pava
Chedi (River Ken Bundelkhand area)	Sothivati-nagar or Shuktimati
Vatsa (River Yamuna, Allahabad and Mirzapur district in UP)	Kaushambi
Kosala (Eastern UP)	Sravasti and Ayodhaya (Saket)
Kuru (Ganga-Yamuna doab. Delhi-Meerut region)	Hastinapur and Indraprastha
Panchala (Ganga-Yamuna doab, Rohilkhand)	Ahichhatra and Kampilya
Matsya (Jaipur-Bharatpur-Alwar district)	Viratnagar/Bairath
Surasenas (Mathura region)	Mathura
Asmaka (River Godavari) (Near Paithan in Maharashtra)	Patna or Patali
Avanti (Malwa)	Ujjain (Northern capital), Mahismati (Southern capital)
Kamboja (Hazara district of Pakistan)	Rajapur or Hataka

JAINISM AND BUDDHISM

- Came into existence around 600 BC.
- The main causes being the reaction against domination of Brahmanas and spread of agricultural economy in the North-East.

Jainism

- Founded by Rishabhadeva (Emblem : Bull) born in Ayodhya.
- There were 24 tirthankaras (great teachers), the 23rd being Parshvanatha and the 24th being the Vardhamana Mahavira.
- Mahavira was born in 540 BC in **Kundagram** near Vaishali.
- Father **Siddhartha** of Jnatrik Kshatriya Clan.
- Mother Trishala—sister of Lichchhavi Chief Chetaka, married to **Yashoda** and had a daughter named Priyadarshini, whose husband Jamali became his first disciple. Mahavira became an ascetic at the age of 30, attained **Kaivalya** (Jina) outside the town of Jimbhikgrama at the age of 42 and died at the age of 72 in 468 BC in **Pavapuri**.
- Five Doctrines of Jainism
  1. Do not commit violence (Ahimsa)
  2. Do not steal (Asteya)
  3. Do not acquire property (Aparigraha)
  4. Do not speak lie (Satya)
  5. Observe continence (Brahmacharya)
- **Triratnas of Jainism** are right knowledge, right faith and right conduct.
- Jainism says salvation is possible only by abandoning all possessions, a long course of fasting, self mortification, study and meditation.
- Jainism recognised existence of God, but lower than **Jina.** It didn't condemn *varna* system unlike Buddhism.
- Jainism could not delink clearly from brahmanical religion, hence failed to attract masses; admitted both men and women. Jain monastic establishments were called **basadis.**
- Jainism was patronised by *Kharavela*–the king of Kalinga; Chandragupta Maurya *became the disciple of Bhadrabahu and spread Jainism in the South.*
- Jainism was divided into two sects during the reign of Chandragupta Maurya, mainly due to famine in Magadha named. **Svetambaras** (wearing white dresses) under Sthulbhadra and **Digambaras** (*naked*) under Bhadrabahu.
- Jaina texts were written in **Prakrit language**.

Councils

First Council (300 BC) At Pataliputra Under Sthulbhadra (Pataliputra) Jaina Canons compiled.

Second Council At Vallabhi (AD 5th Century). Under Kshamasramana (*Vallabhi*) 12 *Angas* and 12 Upangas were compiled in **Ardh Magadhi language**.

Buddhism

Founded by Gautama Buddha, also known as **Siddhartha** or *Sakyamuni* or Tathagata.

- Born in 563 BC in Lumbini in Nepal in Shakya Kshatriya Clan.
- His father Suddhodana was a Shakya ruler and his mother Mahamaya of Kosalan dynasty died early. Brought up by step mother Gautami.
- Married to Yashodhara and had a son Rahul.
- **Triratnas** in Buddhism stand for 3 pillars
  - **Buddha** Its founder
  - **Dhamma** His teachings
  - **Sangha** Order of Buddhist monks and nuns

Buddhism was also divided in two main sects namely **Hinayana** and **Mahayana**.

Phases of Buddha's Life	*Symbols*
Birth	Lotus and Bull
Mahabhinishkraman (Renunciation)	Horse
Nirvana (Enlightenment)	Bodhi Tree
Dharmachakra Pravartana (First Sermon)	Wheel
Mahaparinirvana (Death)	Stupa

The Dhamma

The Four Great Truths

- The world is full of sorrow and misery.
- The cause of all pain and misery is desire.
- Pain and misery can be ended by killing or controlling desire.
- Desire can be controlled by following the Eight-Fold Path.

The Eight-Fold Path

1. Right Understanding	5. Right Efforts
2. Right Thought	6. Right Speech
3. Right Action	7. Right Mindfullness
4. Right Livelihood	8. Right Concentration

Madhya Marga (The Middle Path)

Man should avoid both extremes, i.e. life of comforts and luxury and a life of severe asceticism.

Buddhist Literature

In **Pali language** commonly referred to as **Tripitakas**, *i.e.*, 'three fold basket'.

Vinaya Pitaka

Rules of discipline in Buddhist monasteries.

Sutta Pitaka

It contains collection of Buddha's sermons and teachings. It is largest among all three pitakas.

Abhidhamma Pitaka

Explanation of the philosophical principles of the Buddhist religion. **Mahavamsha** and **Dipavamsa** are the other Buddhist texts of Sri Lanka.

Causes of Decline of Buddhism

Use of Sanskrit, the language of intellectuals, in place of Pali, the language of the common people. Revival of Hinduism.

Buddhist Councils

Buddhist Councils	*Period*	*Place*	*Chairman*	*Patron*
First	483 BC	Rajagriha	Mahakashyapa	Ajatashatru
Second	383 BC	Vaishali	Sabakami	Kalashoka
Third	250 BC	Patliputra	Mogaliputta Tissa	Ashoka
Fourth	AD 72	Kundalvana	Vasumitra, Ashwaghosa	Kanishka

DYNASTIES OF ANCIENT INDIA

Haryanka Dynasty

- **Bimbisara** was the founder, who expanded the Magadha kingdom by annexing Anga, and entering into matrimonial alliances with Kosala and Vaishali. He was contemporary of Buddha. Capital-**Rajgir** (Girivraja).
- **Ajatashatru** came to power by killing his father. Annexed Vaishali, Kosala and Lichchhavi kingdom.
- **Udayin** founded the new capital, **Pataliputra**.

Shishunaga Dynasty

Founded by Shishunaga; Kalashoka or Kakavarin of this dynasty convened the Second Buddhist Council. Their greatest achievement was the destruction of Avanti.

Nanda Dynasty

- Considered **non-Kshatriyan** dynasty, founded by **Mahapadma Nanda**. Alexander attacked during Dhana Nanda's reign. **Cyrus** was the first foreign invader of India.
- **Alexander,** the king of Macedonia, invaded India in 326 BC and fought the Battle of Hydaspes (Jhelum) with **Porus** (Purushottam) of **Paurava dynasty.**

Mauryan Dynasty

Important rulers of Mauryan Dynasty are

Chandragupta Maurya (321-298BC)

The first ruler who overthrew the Nanda dynasty with the help of **Chanakya**.

- He has been called **Sandrocottus** by Greek scholars.
- Chandragupta defeated **Seleucus Nikator,** the general of Alexander (304 BC), who later sent **Megasthenese** the author of **Indica** to Chandragupta's court.
- His mother was **Mura**—a Shudra woman in Nanda's court.
- **Mudrarakshasa** was written by Vishakhadatta and describes about mechanisation of Chanakya against Chandragupta's enemy. Chandragupta maintained six wings of armed forces.
- He adopted Jainism and went to **Sravanabelgola** with **Bhadrabahu**.

Bindusara (298-273 BC)

He was called *Amitraghat* (*i.e.*, slayer of foes) by Greek writers; Greek ambassador, **Deimachos** visited his court; said to conquer the **land between the two seas**—The Arabian Sea and Bay of Bengal.

Bindusara appointed his eldest son Sumana as his viceroy at Taxila and Ashoka at Ujjain.

Ashoka (293-273 BC)

- For the first eight years Ashoka ruled like a cruel king and maintained discipline.
- He was called **Devanamapriya,** Dear to Gods in some of his inscriptions.
- The name **Ashoka** occurs only in copies of Minor Rock Edict I.
- Three languages were used for Ashokan inscription that is Prakrit, Greek and Aramic.
- Most of the Ashokan edicts were written in Brahmi script. It was James Princep who deciphered first the Brahmi script of Ashokan edicts in AD 1837.
- Ashoka was the first king to maintain direct contact with people through inscriptions.
- **Kalinga War** (261 BC) mentioned in 13th Major Rock Edict converted Ashoka to Buddhism under **Upagupta**.
- **Sanchi Stupa** was built by Ashoka.
- The last Mauryan king **Brihadratha,** was killed by Pushyamitra Sunga in 185 BC, who established the Sunga dynasty.
- The **Punch-marked coins** carrying the symbol of the peacock and the hill and crescent, famed the imperial currency of Mauryas.
- The Mauryan artisans started the practice of carving caves of monks to live in. **Barabar Caves** near Gaya is earliest example of such cave.
- **Ringwells** for domestic use of water appeared first under the Mauryas.
- Sri Lanka is called **Tamrapani** in the Ashokan inscription.

The Sunga Dynasty (185-73 BC)

- The Sunga Dynasty was established by **Pushyamitra Sunga**. (who killed last Mauryan King Brihadratha)
- They were basically Brahmins. This period saw the revival of Bhagvatism.
- **Patanjali** wrote 'Mahabhasya' at this time.
- In arts, the **Bharhut stupa** is the most famous monument of the Sunga period.

The Kanva Dynasty (73-28 BC)

- In 73 BC, **Devabhuti**, the last ruler of the Sunga dynasty, was murdered by his minister **Vasudeva**, who usurped the throne and founded the Kanva dynasty which was later replaced by the Satavahanas.

The Indo-Greeks

- The most famous king among the Indo-Greeks was **Menander** (165-145 BC) also called **Milinda,** his capital was **Sakala** (modern Sialkot) in Punjab.
- Converted to Buddhism by Nagasena as per the **Milindapanho**—a Pali text.
- The Greeks were the first to issue coins attributable to the king and also the first to issue gold coins in India; introduced Hellenistic art.

The Shakas

- The most famous ruler was **Rudradaman I** (AD 130-150), who repaired Sudarshana lake in Kathiawar region, issued first ever inscription in Chaste Sanskrit (Junagarh inscription). He defeated the Satavahanas twice.
- **Vikramaditya**, the king of Ujjain, was the only one who defeated the Shakas. To commemorate the victory, he started the **Vikram Samvat** in 57 BC.
- **The Parthians** The most famous king was **Gondophernes** (AD 19-45), in whose reign St Thomas visited India to propagate Christianity.

The Kushanas

- Also called **Yechi** or **Tocharians**, were nomadic people from the Steppes.
- **Kanishka** was the greatest of the Kushanas , who started the **Saka Era** in AD 78.
- Kushanas were the first rulers to issue **gold coins** on a wide scale known for metallic purity.
- In the royal court of **Kanishka**, a host of scholars found patronage, like Parsva, Vasumitra, Asvaghosha, Nagarjuna, Charak (Physician) and Mathara. He also patronised the Greek engineer Agesilaus.

The Satavahanas (or Andhras)

- **Simuka** (60-37 BC) was the founder of the Satavahana dynasty.
- Satavahanas were finally succeeded by the **Ikshvakus** in AD 3rd century.
- Under the Satavahanas, many chaityas (worship halls) and viharas (monastries) were cut out from rocks mainly in North-West Deccan or Maharashtra the famous examples were **Nasik, Kanheri** and **Karle**.
- The official language of the Satavahanas was **Prakrit**.
- The Satavahanas issued **coins** of lead (mainly), copper, bronze and potin.
- Gautamiputra Satakarni was a famous king.

Sangam Age

- Sangam Age corresponds to the post-Mauryan and pre-Gupta periods.
- South India, during the Sangam Age, was ruled by three dynasties- the cheras, cholas and pandyas.

The Pandyas

- Their capital was **Madurai** famous for pearls. The Pandyas were first mentioned by Megasthenese.
- Traded with Roman empire, sent embassies to emperor Augustus.

The Cholas

- The Chola kingdom, also called as Cholamandalam was situated to the North-East of Pandya Kingdom between Pennar and Vellar rivers.
- Their Capital was Kaveripattanam/ Puhar.

The Cheras

- Their capital was **Vanji** (also called Kerala country). It had important trade relations with the Romans.

Sangam Literature

- Sangam was a college or an assembly of Tamil poets, held under **Royal Patronage.**

  Three Sangams were held

  (i) at Madurai chaired by Agastya.

  (ii) at Kapatpuram, chaired by Tolkappiyar.

  (iii) at Madurai, chaired by Nakkirar.
- Kural by Tiruvalluvar is called the '**Fifth Veda**' or **the Bible of Tamil Land.'**

Gupta Period

The important rulers of Gupta period are

Chandragupta I (AD 319-334)

Married a Lichchhavi princess, who strengthened his position and enhanced the prestige of the Guptas.

- He was the first Gupta ruler to acquire the title of **Maharajadhiraja.**
- Chandragupta I was able to establish his authority over Magadha, Prayaga and Saketa.

Samudragupta (AD 335-380)

- He is called the **Napoleon of India** (by VA Smith) on account of his conquests.
- **Meghavarman** the ruler of Sri Lanka, sent a missionary to his court for permission to built a Buddhist temple at Gaya.
- The Allahabad pillar inscription gives detailed information about Samudragupta, it was composed by his court poet **Harisena**.
- He assumed the titles of **Kaviraj** and **Vikrama**.

Chandragupta II (AD 380-414)

- Mehrauli inscription on Iron Pillar near Qutub Minar is related to him.
- His court was adorned by **Navratnas**, the chief being **Kalidasa** and **Amarsimha**.
- **Fa-hien**, Chinese Pilgrim (AD 399-414) visited during his reign.
- Defeated Saka Kshatrapa Rudrasimha III
- Chandragupta II also succeeded in killing Ramagupta, and not only seized his kingdom, but also married his widow Dhruvadevi.
- He was the first Gupta ruler to issue the silver coins in the memory of victory over *Sakas* and to have adopted the titles *Sakari* and *Vikramaditya*.
- The Gupta age is called **golden age** of Indian history and saw the issuance of the largest number of gold coins.

Kumaragupta I (AD 415-455)

- Chandragupta II was succeeded by his son Kumaragupta I.
- Kumaragupta was the worshipper of God *Kartikeya*.
- He founded the **'Nalanda Mahavihara'** which developed into a great centre of learning.

Skandagupta (AD 455-467)

- Skandagupta was the last great ruler of the Gupta dynasty.
- During his reign the Gupta empire was invaded by the Hunas.
- Success in repelling the Hunas seems to have been celebrated by the assumption of the title 'Vikramaditya' (Bhitari Pillar Inscription).

Pushyabhuti Dynasty (AD 606-647)

- The greatest king was **Harshavardhana**, son of Prabhakar Vardhana of Thaneshwar. He shifted the capital to **Kannauj.**
- **Hieun Tsang** visited during his reign.
- He established a large monastery at Nalanda. **Banabhata** adorned his court, wrote Harshacharita and Kadambari. Harsha himself wrote three plays—Priyadarshika, Ratnawali and Nagananda.

Rashtrakutas

- Founded by Dantidurg; Krishna I built the Kailasha temple at **Ellora**. Amoghavarsha, who is compared to Vikramaditya, wrote the first Kannada poetry *Kaviraj Marg*. Rashtrakutas are credited for building cave shrine **Elephanta,** dedicated to *Shiva*.

Gangas

Ruled Orissa; Narsimhadeva constructed the Sun Temple at Konark; Anantvarman built the **Jagannath Temple** at Puri; and Kesaris, who used to rule before Gangas built the **Lingaraja Temple** at Bhubaneshwar.

Pallavas

Founder–**Simhavishnu**; Capital–Kanchi; greatest king **Narsimhavarman**, who founded the town of Mamallapuram (Mahabalipuram) and built rock-cut rathas and even pagodas.

- **Palas,** with their capital at Monghyr is known for Dharmapala, their second king, who founded the Vikramashila University and revived the Nalanda University.
- The greatest ruler of **Pratiharas** was **Bhoja** (also known as Mihir, Adivraha).
- Khajuraho temples were built during the reign of **Chandellas** of Bundelkhand.
- **Chalukyas** of Vatapi-founded by Jayasimha were contemporary to Harshavardhan.
- **Rajputs** divided into four clans: Pratiharas (S Rajasthan), Chauhans (E Rajasthan), Chalukyas/Solankis (Kathiawar), Parmaras (Malwa).

The Cholas

- Founder **Vijayalaya**, Capital **Tanjore**.
- **Aditya I** wiped out the Pallavas and weakened the Pandyas.
- **Purantaka I** captured Madurai, but was defeated by the Rashtrakuta ruler **Krishna** III at the **Battle of Takkolam**.
- **Rajaraja I** (AD 985-1014) led a naval expedition against Shailendra empire (Malaya Peninsula) and conquered Northern **Sri Lanka**; constructed Rajarajeshwari (or Brihadeshvara) Shiva temple at **Tanjore.**
- **Rajendra I** (AD 1014-1044) annexed the whole of Sri Lanka; took the title of **Gangaikonda** and founded **Gangaikonda Cholapuram**.
- **Dancing Figure of Shiva** (Nataraja) belongs to the Chola period. Local self government existed.

MEDIEVAL INDIA

- **Mohammad bin Qasim** invaded India in AD 712 and conquered Sindh.
- Sultan **Mahmud of Ghazni** led about 17 expeditions of India.
- In 1025, he attacked and raided the most celebrated Hindu temple of **Somnath**, situated on the sea coast of Kathiawar.

FOUNDATION OF THE DELHI SULTANATE

- **Mohammad Ghori** invaded India and was defeated by Prithviraj Chauhan in **First Battle of Tarain** (1191).
- Ghori defeated the Rajput king in Second Battle of Tarain (1192) and laid the foundation of the Muslim dominion in India. He may be considered the **'founder of Muslim rule' in India**.

Ilbari Dynasty (AD 1206-1290)

Qutub-ud-in-Aibak

- Capital **Lahore** (initial); **Delhi** (later)
- The founder of the Slave dynasty. Also called **Lakh Baksh** because of his generosity.
- Qutub-ud-din Aibak laid the foundation of **Qutub Minar**, after the name of the famous Sufi saint Khwaja Qutubuddin Bakhtiyar Kaki; built Quwwat-ul-Islam (first mosque in India) and **Adhai Din ka Jhopra** (Ajmer).
- Died while playing Chaugan (polo) at Lahore.

Iltutmish (AD 1210-1236)

- Attack of Mongols; formed **Turkan-e-Chahalgani** or Chalisa (a group of 40 powerful Turkish nobles).
- Divided his empire into **Iqtas** (assignment of land in lieu of salary).
- Introduced 2 types of coins-silver tanka and copper jital.

Razia Sultan (AD 1236-1240)

- First and last Muslim woman ruler of Medieval India.
- She disregarded Purdah, married Altunia, the Governor of Bhatinda.
- Bahram Shah, son of Iltutmish, killed her.

Balban (AD 1266-1286)

- Separated Military Department (*Diwan-e-Ariz*) and Finance Department (*Diwan-e-Wazarat*).
- He declared that king was the deputy of God (Niyabat-e-Khudai) and shadow of God (Zil-e-Illahi) and introduced the practices of **Sijdah** and **Paibos**.

Khalji Dynasty (AD 1290-1320)

- **Jalaluddin Firuz Khalji** was the first ruler, who reviewed that India cannot be a totally Islamic state.
- **Alauddin Khalji** His conquests were that of Gujarat ruled by Vaghela king; Ranthambhor, Chittor and Malwa and later to the South (mainly by Malik Kafur).
- He abolished Zamindari in *Khalisa* land. No iqta was allotted in Doab area.

- Alauddin adopted the policy of **Blood and Iron** in tackling the Mongols.
- He built Khizrabad, **Alai Darwaja** and his capital city **Siri**.
- Also built **Hauz Khas** in Delhi and added entrance door to **Qutub Minar**, introduced market reforms.
- Adopted the title of **Sikandar-i-Sani.**
- Built a permanent army, introduced Chehra and Dagh System.
- First Turkish Sultan' who separated religion from politics.
- His court poets were **Amir Khusrau** and **Mir Hassan Dehlvi.**

Tughlaq Dynasty (AD 1320-1413)

- Founded by **Ghiyasuddin Tughlaq**, who built the fortified city of *Tughlaqabad* and made it his capital.
- He was the first sultan to start irrigation works.
- **Muhammad-bin-Tughlaq** also called the **wise fool king** on account of five experiments, namely (a) Transfer of capital to Daulatabad (b) Taxation in Doab (c) Qarachil expedition (d) Khurasan expedition (e) Token currency.
- The Sultan set-up a separate department for agriculture, *Diwan-i-kohi*. He gave *Sondhar* loans to farmers.
- South Indian states of the Vijayanagara empire, the Bahmani kingdom and the Sultanate of Madura were founded.
- The famous traveller of Morocco, **Ibn-Batuta** visited his court.
- **Firoz Shah Tughlaq** built new towns of Hissar, Firozpur, Fatehabad, Jaunpur and Firozabad (his capital). During his reign two Ashokan pillars, one from Topara in Ambala and the other from Meerut were brought. Built canals was fond of slaves and wrote a book **Fatuhat-e-Firozshahi**.
- He repaired Qutub Minar when it was struck by lightening.
- Firoz Shah Tughlaq also made **Iqtadari system** hereditary and imposed new taxes like **Kharaj** (land tax equal to one-tenth of the producer) and **Zakat** and **Khams** (one-tenth of the booty captured in war).
- He made **Jizya** a separate tax and he imposed this tax upon the **Brahmans** for the first time in the history of Sultanate.
- He introduced the following coins—Aadha, Bhikh, Shashgani and Hasthragani.
- **Timur** Mongol leader of Central Asia, ordered general massacre in Delhi (AD 1398) at the time of Nasiruddin Mahmud (last Tughlaq king).

Sayyids and Lodhis

- **Sayyids** dynasty was founded by Khizr Khan : Successors-Mubarak Shah, Muhammad Shah and Alauddin Alam Shah.
- The **Lodhis** were the first Afghans to rule India.
- **Bahlol Lodhi** (AD 1451-1481) founded the dynasty.
- **Sikander Lodhi** (AD 1418-1517) introduced **Gaz-i-Sikandari**. (unit for measuring cultivated field). He founded Agra in 1504. He wrote the Persian verse 'Gulrukhi'.
- He was succeeded by **Ibrahim Lodhi** (1517-1526), who was defeated by **Rana Sanga** of Mewar in the Battle of Khatoli. Ibrahim Lodhi was also defeated by **Babur** in April, 1526 which led to the establishment of the Mughal rule in India.

PROVINCIAL KINGDOMS

Gujarat

- Broke away from Delhi in AD 1397 under **Zafar Khan**, who assumed the title of **Sultan Muzaffar Shah**.
- His grandson Ahmed Shah I built a new city **Ahmedabad**.
- The next prominent ruler was **Mahmud Beghra**. During his rule, the Portuguese set-up a factory at Diu.

Kashmir

Kashmir was ruled by Hindu rulers until **Shamsuddin Shah** asserted himself in AD 1339. The greatest ruler was **Zain-ul-Abidin** (AD 1420-70), who is called the **Akbar of Kashmir**, built Zaina lank, artificial island in **Wular lake**.

Mewar

- Rajput rule restored by **Rana Hamir** after Alauddin Khilji captured Chittor in AD 1303.
- The greatest was **Rana Kumbha** who built the **Vijay Stambh** at Chittor to commemorate his victory over Mahmud Khalji of Malwa.

Vijayanagara Kingdom
(AD 1336-1565)

- Founded by Harihara I and Bukka I.
- Four dynasties ruled over Vijayanagar-Sangam, Saluva, Tuluva and Aravidu.
- **Devaraya** I built a dam across Tungabhadra river and Italian traveller **Nicolo de Conti** visited his court followed by the Russian merchant **Nikitin**.
- **Devaraya** II, the greatest ruler, who was seen as incarnation of Indra by Commoners; He was also called 'Gajabetekara' and wrote **Mahanataka Sudhanidhi** and commentary on the **Brahma Sutras** in Sanskrit; Persian Ambassador **Abdur Razzaq** visited his court. Krishnadeva Raya (AD 1509-29) was the greatest ruler.
- Krishnadeva Raya was known as **Abhinava Bhoja**, **Andhra Pitamah** and **Andhra Bhoja** because of being a great patron of literature. Eight great poets of Telugu (Ashta Diggaja) adorned his court like Pedanna and Tenalirama.
- Portuguese **Dominigo Paes** and **Barbosa** visited his court.
- **Battle of Talikota** (AD 1565) **Sadasiva**, the last ruler of the Tuluva dynasty was defeated by an alliance of Ahmadnagar, Bijapur, Golconda and Bidar.

Bahmani Kingdom

- **Alauddin Hasan Bahman Shah** (AD 1347-58), also known as **Hasan Gangu,** founded it with capital at **Gulbarg.**
- **Ahmad Shah Wali** transferred the capital from **Gulbarg** to **Bidar**.
- Bahmani kingdom broke up into :
  - **Nizamsahis of Ahmadnagar**
    Founder *Malik Ahmad Bahri*
  - **Adilsahis of Bijapur**
    Founder *Yusuf Adil Shah*
  - **Imadsahis of Berar**
    Founder *Fatullah Khan Imad-ul-Mulk*
  - **Qutubsahis of Golconda**
    Founder *Quli Qutub Shah*
  - **Baridsahis of Bidar**
    Founder *Ali Barid*
- The **Gol Gumbaz** (a tomb with World's second largest dome) was built by Muhammad Adil Shah at **Bijapur**.
- Muhammad Quli Qutubshah founded **Hyderabad** and built **Charminar**.

Mughal Empire
(AD 1526-1707)

Babur (AD 1526-1530)

- Founder of Mughal empire, who introduced gunpowder in India; defeated Ibrahim Lodhi in the **First Battle of Panipat** (AD 1526); Rana Sanga (Sangram Singh) at **Battle of Khanwa** (AD 1527); Medini Rai of Chanderi at **Battle of Chanderi** (AD 1528) and Mahmud Lodi at **Battle of Ghagra** (AD 1529); he wrote **Tuzuk-i-Baburi** in Turkish language.
- Babur declared **Jehad** and adopted the title Ghazi.
- Died in 1530 and was buried at Aram Bagh (Agra). Later his body was taken to Bagh-e Babun (Kabul).

Humayun (AD 1530-1556)

- Built **Dinpanah** at Delhi as his second capital.
- Sher Shah Suri gradually gained power. He fought two battles with Humayun—**Battle of Chausa** (AD 1539) and another **Battle of Kannauj** (AD 1540) culminating into Humayun's defeat.
- Humayun passed 15 years in exile; again invaded India in 1555 with the help of his officer Bairam Khan.
- Died in AD 1556 due to a fall from his library building's stairs; **Gulbadan Begum**, Humayun's half-sister wrote **Humayun-nama**.

Akbar (AD 1556-1605)

- Coronated at the young age of 14 by Bairam Khan; defeated Hemu at the **Second Battle of Panipat** (AD 1556) with the help of Bairam Khan; conquered Malwa (AD 1561) defeating Baz Bahadur followed by Garh-Katanga (ruled by Rani Durgawati), Chittor (AD 1568), Ranthambhor and Kalinjar (AD 1569), Gujarat (AD 1572), Mewar (Battle of Haldighati, AD 1576 Akbar and Rana Pratap), Kashmir (AD 1586), Sindh (AD 1593) and Asirgarh (AD 1603) were also conquered.

- **Buland Darwaza** was constructed at Fatehpur Sikri after victory over Gujarat in AD 1572.
- Married to **Harkha Bai**, daughter of Rajput ruler Bharmal
- **Ralph Fitch** (in AD 1585) was the first Englishman to visit Akbar's court.
- Abolished **Jaziyah** (AD 1564); believed in **Sulh-i-Kul** (peace to all), built Ibadat Khana (Hall of prayer) at Fatehpur Sikri; issued 'Degree of Infallibility (AD 1579); formulated religious order **Din-i-Ilahi** (AD 1582). Birbal was the first to embrace it.
- Land revenue system was called Todar Mal **Bandobast** or **Zabti System** measurement of land, classification of land and fixation of rent; and introduced **Mansabdari System** (holder of rank) to organise nobility and army.
- The Navratnas included Todar Mal, Abul Fazal, Faizi, Birbal, Tansen, Abdur Rahim Khana-i-Khana, Mullah-do-Pyaza, Raja Man Singh and Fakir Aziao-Din

Jahangir (AD 1605-1627)

- Executed the fifth Sikh guru, **Guru Arjan Dev**.
- Greatest failure was loss of Kandahar to Persia in AD 1622.
- Married Mehr-un-Nisa in AD 1611 and conferred the title of **Nurjahan** on her; He established **Zanjir-i-Adal** at Agra Fort for the seekers of royal justice.
- **Captain Hawkins** and **Sir Thomas Roe** visited his court.
- Famous painters in his court-Abdul Hassan, Ustad Mansur and Bishandas.

Shahjahan (AD 1628-1658)

- Annexed Ahmadnagar while **Bijapur** and **Golconda** accepted his overlordship.
- Secured **Kandahar** (AD 1639).
- Two Frenchmen, **Bernier** and **Tavernier** and an Italian adventurer **Manucci** visited his court.
- Built **Moti Masjid** and **Taj Mahal** at Agra, **Jama Masjid** and **Red Fort** at Delhi. His reign is considered the **Golden Age** of the **Mughal architecture**.

Aurangzeb (Alamgir) (AD 1658-1707)

- Aurangzeb became victorious after the brutal war of succession among his brother Dara, Shuja and Murad.
- Rebellions during his rule—**Jat Peasantry** at Mathura, **Satnami peasantry** in Punjab and **Bundelas** in Bundelkhand.
- The annexation of Marwar in AD 1658 led to a serious rift between Rajput and Mughals after the death of Raja Jaswant Singh.
- Ninth Sikh Guru, **Guru Tegh Bahadur** was executed by him in AD 1675.
- Mughal conquests reached territorial climax during his reign.
- It stretched from Kashmir in North to Jinji in South, from the Hindukush in West to Chittagong in East.
- He was called **Darvesh** or a **Zinda Pir**. He forbade **Sati.** Conquered Bijapur (AD 1686) and Golconda (AD 1687) and reimposed Jaziya in AD 1679.
- He built **Biwi ka Makbara** on the tomb of his queen **Rabaud-Durani** at Aurangabad; **Moti Masjid** within Red Fort, Delhi; and the Jami or Badshahi Mosque at Lahore.

Causes behind the fall of Mughal Empire

- Weak and incompetent successors
- Wars of succession
- Aurangzeb's Deccan, religious and Rajput policies
- Jagirdari crisis
- Growth of Marathas and other regional powers
- Foreign invasions of Nadir Shah (1739) and Abdali

Sur Dynasty

- The founder of Sur dynasty was **Farid**.
- Afghan ruler of Bihar, Bahar Khan Lohani gave the title of **Sher Shah** to Farid. Introduced Silver coin called **Rupaya** and Copper coin **Dam.**
- Built his tomb at **Sasaram** and built a new city on the bank of Yamuna river in Delhi (present day **Purana Qila**).

LATER MUGHALS

- **Bahadur Shah I** (1707-12) Original name was Muazzam; Title-Shah Alam I.
- **Jahandar Shah** (1712-13) He ascended the throne with the help of Zulfikar Khan; abolished Jizya.
- **Farrukhsiyar** (1713-19) He lacked the ability and knowledge to rule independently. His reign saw the emergence of the Sayyid Brothers.
- **Muhammad Shah** (1719-48) Nadir Shah invaded India and took away Peacock throne and Kohinoor diamond.
- **Ahmed Shah** (1748-54) Ahmed Shah Abdali (General of Nadir Shah) marched towards Delhi and the Mughals ceded Punjab and Multan.
- **Alamgir** (1754-59) Ahmed Shah occupied Delhi. Later, Delhi was plundered by Marathas.
- **Shah Alam II** (1759-1806) could not enter Delhi for 12 years.
- **Akbar II** (1806-37) pensioner of East India Company. He gave the title 'Raja' to Ram Mohan Roy.
- **Bahadur Shah II** (1837-57) Last Mughal Emperor who was made premier during the 1857 Revolt.

Literature of Mughal Period

Author	*Work*
Babur	Tuzuk-i-Babari
Abul Fazal	Ain-i-Akbari, Akbarnamah
Jahangir	Tuzuk-i-Jahangir
Hamid Lahori	Padshahnama
Darashikoh	Majma-ul-Bahrain
Mirza Md Qasim	Alamgirnama

MARATHAS (AD 1674-1818)

Shivaji (AD 1627-80)

- Born at Shivner to **Shahji Bhonsle** and **Jijabai.** His religious teacher was **Samarth Ramdas** and guardian was **Dadaji Kondadev**.
- **Treaty of Purandar** (AD 1665) between Shivaji and Mughals.
- Coronation at Raigarh (AD 1674) and assumed the title of **Haindava Dharmadharak** (Protector of Hinduism).
- **Ashtapradhan** (eight ministers) helped in administration. These were **Peshwas, Sar-i-Naubat** (Military), **Mazumdar** or Amatya (Accounts); **Waqenavis** (Intelligence); Surunavis (Correspondence); **Dabir or Sumanta** (Ceremonies); **Nyayadhish** (Justice); and **Panditrao** (Charity).
- Successors of Shivaji were Shambhaji, Rajaram and **Shahu** (fought at Battle of Khed in AD 1708).

Peshwas (AD 1719-18)

- **Balaji Vishwanath** was the first Peshwas, who concluded an agreement with the Sayyid Brothers (the king makers in history) by which Mughal emperor Farukh Siyyar recognised Shahu as the king of Swarajya.
- **Baji Rao** considered as the "greatest exponent of guerilla tactics after Shivaji"; Maratha power reached its zenith and system of confederacy began; defeated Siddis of Janjira; Conquest of Bassein and Salsette from Portuguese.
- **Balaji Baji Rao** known as Nana Sahib; **Third Battle of Panipat** (AD 1761) between Marathas and Ahmed Shah Abdali gave a big jolt to the Maratha empire.

SIKH GURUS

- **Guru Nanak Ji** (1469-39) founded Sikh religion.
- **Guru Angad** (1539-52) invented Gurmukhi.
- **Guru Amardas** (1552-74) struggled against sati system, and purdah system and established 22 **Gadiyans** to propagate religion.
- **Guru Ramdas** (1574-81) founded Amritsar in 1577. Akbar granted the land.
- **Guru Arjan Dev** (1581-1606) founded **Swarn Mandir** (Golden Temple) and composed **Adi Granth** later expanded into the Guru Granth Sahib.
- **Guru Hargobind Singh** (1606-44) established **Akal Takht**, and fortified Amritsar.
- **Guru Har Rai** (1644-61) provided care to Dara Shikoh.
- **Guru Harkishan** (1661-64)
- **Guru Tegh Bahadur** (1664-75)
- **Guru Gobind Singh** (1675-1708) was the last Guru who founded the Khalsa. After him Sikh guruship ended.

MODERN INDIA

ADVENT OF THE EUROPEANS

Portuguese

- **Vasco-da-Gama** reached the port of Calicut in 1498 during the reign of king Zamorin. (Hindu ruler of Calicut).
- **Settlements** Daman, Salsette, Chaul and Bombay (West coast), San Thome (near Madras) and at Hooghly.
- **Alfonso de Albuquerque**, the second Governor of India (first being Francisco de Almeida) arrived in 1509 and captured Goa in AD 1510.

Dutch

- Dutch East India Company was formed in AD 1602.
- Dutch were defeated by English at the **Battle of Bedara** in AD 1759 and as per agreement, the Dutch gained the control over Indonesia and the British over India, Sri Lanka and Malaya.
- **Settlements** They set-up their first factory at Masulipatnam in 1605. Their other factories were at Pulicat, Chinsura, Patna, Balasore, Naga pattanam, Cochin, Surat, Karaikal and Kasimbazar.

English

- The English East India Company was formed in 1599 under a charter granted by Queen Elizabeth in 1600. Jahangir granted a farman to **Captain William Hawkins** permitting the English to erect a factory at Surat (1613).
- In 1615, **Sir Thomas Roe** succeeded in getting an imperial farman to trade and establish factory in all parts of the Mughal Empire by ruler Jahangir.
- In 1690, a factory was established at Suttanati by **Job Charnock**. In 1698, following the acquisition of zamindari of three villages of **Suttanati**, **Kalikata** and **Govindpur,** the city of Calcutta was founded. Fort William was set-up in 1700.
- In 1717, John Surman obtained a farman from Farrukhsiyar, which gave large concessions to the company. This farman has been called the Magna Carta of the Company.
- **Battle of Plassey** (1757) English defeated Sirajuddaula, the nawab of Bengal.
- **Battle of Buxar** (1764) Captain Munro defeated joint forces of Mir Qasim (Bengal), Shujauddaula (Awadh) and Shah Alam II (Mughal).

Danes

- **The Danish East India Company** was formed in 1616.
- The Danish colony 'Tranquebar' was established on Southern Coromondel coast of India.
- **Settlements** Serampur (Bengal) and Tranquebar (Tamil Nadu) sold their settlements to the English in 1845.

French

- **The French East India Company** was formed by Colbert under state patronage in 1664. The First **French factory** was established at Surat by Francois Caron in 1668. A factory at Masulipatnam was set-up in 1669.
- French were defeated by English in **Battle of Wandiwash** (1760).

GOVERNOR-GENERALS OF BENGAL

Warren Hastings (AD 1774-85)

- Brought the **dual government** to an end by the **Regulating Act**, 1773.
- The Act of 1781 made clear demarcation between the jurisdiction of the Governor General-in-Council and Supreme Court at Calcutta.
- **Pitt's India Act** (1784), Rohilla War (1774), First Maratha War (1775-1782) and Treaty of Salbai with Marathas (1782) and Second Mysore War (1780-84). Foundation of Asiatic Society of Bengal (1784) in Calcutta by **Sir William Jones**.
- English translations of **Bhagavad Gita** by Charles Wilkins in 1785.

Lord Cornwallis (AD 1786-93)

- **Third Mysore War** (1790-92) and **Treaty of Seringapatnam** (1792).
- Introduced Permanent Settlement in Bengal and Bihar (1793).
- He is called the **Father of Civil Services** in India, introduced judicial reforms by separating revenue administration from judicial administration and established a system of circles (*thanas*, headed by a *Daroga* (an Indian).
- Translation of *Abhigyan Shakuntalam* in English by **William Jones** in 1789.

Sir John Shore (AD 1793-98)

- Played an important role in the introduction of Permanent Settlement.
- **Battle of Kharda** between the Nizams and the Marathas (1795).

Lord Wellesley (AD 1798-1805)

- Introduction of the **Subsidiary Alliance** (1798), first alliance with Nizam of Hyderabad followed by Mysore, Tanjore, Awadh, the Peshwa, the Bhonsle and the Scindia.
- **Treaty of Bassein** (1802) and the Second Maratha War.

George Barlow (1805-07)

- Vellore Mutiny (1806)

Lord Minto I (AD 1807-13)

- Concluded the **Treaty of Amritsar** with Maharaja Ranjit Singh (1809). **Charter Act of 1813** was passed.

Lord Hasting (AD 1813-23)

- **Anglo Nepal War** (1814-1816) and Treaty of Sagauli (1816).
- **Third Maratha War** (1817-18) dissolution of Maratha confederacy and creation of Bombay Presidency.
- Pindari War and establishment of **Ryotwari System** by Thomas Munro (1820).

Lord Amherst (AD 1823-28)

- **First Burmese War** (1824-26), **Treaty of Yandaboo** (1826) and capture of Bharatpur (1826).

GOVERNOR-GENERALS OF INDIA

Lord William Bentinck (AD 1828-35)

- **Charter Act of 1833** was passed and he was made the **first Governor General of India**. Before him, the designation given was **Governor General of Bengal**.
- Carried out social reforms like prohibition of sati (1829) and elimination of thugs (1830). On Macaulay's recommedations, English was made the medium of higher education. Suppressed female infanticide and child sacrifice.

Lord Metcalfe (AD 1835-36)

Known as **liberator of the press** in India.

Lord Auckland (AD 1836-42)

First Afghan War (1838-42), a disaster for the English.

Lord Ellenborough (AD 1842-44)

Brought an end to the Afghan war. War with Gwalior (1843), **Annexation of Sind** by Charles Napier (1843).

Lord Hardinge (AD 1844-48)

First Anglo-Sikh War (1845-46) and Treaty of Lahore (1846). Gave preference to English educated persons in employment.

Lord Dalhousie (AD 1848-56)

- Introduction of **Doctrine of Lapse** and annexation of Satara (1848), Jaitpur and Sambhalpur (1849), Baghat (1850), Udaipur (1852), Jhansi (1853), Nagpur (1854) and Awadh (annexed in 1856 on account of maladministration).
- Laid down the **first railway line** between Bombay and Thane (1853), Telegraph line between Calcutta and Agra and **Postal** reforms (first issue of the Indian stamp in Karachi in 1854) with the Post Office Act.
- **Widow Remarriage Act**, 1856 (the main force being Ishwar Chand Vidyasagar).
- Started **Public Works Department**, Grand Trunk Road work and harbour of Karachi, Bombay and Calcutta developed.
- Charter Act, 1853-Selection to Civil Service through competitive examination.
- Started Engineering College at Roorkee; made Shimla, the summer capital of India.

VICEROYS OF INDIA

Lord Canning (AD 1856-62)

- The **last Governor General** and the **first Viceroy**. Withdrew Doctrine of Lapse.
- Revolt of 1857, Mutiny took place. Indian Penal Code 1860 was passed.
- Passed the Act, 1858, which ended the rule of the East India Company. The Universities of Calcutta, Bombay and Madras were established in 1857.

Lord Elgin (AD 1862)

- Wahabi Movement

Lord John Lawrence (AD 1864-69)

- Established the **High Courts** at Calcutta, Bombay and Madras in 1865.
- Telegraphic communication was opened with Europe. Created the Indian Forest Department.

Lord Mayo (AD 1869-72)

- Organised the Statistical Survey of India and for the **first time** in Indian history, a **census** was held in 1871.
- Started the process of financial decentralisation in India. Established the Department of Agriculture and Commerce.
- Established the Rajkot College at Kathiawar and Mayo College at Ajmer for the Indian princes.
- He was the only viceroy to be murdered in office by a Pathan convict in the Andamans in 1872.

Lord Northbrooke (AD 1872-76)

Kuka Rebellion in Punjab, Famine in Bihar.

Lord Lytton (AD 1876-80)

- Known as the *'Viceroy of Reverse Character'*.
- **Royal Titles Act of 1876** and the assumption of the title of 'Empress of India' by Queen Victoria, the Delhi Durbar in January 1877.
- **Vernacular Press Act** (also called the 'Gagging Act' to restrain the circulation of printed matter) and the **Arms Act** (made it mandatory for Indians to acquire license in arms) of 1878.

Lord Ripon (AD 1880-84)

- **First Factory Act** of 1881 prohibited Child Labour under the age of 7. **Local Self-Government** was introduced in 1882.
- Repealed the **Vernacular Press Act** in 1882. Finances of the centre were divided.
- Lord Ripon is regarded as '**the founding father of local self governance**' in India.
- An Education Commission was appointed under **Sir William Hunter** in 1882 to improve primary and secondary education.
- The **Ilbert Bill Controvers**y (1883) enabled Indian district magistrates to try European criminals.

Lord Dufferin (AD 1884-88)

Third Burmese War (AD 1885-86). Establishment of the **Indian National Congress** in 1885.

Lord Lansdowne (AD 1888-94)

- **Factory Act of 1891** granted weekly holiday and stipulated working hours for women and children.
- Civil services were divided into Imperial, Provincial and Subordinate Services.
- **Indian Councils Act** of 1892.
- The **Durand Commission** defined the Durand Line between British India and Afghanistan (now between Pakistan and Afghanistan) in 1893.

Lord Elgin II (AD 1894-99)

- Southern uprisings of 1899. **Great famine** of 1896-1897 and **Lyall Commission** on famine was established.

Lord Curzon (AD 1899-1905)

- A Commission was appointed under **Sir Thomas Raleigh** in 1902 to suggest reforms regarding universities, the **Indian Universities Act of 1904** was passed on the basis of its recommendations.
- **Ancient Monuments Preservation Act** of 1904. Thus, Archaeological Survey of India was established.
- **Agricultural Research Institute** was established at Pusa in Delhi. Partitioned Bengal in 1905.

Lord Minto (AD 1905-10)

Swadeshi Movement (1905-08); foundation of Muslim League (1906); Surat Session and split in the Congress (1907). Morley-Minto Reforms (1909).

Lord Hardinge (AD 1910-16)

Capital shifted from Calcutta to Delhi (1911); Delhi Durbar; Partition of Bengal was cancelled. The **Hindu Mahasabha** was founded in 1915 by Pandit Madan Mohan Malaviya.

Lord Chelmsford (AD 1916-21)

- Gandhi returned to India (1915) and founded the **Sabarmati Ashram** (1916), Champaran Satyagraha (1917), Satyagraha at Ahmedabad (1918), Kheda Satyagraha (1918).
- **August Declaration** (1917) by Montague, the then Secretary of State, and Montford reforms or the Government of India Act of 1919.
- **Rowlatt Act** (March, 1919) and the **Jallianwala Bagh Massacre** (13th April, 1919).
- **Khilafat Committee** was formed and Khilafat Movement started (1919-20).
- **Non-Cooperation Movement** started (1920-22). Women's University was founded at Poona (1916).

Lord Reading (AD 1921-26)

- Repeal of Rowlatt Act. Chauri-Chaura incident. RSS founded in 1925. Suppressed Non-Cooperation Movement. Formation of Swaraj Party.
- Moplah Rebellion (1921) took place. **Kakori Train** Robbery on 1st August, 1925. **Communal Riots** of 1923-25 in Multan, Amritsar, Delhi etc.

Lord Irwin (AD 1926-31)

- **Simon Commission** visited India in 1927. Congress passed the Indian Resolution in 1929.
- Dandi March (12th March, 1930). Civil Disobedience Movement (1930).
- **First Round Table Conference** was held in England in 1930. Gandhi-Irwin Pact.
- Lahore Session of Congress and **Poorna Swaraj Declaration** (1925).

Lord Willingdon (AD 1931-36)

- **Second Round Table Conference** in London in 1931 and **third** in 1932.
- **Government of India Act** (1935) was passed. Communal Awards (16th August, 1932) assigned separate electorate for Gandhiji went on a **epic fast** to protest against this division.

Lord Linlithgow (AD 1936-43)

- Congress Ministries resignation celebrated as **'Deliverance Day'** by the Muslim League (1939), the **Lahore Resolution** (23rd March, 1940) of the Muslim League demanding separate state for the Muslims. (It was at this session that Jinnah propounded his **Two-Nation Theory**). Outbreak of World War II in 1939. **Cripps Mission** in 1942. **Quit India Movement** (8th August, 1942).

Lord Wavell (AD 1943-47)

- **Cabinet Mission Plan** (16th May, 1946).
- First meeting of the Constituent Assembly was held on 9th December, 1946.
- Arranged the **Shimla Conference** on 25th June, 1945 with the failure of talks between the Indian National Congress and Muslim League.
- Election to the Constituent Assembly were held and an interim government was appointed under Nehru.

Lord Mountbatten (March to August, 1947)

- **Last Viceroy** of **British India** and the **first Governor-General** of **free India**.
- Partition of India decided by the 3rd June Plan or **Mountbatten Plan**.
- Retired in June, 1948 and was succeeded by **C Rajagopalachari**, the first and the last Indian Governor-General of Free India.
- **Indian Independence Act** was passed by the British Parliament on 4th July, 1947, by which India became independent on 15th August, 1947.

THE REVOLT OF 1857

- Started at Meerut on 10th May, 1857.
- **Political Causes** The policy of Doctrine of Lapse.
- **Economic Causes** Heavy taxation, evictions, Discriminatory Tariff Policy against Indian products and destruction of traditional handicrafts that hit peasants, artisans and small zamindars.
- **Military Discrimination** as Indian soldiers were paid low salaries, they could not rise above the rank of subedar and were racially insulted.
- **Grievances of Sepoys** The introduction of Enfield rifle, and its cartridge of which was greased with animal fat, provided the spark.
- A rebellion broke out among Sepoys of Meerut on 10th May, 1857 which later spread to other parts of the country.
- British social reforms (widow remarriage, abolition of sati, education for girls, Christian missionaries).

Centres of Revolt and the Leaders

Centre of Revolt	*Leader*	*British Suppressor*
Delhi	Bahadur Shah II, Bakht Khan	John Nicholson, Hudson
Banaras	Liaquat Ali	James Neill
Kanpur	Nana Saheb, Tantia Tope, Azimullah Khan	Campbell, Havelock
Lucknow	Hazrat Mahal (Begum of Awadh)	Havelock, James Neill, Campbell
Jhansi	Rani Laxmi Bai	Sir Hugh Rose
Bareilly	Khan Bahadur Khan	Sir Colin Campbell
Awadh (Bihar)	Veer Kunwar Singh	William Taylor and Vincent Eyer

Causes of Failure

- The Nizam of Hyderabad, the Raja of Jodhpur, Scindia of Gwalior, the Holkar of Indore, the rulers of Patiala, Sindh and Kashmir and the Rana of Nepal provided active support to the British.
- Comparative lack of efficient leadership.

Impact of the Revolt

- The control of Indian administration was passed on to the **British Crown** by the Government of India Act, 1858.
- Reorganisation of the army.
- After the revolt, the British pursued the Policy of **Divide and Rule.**

CHIEF NATIONAL ACTIVITIES

The Indian National Congress

- It was formed in 1885 by **AO Hume** a retired Civil Servant.
- The first session was held in Bombay under Presidentship of WC Bannerjee in 1885, attended by 72 delegates from all over India.
- The first two decades of INC are described in history as those of moderate demands and a sense of confidence in British justice and generosity.
- **Moderate leaders** Dada Bhai Naoroji, Badruddin Tayabji, Gopal Krishna Gokhale, Surendranath Bannerjee and Anand Mohan Bose.

Partition of Bengal (1905)

- The partition was announced by **Lord Curzon** on 16th October, 1905 through a royal proclamation, reducing the old province of Bengal in size by creating East Bengal and Assam out of the rest of Bengal.

Swadeshi Movement (1905)

This movement had its origin in the anti-partition movement of Bengal. Lal, Bal, Pal and Aurobindo Ghosh played an important role. INC took the Swadeshi call first at the Banaras Session, 1905 presided over by GK Gokhale.

Muslim League (1906)

- It was set-up in 1906 by Aga Khan, Nawab Salimullah of Dhaka and Nawab Mohsin-ul- Mulk.
- The league supported the **Partition of Bengal** and opposed the **Swadeshi Movement**, demanded special safeguards to its community and a separate electorate for Muslims.

- This led to communal differences between the Hindus and the Muslims.

Demand for Swaraj
(Calcutta Session in Dec, 1906)

- The INC, under the leadership of Dadabhai Naoroji, adopted *'Swaraj'* (Self-government) as the goal of Indian People.

Surat Session (1907)

- The INC split into two groups: the **Extremists** and the **Moderates**, due to the debate on nature of **Swadeshi Movement**.
- Extremists were led by Lal, Bal, Pal while the Moderates by GK Gokhale.

Morley-Minto Reforms (1909)

- The reforms envisaged a separate electorate for Muslims, besides other constitutional measures.
- Lord Minto came to be known as the Father of Communal Electorate.

Ghadar Party (1913)

- Formed by Lala Hardayal, Taraknath Das and Sohan Singh Bhakna. Headquarter—San Francisco.
- The name was taken from a weekly paper, **Ghadar**, which had been started on 1st November, 1913 to commemorate the 1857 Revolt.

Home Rule Movement (1916)

- Started by BG Tilak (April, 1916) at Poona and Annie Besant and S Subramania Iyer at Adyar, near Madras (September, 1916).
- **Objective** Self-government for India in the British Empire.
- During this movement, Tilak raised the slogan **Swaraj is my Birth Right and I shall have it**.

Lucknow Pact (1916)

Pact between INC and Muslim League following a war between Britain and Turkey leading to anti-British feelings among Muslims. Both organisations jointly demand dominion status for the country congress accepted separate electorate for Muslims.

August Declaration (1917)

- After the Lucknow Pact, the British policy was announced which aimed at "increasing association of Indians in every branch of the administration for progressive realisation of responsible government in India as an integral part of the British empire". This came to be called the August Declaration.
- **The Montague—Chelmsford reforms or the Act of 1919** was based on this declaration.

Rowlatt Act (18th March, 1919)

- This gave unbridled powers to the government to arrest and imprison suspects without trail. This law enabled the government to suspend the right of **Habeas Corpus**, which had been the foundation of civil liberties in Britain.
- **Rowlatt Satyagraha** was started against the act. This was the first countrywide agitation by Gandhiji.

Jallianwala Bagh Massacre
(13th April, 1919)

- People were agitated over the arrest of **Dr Saifuddin Kitchlew** and **Dr Satya Pal** on 10th April, 1919.
- **General Dyer** fired at people who assembled in the Jallianwala Bagh, Amritsar. Michael O' Dwyer was Lt. Governor of Punjab that time. The Hunter Commission was appointed to enquire into it.
- Rabindra Nath Tagore returned his knighthood in protest.
- Sardar **Udham Singh** killed Michael O' Dwyer in Caxton Hall, London on March 13, 1940.

Khilafat Movement (1920)

- Muslims were agitated by the treatment done with Turkey by the British in the treaty that followed the **First World War**.
- Ali brothers, **Mohd Ali** and **Shaukat Ali** started this movement. It was jointly led by the Khilafat leaders and the Congress.

Non-Cooperation Movement (1920)

- Congress passed the resolution in its Calcutta Session in September, 1920.
- It was the first mass-based political movement under Gandhiji.
- The movement envisaged resignation from nominated offices and posts in the local bodies.

- Refusal to attend government *durbars* and boycott of British courts by the lawyers.
- Refusal of general public to offer themselves for military and other government jobs and boycott of foreign goods.

Chauri-Chaura Incident (1922)

- The Congress Session at Allahabad in December 1921, decided to launch a **Civil Disobedience Programme**. Gandhiji was appointed its leader.
- But before it could be launched, a mob of people at Chauri-Chaura (near Gorakhpur) clashed with the police and burnt 22 policemen on 5th February, 1922. This compelled Gandhiji to withdraw the Non-Cooperation Movement on 12th February, 1922.

Swaraj Party (1923)

- Motilal Nehru, CR Das and NC Kelkar (called Pro-changers) demanded that the nationalist should end the boycott of the Legislative Councils, enter them and expose them.
- They formed Swaraj Party for this purpose with CR Das as the President.

Simon Commission (1927)

- It was constituted by John Simon, to review the political situation in India and to introduce further reforms and extension of parliamentary democracy.
- Indian leaders opposed the commission, as there were no Indians in it, they shouted **Simon Go Back**.
- The government used brutal repression and at Lahore, **Lala Lajpat Rai** was severely beaten in lathi- charge and later succumbed to death.

The Nehru Report (1928)

- After boycotting the Simon Commission, all political parties constituted a committee under the chairmanship of **Motilal Nehru** to evolve and determine the principles for the Constitution of India.

Lahore Session (1929)

- On 19th December, 1929, under the presidentship of **JL Nehru**, the INC, at its Lahore Session, declared **Poorna Swaraj** (complete independence) as its ultimate goal .
- The tri-coloured flag adopted on 31st December, 1929, was unfurled and 26th January, 1930 was fixed as the **First Independence Day**, to be celebrated every year. Later, this day was chosen as the **Republic Day of India**.

Dandi March (1930)

- Also called the **Salt Satyagraha**.
- Gandhiji started his march from Sabarmati Ashram on 12th March, 1930 for the small village Dandi to break the Salt Law.
- He picked a handful of salt and inaugurated the **Civil Disobedience Movement**.

Civil Disobedience Movement

- Countrywide mass participation by women.
- The Garhwal soldiers refused to fire on the people at Peshawar.

First Round Table Conference (1931)

- It was the first conference arranged between the British and Indians as equals. It was held on 12th November, 1930 in London to discuss Simon Commission.
- Hindu Mahasabha and Muslim League participated in it. The conference failed due to absence of the Indian National Congress.

Gandhi Irwin Pact (1931)

- The government represented by Lord Irwin, and INC led by Gandhiji signed a pact on 5th March, 1931.
- In this, the INC called off the Civil Disobedience Movement and agreed to join the Second Round Table Conference.

- The government allowed the villagers on the coast to make salt for consumption and released the political prisoners. The **Karachi Session of 1931** of Congress endorsed the Gandhi Irwin Pact.

Second Round Table Conference (1931)

- Gandhiji represented the INC and went to London to meet British Prime Minister Ramsay McDonald.
- The conference however failed as Gandhiji could not agree with British Prime Minister on his policy of Communal Representation and refusal of the British Government on the basic Indian demand for freedom.

The Communal Award (16th August, 1932)

- Announced by **Ramsay McDonald**. It showed **divide** and **rule policy of the British**.
- It envisaged communal representation of depressed classes, Sikhs and Muslims.
- Gandhiji opposed it, and started fast unto death in Yervada jail Pune (Maharashtra).

Poona Pact/ Gandhi- Ambedkar Pact (25th September, 1932)

- The idea of separate electorate for the depressed classes was abandoned, but seats reserved for them in the Provincial Legislature were increased.
- Thus, Poona Pact agreed upon a joint electorate for upper and lower castes.

Third Round Table Conference (1932)

- Proved fruitless as most of the national leaders were in prison.

Demand for Pakistan

- In 1930, **Iqbal** suggested that the North-West provinces and Kashmir should be made Muslim states within the federation.
- **Chaudhary Rehmat Ali** gave the term **Pakistan** in 1933.
- Muslim League first passed the proposal of separate Pakistan in its Lahore Session in 1940 (called **Jinnah's Two-Nation Theory**). It was drafted by **Sikandar Hayat Khan**, moved by Fazlul Haq and seconded by Khaliquzzamah.
- In December 1943, the Karachi Session of the Muslim League adopted the slogan **Divide and Quit**.

August Offer (8th August, 1940)

- It offered (i) Dominion status in the unspecified future, (ii) A post-war body to enact the Constitution (iii) To expand the Governor-General's Executive Council to give full weightage to minority opinion.
- This was rejected by the INC, but was accepted by the Muslim League.

The Cripps Mission (1942)

- The British Government with a view to get cooperation from Indians in the Second World War, sent **Sir Stafford Cripps** to settle terms with Indian leaders.
- He offered dominion status to be granted after war.
- Congress rejected it. Gandhiji termed it as '*a post - dated cheque on a crashing bank*'.

The Revolt of 1942 and the Quit India Movement

- Also called the **Wardha Proposal,** a Leaderless Revolt.
- The resolution was passed on 8th August, 1942, at Bombay. Gandhiji gave the slogan **Do or Die**.
- On 9th August, the Congress was banned and its important leaders were arrested. Gandhiji was kept at the **Aga Khan Palace**, Pune.
- The people became violent. The movement was, however, crushed by the government.

Indian National Army (INA)

- **Subhash Chandra Bose** escaped to Berlin in 1941 and set-up the Indian League there. In July 1943, he joined the INA at Singapore. Ras Bihari Bose handed over the leadership to him.
- INA had three fighting brigades, named after Gandhi, Azad and Nehru. **Rani of Jhansi Brigade** was an exclusive women force. INA had its headquarters at Rangoon and Singapore.

The Cabinet Mission Plan (1946)

- Members were Pethick Lawrence, Stafford Cripps and AV Alexander. Lord Wavell was the Viceroy of India that time.
- *Main proposals*
    1. Rejection of demand for a full-fledged Pakistan.
    2. Loose union under a Centre with Centre's control over defence and foreign affairs.
    3. Provinces were to have full autonomy and residual powers.
    4. Provincial legislatures would elect a Constituent Assembly.

The Muslim League accepted it on 6th June, 1946. The Congress also partially accepted this plan.

Formation of Interim Government (2nd September, 1946)

- It came into existence on 2nd September, 1946 in accordance with Cabinet Mission's proposals and was headed by **JL Nehru.** Muslim League refused to join it initially.
- **Prime Minister Attlee** on 20th February, 1947 announced that British would withdraw from India by 30th June, 1948.

Formation of Constituent Assembly (December, 1946)

- The Constituent Assembly met on 9th December, 1946 and Dr Rajendra Prasad was elected as its President.

Jinnah's Direct Action Resolution (16th August, 1946)

- Provoked by the success of the Congress in the voting for Constituent Assembly Jinnah withdrew his acceptance to the Cabinet Mission Plan.
- Muslim League passed a Direct Action Resolution, which condemned both the British Government and the Congress (16th August, 1946). It resulted in heavy communal riots.
- Jinnah celeberated **Pakistan Day** on 27th March, 1947.

Mountbatten Plan (also called 3rd June Plans) (3rd June, 1947)

The plan formulated by Lord Mountbatten outlined that

- India was to be further divided into India and Pakistan.
- There would be a separate Consitutional Assembly for Pakistan to frame its Constitution.
- The princely states would enjoy the liberty to either join India or Pakistan, or could even remain independent.
- Bengal and Punjab will be partitioned and a referendum in NWFP and Sylhet district of Assam would be held. A separate state of Pakistan would be created. **Boundary Commission** was to be headed by Radcliffe.

Partition and Independence (August, 1947)

- **Indian Independence Act**, 1947 implemented on 15th August 1947, abolished the sovereignty of British Parliament. Dominions of **India** and **Pakistan** were created. Each dominion was to have a Governor-General. Pakistan was to comprise Sind, British Baluchistan, NWFP, West Punjab and East Bengal.
- **Sardar Vallabhbhai Patel**, the first Home Minister, integrated all the states by 15th August, 1947. Kashmir, Hyderabad, Junagarh, Goa (with Portuguese) and Pondicherry (with French) later acceded to Indian Federation.

Socio-Religious Reform Movements

Religious Institution	*Founder*	*Ideas*
Brahmo Samaj was founded in Calcutta (1828)	*Raja Ram Mohan Roy Author of Gift to Monotheists and Percepts of Jesus and the Journals Sambad Kaumudi and Mirat-ul Akbar*	Propagated monotheism, opposed sacrifices, idolatory, superstition and sati.
Young Bengal Movement (1826-31)	*Henry Louis Vivian Derozio, probably the first modern nationalist poet brought out journal 'Jananresan'*	Opposed the vices in society and believed in truth, freedom and right.
Tattavabodhini Sabha (1839)	*Debendranath Tagore brought out the journal Tattavabodhini Patrika*	Propagated Brahmo Samaj idea, eventually founding Adi Brahmo Samaj (1866).
Dharma Sabha (1820), Rohilkhand	*Radhakant Deb*	Emerged to counter Brahmo Samaj and propagated orthodoxy.
Wahabi Movement (1820), Rohilakhand	*Syed Ahmed of Rai Bareilly*	Popularised the teachings of Waliullah, stressed the role of individual conscience in religion.
Namdhari or Kuka Movement (1841-71)	*Bhai Balak Singh and Baba Ram Singh*	For political and social reforms among Sikhs.
Paramhans Mandali (1849)	*Dadoba Pandurang*	Emphasised the unity of God, against caste rules.
Rahnumai Mazdayasanan Sabha (1851)	*SS Bengali, Dadabhai Naoroji and others*	To improve the social condition of Parsis and restore the purity of Zorastrianism. Their journal was Rast Gotar.
Prarthana Samaj (1867), Bombay	*Atmaram Pandurang*	Monotheism, upliftment of women, abolition of caste discrimination.
Indian Reform Association (1870), Calcutta	*Keshab Chandra Sen*	Opposed child marriage, advocated widow remarriage and inter-caste marriages.
Arya Samaj (1875), Bombay	*Dayanand Saraswati (original name Mulshankar)*	Gave the slogan **Go Back to the Vedas** and within a revivalist framework denounced rites, idolatory, Brahmins's supremacy etc.
Aligarh Movement (1875) grew into Mohammedan Anglo-Oriental College (1875) and later Aligarh Muslim University	*Syed Ahmed Khan, his journal Tahzib-al-Akhlaq*	Religious reform through emphasis on principle of equality in religion, favoured scientific and national outlook.
The Theosophical Society (1875), New York (later shifted to Adyar)	*Madam HP Blavatsky and Col HS Olcott*	Drew inspiration from Upanishads, philosophy of the *Vedanta* and transmigration of the souls.
Deccan Education Society (1884), Pune	*MG Ranade, VG Chiplinkar and GG Agarkar*	To contribute to education and culture in Western India established **Fergusson College**, Pune (1885).
Seva Sadan (1885), Bombay	*Behramji M Malabari*	Against child marriages, and forced widowhood.
Deva Samaj (1887), Lahore	*Shiv Narain Agnihotri*	Favoured a code of conduct against bribe- taking, gambling, etc.
Madras Hindu Association (1892)	*Veresalingam Pantulu*	Social Purity Movement and against Devadasi system.
Ramkrishna Mission (1897), Belur	*Vivekananda (original name Narendranath Dutta)*	Revive Hinduism, against caste restrictions, superstition in Hinduism and overhaul of education system.

Religious Institution	*Founder*	*Ideas*
Servants of Indian Society (1905), Bombay	*Gopal Krishna Gokhale*	Famine relief and improving tribal conditions, in particular.
Bharat Stri Mahamandal (1910), Calcutta	*Sarlabai Devi Chaudhrani*	Women's education and emancipation.
Social Service League (1911)	*NM Joshi*	Improving the condition of the masses.
Women's Indian Association (1917), Madras	*Annie Besant*	Upliftment of Indian women.

Popular Names of Personalities

Popular Name	*Personality*	*Popular Name*	*Personality*
Andhra Kesari	T Prakasam	JP	Jayaprakash Narayan
Babuji	Jagjiwan Ram	Lady with the Lamp	Florence Nightingale
Bapu	Mahatma Gandhi	Lion of the Punjab	Lala Lajpat Rai
CR	C Rajagopalachari	Little Corporal	Napoleon
Desh Bandhu	Chitranjan Das	Lokmanya	Bal Gangadhar Tilak
Grand Old man	Dadabhai Naoroji	Jawan	Indian soldier
Lal, Bal, Pal	Lala Lajpat Rai, Bal Gangadhar Tilak, Bipin Chandra Pal	Mahamanya	Pandit Madan Mohan Malaviya
		Man of Blood	Bismarck
Guru ji	MS Golvalkar	Netaji	Subhash Chandra Bose
Gurudev	Rabindranath Tagore	Nightingale of India	Sarojini Naidu
Iron Man	Vallabhbhai Patel	Pandit ji	Jawaharlal Nehru
Sparrow	Major Rajender Singh	Shastri ji	Lal Bahadur Shastri

Crematoriums of Famous Persons

Crematorium	*Famous Person(s)*	*Crematorium*	*Famous Person (s)*
Raj Ghat	Mahatma Gandhi	Shanti Van	Jawaharlal Nehru
Vijay Ghat	Lal Bahadur Shastri	Shakti Sthal	Indira Gandhi
Kisan Ghat	Ch Charan Singh	Abhay Ghat	Morarji Desai
Veer Bhumi	Rajiv Gandhi	Samata Sthal	Jagjivan Ram
Ekta Sthal	Giani Zail Singh, Chandra Shekhar	Karma Bhumi	Dr Shankar Dayal Sharma
Uday Bhoomi	KR Narayana	Mahaprayan Ghat	Dr Rajendra Prasad

Newspapers and Journals

Name	*Published by*
Bengal Gazette	JA Hickey
Kesari	BG Tilak
Maratha	BG Tilak
Amrita Bazar Patrika	Sisir Kumar Ghosh and Motilal Ghosh
Vande Mataram	Aurobindo Ghosh
Yugantar	Bhupendranath Dutta and Barinder Kumar Ghosh
Bombay Chronicle	Firoz Shah Mehta

Books and Authors

Book	*Author*
Ghulam Giri	Jyotiba Phule
Pather Panchali	B.Bhushan Bannerji
Satyarth Prakash	Swami Dayanand
Anand Math	Bankim Chandra Chatterji
Unhappy India	Lala Lajpat Rai
India Divided	Rajendra Prasad
The Discovery of India	Jawaharlal Nehru

ART AND CULTURE

Classical Dancers of India

Dance	*Dancer*
Bharatanatyam	Bala Saraswati, CV Chandrasekhar, Leela Samson, Mrinalini Sarabhai, Padma Subramanyam, Rukmini Devi, Sanyukta Panigrahi, Sonal Mansingh, Yamini Krishnamurti
Kathak	Bharti Gupta, Birju Maharaj, Damayanti Joshi, Durga Das, Gopi Krishna, Kumudini Lakhia, Sambhu Maharaj, Sitara Devi
Kuchipudi	Josyula Seetharamaiah, Vempathi Chinna Sathyam
Manipuri	Guru Bipin Sinha, Jhaveri Sisters, Nayana Jhaveri, Nirmala Mehta, Savita Mehta
Odissi	Debaprasad Das, Dhirendra Nath Patnaik, Indrani Rahman, Kelucharan Mahapatra, Priyambada Mohanty
Kathakali	Mrinalini Sarabhai, Guru Shankaran, Namboodripad, Thottam Shankaran, Kutti Nayyar, Shankar Kurup, KC Pannikar, TT Ram Kulti
Mohiniattam	Protima Devi, Sanyukta Panigrahi, Sonal Mansingh, Pankaj Charan Das, Kelucharan Mahapatra, Madhvi Mudgal, etc

State and Folk Dances

Andhra Pradesh	Kuchipudi, Ghantamardala, Ottam Thedal, Veedhi Natakam
Assam	Bihu, Bichhua, Natpuja, Maharas, Kaligopal, Bagurumba, Khel Gopal, Canoe, Jhumura Hobjanai
Bihar	Jata-Jatin, Bakho-Bakhain, Panwariya, Sama-Chakwa, Bidesia
Gujarat	Garba, Dandiya Ras, Tippani Juriun, Bhavai
Haryana	Jhumar, Phag, Daph, Dhamal, Loor, Gugga, Khor, Gagor
Himachal Pradesh	Jhora, Jhali, Chharhi, Dhaman, Chhapeli, Mahasu, Nati, Dangi
Jammu and Kashmir	Rauf, Hikat, Mandjas, Kud Dandi Nach, Damali
Karnataka	Yakshagan, Huttari, Suggi, Kunitha, Karga, Lambi
Kerala	Kathakali (Classical), Ottam Thulal, Mohiniattam, Kaikottikali
Maharashtra	Lavani, Nakata, Koli, Lezim, Gafa, Dahikala Dasavtar or Powada
Odisha	Odissi (Classical), Savari, Ghumara, Painka, Munari, Chhau
Paschim Banga	Kathi, Gambhira, Dhali, Jatra, Baul, Marasia, Mahal, Keertan
Punjab	Bhangra, Giddha, Daff, Dhaman, Bhand, Naqual
Rajasthan	Ghumar, Chakri, Ganagor, Jhulan Leela, Jhuma, Suisini, Ghapal, Kalbeliya
Tamil Nadu	Bharatanatyam, Kumi, Kolattam, Kavadi
Uttar Pradesh	Nautanki, Raslila, Kajri, Jhora, Chappeli, Jaita
Uttarakhand	Garhwali, Kumayuni, Kajari, Jhora, Raslila, Chappeli

Instruments and Vocalists

Carnatic	MS Subbalakshmi, Balamuralikrishna, Bombay Jaishri, HK Raghavendra, Aryakudi Ramanujan Iyenegar Venkataram, Sitarajam, Mani Krishnaswamy, Akhil Krishnan, ML Vasanthakumari, MD Ramanathan, GN Balasubramaniam
Dhrupad	Ustad Rahim Fahim-ud-din Dagar, Zahir-ud-din Dagar, Wasif-ud-din Dagar, Bundecha Bandhu, Pt Abhay Narayan Mallick, Pt Ritwik Sanyal, Uday Bhawalkar
Hindustani	Shubha Mudgal, Madhup Mudgal, Mukul Shivputra, Pandit Jasraj, Parveen Sultana, Naina Devi, Girija Devi, Ustad Ghulam Mustafa Khan, Gangubai Hangal, Krishna Hangal, V Rajput, Kumar Gandharva, Faiyyaz Khan, Mallikariun Mansur.
Thumri	Ustad Bade Ghulam Ali Khan, Ustad Mazhar Ali Khan, Ustad Zawad Ali Khan, Poornima Chaudhary, Shanti Heerananda, Naina Devi, Rita Ganguly

Musical Instruments and Instrumentalists

Instruments	*Instrumentalists*
Stringed Instruments	
1. Been	Asad Ali Khan, Zia Moin-ud-din Khan
2. Santoor	Shiv Kumar Sharma
3. Sarod	Buddhadev Dasgupta, Ali Akbar Khan, Amjad Ali khan, Bahadur Khan, Sharan Rani, Zarin S Sharma
4. Sarangi	Ustad Binda Khan
5. Sitar	Ravi Shankar, Hara Shankar Bhattacharya, Nikhil Banerjee, Vilayat Khan, Mustaq Ali Khan
6. Surb Ahar	Sajjad Hussain, Annapurna
7. Veena	Doraiswamy Iyengar, Chittibabu, Emani Sankara Shastri, Dhanammal, S Bala Chandran, KR Kumaraswamy
8. Violin	Gajanan Rao Joshi, MS Gopal Krishnan, TN Krishnan, Baluswamy, Dikshitar, Dwaran Venkataswamy Naidu Lalyuli G Jayaraman, Mysore T Chowdiah, VG Jog
Wind Instruments	
9. Flute	TR Mahalingam, N Ramani, Hari Prasad Chaurasia, Pannalal Ghosh
10. Nadaswaran	Sheikh Chinna Moula, Neeruswamy Pillai, Rajaratanam Pillai
11. Shehnai	Bismillah Khan
Percussion (Striking Thumping) **Instruments**	
12. Mridangam	Palghat Mani Iyer, Karaikudi R Mani, Palghat Raghu
13. Pakhawag	Pt Ayodhya Prasad, Gopal Das, Babu Ram Shanker Pagaldas
14. Tabla	Zakir Hussain, Nikhil Ghosh, Kishan Maharaj, Alla Rakha Khan, Pandit Samta Prasad, Kumar Bose, Latif Khan
15. Kanjira	Pudukkotai Dakshinamurthi Pillai

Cultural Institutions

Institutions	*Headquarters*
Anthropological Survey of India, 1945	Kolkata
Archaeological Survey of India, 1861	New Delhi
Asiatic Society, 1784 (Sir William Jones)	Kolkata
Indira Gandhi National Centre for Arts, 1985	New Delhi
Lalit Kala Akademi (National Academy of Fine Arts), 1954	New Delhi
National Archives of India, 1981	New Delhi
National School of Drama, 1959	New Delhi

Institutions	*Headquarters*
Sahitya Academy, 1954	New Delhi
Sangeet Natak Academy, 1953	New Delhi
Library of Tibetan Works and Archives	Dharmashala
Science City	Kolkata
Victorial Memorial Hall	Kolkata
Birla Industrial and Tech Museum	Kolkata
Central Institute of Buddhist Studies	Leh
Nava Nalanda Mahavihara	Nalanda (Birla)
National Gallery of Modern Art	New Delhi

GEOGRAPHY

WORLD GEOGPRAHY

UNIVERSE

- The study of universe is known as **Cosmology**. The universe is commonly defined as the totality of everything that exists including all physical matter and energy, the planets, stars, galaxies and the contents of intergalactic space.
- **Galaxy** A galaxy is a vast system of billions of stars, dust and light gases bound by their own gravity. There are 100 billion galaxies in the universe and each galaxy has, on average, 100 billion stars.
- Our galaxy is **Milky Way Galaxy** (or the **Akash Ganga**) formed after the Big Bang.
- **Andromeda** is the nearest galaxy to the Milky Way.
- **The Big Bang Theory** Big Bang was an explosion of concentrated matter in the universe that occurred 15 billion years ago, leading to the formation of galaxies of stars and other heavenly bodies.
- It is believed that universe should be filled with radiation called the "cosmic microwave background." NASA has launched two mission to study these radiation, i.e. the Cosmic Background Explorer (COBE) and the Wilkinson Microwave Anistropy Probe (WMAP).
- **Stars** are heavenly bodies made up of hot burning gases and they shine by emitting their own light.
- **Black Hole** Stars having mass greater than three times that of the Sun, have very high gravitational power, so that even light can not escape from its gravity and hence called black hole.
- **Comets** Made up of frozen gases. They move around the Sun in elongated elliptical orbit with the tail always pointing away from the Sun.
- **Constellations** The sky is divided into units to enable the astronomers to identify the position of the stars. These units are called constellations. There are 88 known constellations.
- **Satellites** are the heavenly bodies that revolve around the planets. Moon is the natural satellite of the Earth.

Facts about the Moon

Diameter	3476 km
Average distance from Earth	384365 km
Rotation Speed	27 days, 7 h, 43 min and 11.47 sec
Revolution Speed	27 days, 7 h, 43 min and 11.47 sec
Time taken by moonlight to reach the Earth	1.3 sec

Solar System

- The solar system consists of the Sun, eight planets and their satellites (or moons) and thousands of other smaller heavenly bodies such as asteroids, comets and meteors.

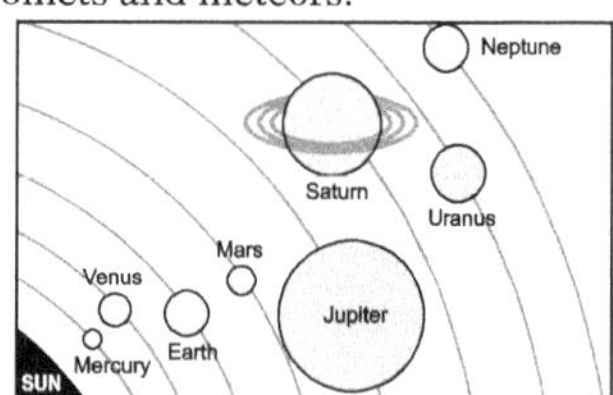

- The **Sun** is at the centre of the solar system and all these bodies revolve around it. It is the nearest star to the Earth.

Facts about the Sun

Average distance from the Earth	149598900 km
Diameter	1391980 km
Temperature of the Core	15000000°C
Rotation Speed	25.38 days (with respect to equator); 33 days (with respect to poles)
Time taken by Sunlight to reach the Earth	8 min and 16.6 sec

Important Facts about Universe

Biggest Planet	*Jupiter*
Biggest Satellite	*Ganymede (Jupiter)*
Blue Planet	*Earth*
Green Planet	*Uranus*
Brightest Planet	*Venus*
Brightest Planet outside Solar System	*Sirius (Dog Star)*
Closest Star of Solar System	*Proxima Centauri*
Coldest Planet	*Neptune*
Evening Star	*Venus*
Farthest Planet from Sun	*Neptune*
Planet with maximum number of satellites	Saturn (Overtaking Jupiter)
Fastest revolution in Solar System	*Mercury*
Hottest Planet	*Venus*
Densest Planet	*Earth*
Fastest rotation in Solar System	*Jupiter*
Morning Star	*Venus*
Nearest Planet to Earth	*Venus*
Nearest Planet to Sun	*Mercury*
Red Planet	*Mars*
Slowest Revolution in Solar System	*Neptune*
Slowest Rotation in Solar System	*Venus*
Smallest Planet	*Mercury*
Smallest Satellite	*Deimos (Mars)*
Earth's Twin	*Venus*
Only Satellite with an atmosphere like Earth	*Titan*

Asteroids (or Planetoids)

Small planetary bodies that revolve around the Sun and found in between the orbits of Mars and Jupiter. Also known as minor planets.

Meteors and Meteorites

- Meteors are also called as **shooting stars**.
- **Meteors** are fragments of rocks coming towards the Earth.
- They are formed due to collision among the asteroids.
- Meteors that do not burn up completely in Earth's atmosphere and land on the Earth, are called **meteorites**.
- Meteorites are composed of various proportions of a nickel-iron alloy (10% nickel and 90% iron) and silicate minerals.

Classification of Planets

Inner Planets Include Mercury, Venus, Earth and Mars.

Outer Planets Include Jupiter, Saturn, Uranus and Neptune.

Inner Planet	*Outer Planet*
They are called as Terrestrial or Rocky planets.	They are called as Jovian or Gaseous planets.
They are nearer to the Sun.	They are far away from the Sun.

Dwarf Planet According to International Astronomical Union (IAU), it is a celestial body in direct orbit of the Sun, that is massive enough that its shape is controlled by gravitational forces, but has not cleared its neighbourhood. *e.g.*, Pluto, Ceres, Eris, Makemake and Haumea.

> **A light year** is the distance light travels in one year at the speed of 3×10^8 m/s.
>
> **Astronomical unit** mean distance between Earth and Sun.

Earth

- The Earth is an **oblate spheroid**. It is almost spherical, flattened a little at the poles with a slight bulge at the centre (equator).
- **Perihelion** Nearest position of the Earth to the Sun.
- **Aphelion** Farthest position of the Earth from Sun.
- The Earth's interior is composed of three major layers: the **crust**, the **mantle** and the **core**.

- Eduard Suess has explained the interior of Earth on the basis of chemical composition as SIAL, SIMA and NIFE.
- **SIAL** (Silicon-Aluminium) Upper part of the crust.
- **SIMA** (Silicon-Magnesium) Lower part of the crust.
- **NIFE** (Nickel-Iron) Outer part of the core.
- **Rotation of the Earth** Earth spins on its imaginary axis from West to East in one day. Result in causation of day and night, tides.
- **Revolution of the Earth** Earth's motion in elliptical orbit around the Sun in one year. Result in Change of seasons.

Statistics Data of the Earth

Age	4550 million years
Mass	5.976×10^{24} kg
Volume	1.083×10^{12} km^3
Mean Density	5.513 g/cm^3
Total Surface Area	510 million sq km
Land Area	29.2% of the total surface area
Water Area	70.8% of the total surface area
Rotation Speed	23 hr, 56 min and 4.100 sec
Revolution Speed	365 days, 5 hr and 45.51 sec
Dates when days and nights are equal	March 21 *(Vernal Equinox)*; 23rd September, *(Autumnal Equinox)*
Longest day	21st June, *(Summer Solstice)* Sun is vertically overhead at Tropic of Cancer
Shortest night	22nd December, *(Winter Solstice)* Sun is vertically overhead at Tropic of Capricorn
Escape velocity	11.2 km/sec
Mean surface temperature	14°C

Latitudes

Imaginary lines drawn on the Earth's surface parallel to the equator. Equator (0°) is the biggest latitude that divides Earth in two equal hemispheres (North and South).

Tropic of Cancer	23.5°N
Tropic of Capricorn	23.5°S
Arctic Circle	66.5°N
Antarctic Circle	66.5°S

- Each degree of latitude equals 111 km.
- The most important line of latitude is the Equator.

Longitudes (Meridians)

- Meridians are a series of semicircles that run from pole to pole passing through the equator.
- **Prime Meridian** passes through Greenwich near London, divides the Earth in Eastern and Western hemisphere. Its value is 0°.
- Longitude has very important function *i.e.*, it determines local time in relation to **Greenwich Mean Time** (GMT).
- 1° change of longitude corresponds to 4 minutes difference in time.

International Date Line (IDL)

- It is the longitude where the date changes by exactly one day when it is crossed.
- 180°East and 180° West meridians is the same line, which is called the International Date Line.
- Crossing Date line from West to East — addition of 1 day
  Crossing Date line from East to West — subtraction of 1 day
- Recently Samoa island decided to shift itself on west side of IDL.

Indian Standard Time (IST)

- The Earth takes approximately 24 hours to complete one rotation *i.e.*, it takes 24 hours to complete 360° of its rotation.
- Indian Standard Time is calculated on the basis of 82.5°E longitude which passes through Uttar Pradesh, Madhya Pradesh Odisha, Chhattisgarh and Andhra Pradesh.
- IST is 5 hr 30 min ahead of GMT.

Eclipses

When the light of the Sun or the Moon is blocked by another body, the Sun or the Moon is said to be in eclipse.

- **Solar Eclipse** It is caused, when the Moon revolving around the Earth comes in between the Earth and the Sun, thus making a part or whole of the Sun invisible from a particular part of the Earth. Thus, the eclipse can be partial or complete.
- **Lunar Eclipse** When the Earth comes between the Moon and the Sun, the shadow cast by the Earth on the Moon results in a lunar eclipse.

ROCKS

Rocks are made up of individual substances, called minerals, found mostly in solid state. *Rocks are classified into three major types*

- **Igneous rocks** are formed by the solidification of the molten magma, *e.g.*, Mica, Granite etc.
- **Sedimentary rocks** are formed due to accumulation of rock particles and organic matter in layers, under tremendous pressure, *e.g.*, Gravel, Peat, Gypsum etc.
- **Metamorphic rocks** were originally igneous or sedimentary but later changed due to pressure, heat or action of water, *e.g.*, Gneiss, Marble, Quartzite etc.

Type of Rock	*Original Rock*	*Metamorphic Rock*
Igneous	Granite	Gneiss
Igneous	Basalt	Green-stone
Sedimentary	Limestone	Marble
Sedimentary	Coal	Graphite, Coal
Sedimentary	Sandstone	Quartzite
Sedimentary	Shale/Clay	Slate, Mica, Schist

Weathering

The process by which rocks are chemically or physically disintegrated into fragments.

EARTHQUAKES

- Any sudden disturbance below the Earth's surface may produce **vibrations** or shaking in Earth's crust and some of these vibrations, when reach the surface, are known as earthquakes.
- The magnitude of an earthquake is measured by **Richter Scale**.
- The intensity of earthquake waves is recorded by **Seismograph**.
- Intensity of shaking is measured on the modified **Mercalli Scale**.
- **Focus** is the point beneath the Earth where earthquake originates.
- **Epicentre** is the point just above the focus on the Earth's surface.

VOLCANISM

- Sudden eruption of hot magma (molten rock), gases, ash and other material from inside the Earth to its surface.

Types of Volcanoes

- **Active** Which erupts frequently, *e.g.*, Mauna Loa *(Hawaii)*, Etna *(Sicily)*, Vesuvius *(Italy)*, Stromboli *(Mediterranean Sea)*.
- **Dormant** Not erupted for quite sometime, *e.g.*, Fujiyama *(Japan)*, Krakatoa *(Indonesia)*, Barren Island *(India)*.
- **Extinct** Not erupted for several centuries. *e.g.*, Arthur's Seat, Edinburgh, Scotland.
- **Ring of Fire** Hundreds of active volcanoes found on the land near the edges of the Pacific Ocean.

Tsunami

Large ocean wave that is caused by sudden motion on the ocean floor. Motion could be an earthquake, volcanic eruption or underwater landslide.

LANDFORMS

There are three major landforms mountains, plateaus and plains.

Mountains

An uplifted portion of the Earth's surface is called a hill or a mountain.

Mountains are classified into following four types

- **Fold Mountains** These are formed by folding of crustal rocks by compressive forces. *e.g.*, Himalayas (Asia), Alps (Europe).
- **Block Mountains** When great blocks of the Earth's crust are raised or lowered during the last stage of mountain building, block mountains are formed, *e.g.*, Vosges in France, Black Forest mountains in Germany.
- **Volcanic Mountains** These are formed by the matter thrown out from the volcanoes, and are also known as mountains of accumulation, *e.g.*, Mt Mauna Loa in Hawaii, Mt Popa in Myanmar.
- **Residual or Dissected Mountains** They are known as relict mountains or mountains of circum-denudation. They owe their present form to erosion by different agencies, *e.g.* Nilgiris, Girnar and Rajmahal.

Major Mountain Ranges

Range	*Location*	*Length (km)*
Andes	South America	7200
Himalayas, Karakoram and Hindukush	South Central Asia	5000
Rockies	North America	4800
Great Dividing Range	East Australia	3600
Atlas	North-West Africa	1930
Western Ghats	Western India	1610
Caucasus	Europe	1200
Alaska	USA	1130
Alps	Europe	1050

Major Mountain Peaks

Mountain Peak	*Location*
Mt Everest *(Highest in the world)*	Nepal-Tibet
K2 *(Godwin Austin)*	India *(PoK)*
Dhaulagiri	Nepal
Annapurna	Nepal
Gurla Mandhata	Tibet
Tirich Mir	Pakistan
Aconcagua	Argentina
Cotopaxi	Ecuador
Kilimanjaro	Tanzania

Plateaus

Plateaus are flat, table like, upland areas with rough top surface and steep side walls.

Famous Plateaus of the World

Plateau	*Situation*
Tibetan Plateau	Between Himalayas and Kunlun Mountains
Deccan Plateau	Southern India
Arabian Plateau	South-West Asia
Plateau of Brazil	Central-Eastern South America
Plateau of Mexico	Mexico
Plateau of Columbia	USA
Plateau of Madagascar	Madagascar
Plateau of Alaska	North-West North America
Plateau of Bolivia	Andes Mountains
Great Basin Plateau	South of Columbia Plateau, USA
Colorado Plateau	South of Great Basin Plateau, USA

Plains

A relatively low-lying and flat land surface with least difference between its highest and lowest points is called a Plain.

ATMOSPHERE

- The **vast expanse of air,** which envelops the earth all around is called the atmosphere. It extends to thousands of kilometres.
- It protects the Earth's surface from the Sun's harmful **ultraviolet rays**.

Structure of Earth's Atmosphere

Layer	*Height (km)*	*Feature*
Troposphere	0-18 km	Contains 75% of the gases in the atmosphere. As height increases, temperature decreases *(about 6.5°c/km ascent)*.
Stratosphere	18-50 km	This layer contains the ozone layer. The temperature remains fairly constant in the lower part but increases slowly with increase in height due to presence of ozone gas. At upper layer temperature is almost 0^0C.
Mesosphere	50-80 km	This is the coldest region of the atmosphere. The temperature drops to about – 100°C.
Ionosphere	80-600 km	Radio waves are bounced off the ions and reflect waves back to the Earth. This generally helps radio communication.
Exosphere	Above 600 km	Upper part of exosphere is called Magnetosphere. The temperature keeps on rising constantly at high rate.

- It also regulates temperature, preventing the Earth from becoming too **hot** or too **cold**.
- The **major constituents of air** in the atmosphere are Nitrogen (78%), Oxygen (21%), Argon (0.93%) and Carbon dioxide (0.03%).
- Besides water vapour, dust particles, smoke, salts and other impurities are present in air in varying quantities.

Greenhouse Effect and Global Warming

- A **greenhouse gas** (sometimes abbreviated GHG) is a gas in the atmosphere that absorbs and emits radiation within the thermal infrared range. This process is the fundamental cause of the greenhouse effect.
- The primary greenhouse gases in the Earth's atmosphere are water vapour, carbon dioxide, methane, nitrous oxide and ozone.
- In the **solar system**, the atmosphere of Venus, Mars and Titan also contain gases that cause greenhouse effects.
- **Global warming** is the increase of Earth's average surface temperature due to effect of greenhouse gases, such as carbon dioxide emissions from burning fossil fuels or from deforestation. This is a type of greenhouse effect.

Pressure System of Earth

- The pressure exerted by the atmosphere due to its weight, above a unit area of the Earth's surface is called **atmospheric pressure**. It is measured by **Mercury Barometer**.
- Major pressure belts of the Earth are equatorial low, sub-tropical high, sub-polar low and polar high.

Winds

Due to horizontal differences in air pressure, air flows from areas of high pressure to areas of low pressure. **Horizontal movement** of the air is called wind.

The types of winds are given below

- **Planetary Winds** The winds blowing throughout the year from one latitude to another in response to latitudinal differences in air pressure are called planetary or prevailing winds.
- Planetary winds are divided into three types they are Trade winds, Westerlies and Polar winds.
  (i) **Trade Winds** They blow from the Sub-tropical High Pressure Belt to the Equatorial Low Pressure Belt in the tropics between 30° North and 30° South latitudes.
  (ii) **Westerlies** They blow from Sub-tropical High Pressure Belt to the Sub-Polar Low Pressure Belt in the temperate latitudes between 30°and 60°, on the either side of the Equator.
  These are also called **Roaring Forties**, the **Furious Fifties** and **Shrieking** or **Screaming sixties**.
  (iii) **Polar Winds** They blow from the Polar High Pressure Belt to the Sub-Polar Low Pressure Belt between 60° latitude and the Pole on both sides of the Equator.
- **Periodic Winds** They change their direction periodically with the change in pressure and temperature, e.g., Monsoon, Land and Sea Breeze.
- **Local Winds** Local winds develop as a result of local differences in temperature and pressure. e.g., Fohn, Chinook, Loo.
- **Cyclones** Rapid inward circulation of airmasses with a low pressure at centre. It is anticlockwise in the Northern Hemisphere and clockwise in the Southern Hemisphere.
- **Anticyclones** Rapid outward movement of air masses with a high pressure at centre.
- **Hurricane** This is also known as tropical cyclone or tropical storm. This is a disturbance of about 650 km across, spinning around a central area of very low pressure, with (with wind speed above) 140 km/h.

List of Local Winds

Name	*Nature of Wind*
Chinook	Hot, dry wind in Rockies, also called 'Snow Eater'.
Fohn	Hot, dry wind in the Alps.
Khamsin	Hot, dry wind in Egypt.
Sirocco	Hot, moist wind from Sahara to Mediterranean Sea. It is also known as Blood rain.
Solano	Hot, moist wind from Sahara towards Iberian Peninsula.
Harmattan	Hot, dry wind blowing outwards from the interior of Western Africa. Also called Guinea Doctor.
Bora	Cold, dry wind blowing outwards from Hungary to the North of Italy *(near Adriatic Sea)*.
Mistral	Very cold wind, which blows from the Alps over France.
Punas	Cold, dry wind blowing down towards the Western side of Andes.
Blizzard	Very cold winds in Tundra region.
Purga	Cold wind in Russian Tundra.
Levanter	Cold wind in Spain.
Norwester	Hot wind in New Zealand.
Santa Ana	Hot wind in South California in USA.

Major Rivers of the World

River	*Origin*
Nile	Victoria lake
Amazon	Andes *(Peru)*
Yangtze	Tibetan Kiang Plateau
Mississippi Missouri	Itaska Lake *(USA)*
Yenisei	Tannu-Ola Mountains
Huang Ho	Kunlun Mountains
Ob	Altai Mountains, Russia
Congo	Lualaba and Luapula rivers
Amur	North East China
Lena	Baikal Mountains
Mekong	Tibetan Highlands
Niger	Guinea

Cyclones of the World

Typhoons	China Sea
Tropical Cyclones	Indian Ocean
Hurricanes	Caribbean Sea
Tornadoes	USA
Willy Willies	Northern Australia

Important Canals of the World

Panama	Pacific Ocean with Caribbean Sea
Suez	Mediterranean Sea to Red Sea
Erie	Atlantic Ocean to Great Lakes
Kiel	North Sea to Baltic Sea

Deepest Point of Oceans

Oceans	*Deepest Point*
Pacific	Mariana Trench
Atlantic	Puerto Rico Trench
Indian	Java Trench
Arctic	Eurasian Basin

Important Straits of the World

Strait	*Water Bodies joined*	*Area*
Bab-el-Mandeb	Red Sea and Arabian Sea	Arabia and Africa
Bering	Arctic Ocean and Bering Sea	Alaska and Asia
Bosphorus	Black Sea and Marmara Sea	Turkey
Dover	North Sea and Atlantic Ocean	England and Europe
Florida	Gulf of Mexico and Atlantic Ocean	Florida and Bahamas Islands
Gibralter	Mediterranean Sea and Atlantic Ocean	Spain and Africa (Morocco)
Malacca	Java Sea and Bay of Bengal	India and Indonesia
Palk	Bay of Bengal and Indian Ocean	India and Sri Lanka
Magellan	South Pacific and South Atlantic Ocean	Chile
Sunda	Java Sea and Indian Ocean	Indonesia

Important Lakes of the World

Lake	*Location*
Caspian Sea	Asia
Superior	Canada and USA
Victoria	Africa
Huron	Canada and USA
Michigan	USA
Tanganyika	Africa
Baikal	Russia
Great Bear	Canada
Aral	Kazakshtan
Great Slave	Canada

Waterfalls

Waterfall	*Location*
Angel Falls	Venezuela
Tugela Falls	South Africa
Monge	Norway
Yosemite	United States
Catarata Yumbilla	Peru

Riverside Cities

Town	*River*
Akyab *(Myanmar)*	Irrawaddy
Baghdad *(Iraq)*	Tigris
Basara *(Iraq)*	Tigris and Euphrates
Belgrade	Danube
Berlin *(Germany)*	Spree
Bristol *(UK)*	Avon
Budapest *(Hungary)*	Danube
Cairo *(Egypt)*	Nile
Canton	Si-Kiang
Glasgow *(Scotland)*	Clyde
Hamburg *(Germany)*	Elbe
Jamshedpur	Subarnarekha
Kabul	Kabul
Karachi	Indus
Khartoum *(Sudan)*	Nile
Lahore	Ravi
Lisbon *(Portugal)*	Tangus
London *(UK)*	Thames
Lucknow	Gomti
Montreal *(Canada)*	Ottawa
New Castle *(UK)*	Tyre
New Orleans *(USA)*	Mississippi
New York *(USA)*	Hudson
Paris *(France)*	Seine
Philadelphia *(USA)*	Delaware
Rome *(Italy)*	Tiber
Shanghai	Yang-tse-Kiang
Srinagar	Jhelum
Warsaw *(Poland)*	Vistula
Washington DC	Potomac
Yangon *(Myanmar)*	Irawady

Great Deserts of the World

Name	*Country/Region*
Sahara *(Libyan, Nubian)*	North Africa
Australian *(Gibson, Simpson)*, Victorian Great Sandy)	Australia
Arabian *(Rub al Khali, An-Nafud)*	Arabia
Dasht-e-Lut *(Barren Desert)*	Iran
Dasht-e-Kavir *(Salt Desert)*	Iran
Desierto de Sechura	Peru
Atacama	North Chile
Patagonia	Argentina
Kalahari	Botswana
Namib	Namibia

Major Islands of the World

Rank	*Name*	*Area* (km^2)	*Country/Area*
1.	Greenland	2,175,600	Denmark
2.	New Guinea	785,753	Melanesia
3.	Borneo	748,168	Indonesia, Malaysia
4.	Madagascar	587,713	Madagascar
5.	Baffin Island	503,944	Canada
6.	Sumatra	443,066	Indonesia

Minerals of the World

Mineral	*Leading Producer*
Gold	China
Bauxite	Australia
Copper	Chile
Platinum	South Africa
Chromium	South Africa
Vanadium	China
Antimony	China
Tungsten	China
Phosphate	China
Manganese	China
Diamond	Russia (Botswana, in term of value)
Iron ore	China
Petroleum	USA

Famous Grasslands of the World

Grassland	Country
Steppe	Eurasia
Pustaz	Hungary
Prairie	USA
Pampas	Argentina and Uruguay *(South America)*
Veld	South Africa
Downs	Australia
Canterbury	New Zealand

Agriculture

Agricultural Produce	Leading Producer
Coffee	Brazil
Rubber	Thailand
Tea	China
Oil Palm	Indonesia
Cocoa	Ghana
Coconut	Indonesia
Date Palm	Egypt
Cotton	China
Wheat	China
Maize	USA
Fruits and Vegetables	China
Wool	Australia
Rice	China
Cloves	Zanzibar

Important International Boundary Lines

Name	In Between
Radcliffe Line (1947)	India and Pakistan (Indo-Pak)
McMahon Line (1914)	India and China (Indo-China)
Durand Line (1893)	Pakistan and Afghanistan
Hindenburg Line	Germany and Poland
Maginot Line	France and Germany
Oder Neisse Line	Germany and Poland
Siegfried Line	Fortification between Germany and France
38th Parallel Line	North and South Korea
49th Parallel Line	USA and Canada
24th Parallel Line	Pakistan claims that it is the boundary between India and Pakistan in Rann of Kachchh
17th Parallel Line	North Vietnam and South Vietnam

Highest and Lowest Points of the Continent

Continent	Highest (m)	Lowest (m)
Asia	Mt Everest (8850)	Dead Sea (–396)
Africa	Mt Kilimanjaro (5895)	Lake Assal (–151)
North America	Mt Mckinley (6190)	Death Valley (–87)
South America	Mt Aconcagua (6962)	Valdes Peninsula (–40)
Antarctica	Vinson Massif (4897)	Bentley Subglacial Trench (–2538)
Europe	Mt El' brus (5642)	Caspian Sea (–28)
Australia	Mt Kosciuszko (2228)	Lake Eyre (–16)

Important Industrial Cities

City	Industry
Anshan (China)	Iron and Steel
Baku (Azerbaijan)	Petroleum
Belfast (Ireland)	Ship-building
Birmingham (UK)	Iron and Steel
Chicago (USA)	Meat Packing
Detroit (USA)	Automobile
Havana (Cuba)	Cigars
Hollywood (USA)	Films
Johannesburg (South Africa)	Gold Mining
Kansas City (USA)	Meat Packing
Kawasaki (Japan)	Iron and Steel
Kimberley (South Africa)	Diamond Mining
Krivoi Rog (Ukraine)	Iron and Steel
Leeds (UK)	Woollen Textiles
Leningard (Russia)	Ship-building
Los Angeles (USA)	Petroleum
Lyon (France)	Silk Textiles
Magnitogorsk (Russia)	Iron and Steel
Manchester (UK)	Cotton Textile
Milan (Italy)	Silk Textile
Multan (Pakistan)	Pottery
Munich (Germany)	Lenses
Nagoya (Janpan)	Automobiles
Philadelphia (USA)	Locomotives
Pittsburg (USA)	Iron and Steel
Plymouth (USA)	Ship-building
Rourkela (India)	Iron and Steel
Sheffield (UK)	Cutlery
Vladivostok (Russia)	Ship-building
Wellington (New Zealand)	Dairy Products

INDIAN GEOGRAPHY

INDIA

- India is the **seventh largest country** in the world with an area of 3287263 sq km, which is 2.42% of world's area.
- India is the **second most populous** country in the world with a population of 1.21 billion, which is 17.44% of the world.
- Indian subcontinent is located in the Northern and Eastern hemisphere.
- India shares **longest boundary** with Bangladesh (4096 km), followed by China (3488 km), Pakistan (3323 km), Nepal (1751 km), Myanmar (1643 km), Bhutan (699 km) and Afghanistan (106 km).
- In India, the **Tropic of Cancer** (23.5° N latitude) passes through **8 states** (Gujarat, Rajasthan, Madhya Pradesh, Chhattisgarh, Jharkhand, West Bengal, Tripura and Mizoram).
- **Islands** Andaman and Nicobar Islands in the Bay of Bengal; Lakshadweep, Amindivi and Minicoy in the Arabian Sea.
- **Ocean** India lies midway between the Far East and Middle East. The trans-Indian Ocean routes connecting the industrially developed countries of Europe in the West and the under developed countries of East Asia pass close by Indian subcontinent.
  It is surrounded by Arabian Sea in the South-West and Bay of Bengal in the South-East.

Indian States UTs Situated on the Border

Country	*Border*
Pakistan (4)	Gujarat, Rajasthan, Punjab, Jammu and Kashmir
Afghanistan (1)	Ladakh
China (5)	Ladakh, Uttarakhand, Himachal Pradesh, Sikkim, Arunachal Pradesh
Nepal (5)	Uttar Pradesh, Uttarakhand, Bihar, West Bengal, Sikkim
Bhutan (4)	Sikkim, West Bengal, Assam, Arunachal Pradesh
Bangladesh (5)	West Bengal, Assam, Meghalaya, Tripura, Mizoram

Highest Peaks of India

Highest Peak	*Height (in m)*	*State/UTs*
Mt K2	8611	PoK (India)
Kanchenjunga	8586	Sikkim
Nanda Devi	7817	Uttarakhand
Kamet	7756	Uttarakhand
Saltoro Kangri	7742	Jammu and Kashmir
Kangto	7090	Arunachal Pradesh
Reo Purgyil	6816	Himachal Pradesh
Saramati	3841	Nagaland
Sandakphu	3636	West Bengal
Khayang	3114	Manipur
Anaimudi	2695	Kerala
Dodda Betta	2636	Tamil Nadu

Important Facts

Latitudinal extent	8°4' North to 37° 6' North
Longitudinal extent	68°7' East to 97° 25' East
North-South extent	*3214 km*
East-West extent	2933 km
Land Frontiers	15200 km
Total Coastline	7516.6 km
Number of States	28
Union Territories	8 (After bifurcation of J & K in Jammu and Kashmir and Ladakh and merger of Dadar and Nagar Haveli with Daman and Diu)
Land Neighbours	Pakistan, Afghanistan, China, Nepal, Bhutan, Bangladesh and Myanmar
Longest Coastline	Gujarat
Active volcano	Barren Island in Andaman and Nicobar Islands
Southern most point	Indira Point or Pygmalion point in Great Nicobar
Southern most tip	Kanyakumari
Northern most point	Indira Col
Western most point	West of Ghaur Mota in Gujarat
Eastern most point	Kibithu (Arunachal Pradesh)

Bhangar and Khadar

Bhangar	*Khadar*
▪ These are low plains. Formed of older alluvium	▪ The deposit of fresh alluvium every year brought by the Himalayas rivers makes this belt of Northern plains.
▪ This belt ends in Khadar.	▪ This belt ends in Terai.

Terai and Bhabar

Terai	*Bhabar*
▪ Terai is a broad long zone South of Bhabar plain.	▪ Bhabar is a long narrow plain along the foothills.
▪ It is a marshy damp area covered with thick forest.	▪ It is a pebble studded zone of porous beds.
▪ It is 20-30 km wide.	▪ It is 9-16 km wide.
▪ It is suitable for agriculture.	▪ It is unsuitable for agriculture.

South to North Doabs

Doab	*Region*
▪ Bist Doab	▪ Between Beas and Sutlej
▪ Bari Doab	▪ Between Beas and Ravi
▪ Rechna Doab	▪ Between Ravi and Chenab
▪ Chaj Doab	▪ Between Chenab and Jhelum
▪ Sind Sagar Doab	▪ Between Jhelum and Indus

The Coastal Plains

Eastern Coast	*Western Coast*
Smooth outline	Dissected outline
Occurence of deltas	Occurence of estuaries
Broad	Narrow
Long rivers	Small rivers

Eastern *and* Western Ghats

Eastern Ghat	*Western Ghat*
Located East to Deccan Plateau.	Located West to Deccan Plateau.
They are parallel to Eastern Coast, *i.e.*, Coromandal, Northern Circar, etc.	They are parallel to Western Coast, *i.e.*, Konkan, Kannad, Malabar etc.
Mahanadi, Cauveri, Godavari, Krishna etc rivers are drawn in this land form.	Narmada, Tapi, Sabarmati and Mahi etc rivers are drawn in this land.
Jindhagada with an altitude of 1690 m is the highest peak.	Anaimudi with an altitude of 2695 m is the highest peak.

Important Indian Towns on Rivers

Town	*River*
Jamshedpur	Subarnarekha
Delhi	Yamuna
Kanpur	Ganga
Surat	Tapti
Ferozpur	Sutlej
Prayagraj	At the confluence of the Ganga, Yamuna and Saraswati
Varanasi	Ganga
Haridwar	Ganga
Badrinath	Alaknanda
Ludhiana	Sutlej
Srinagar	Jhelum
Ayodhya	Saryu
Ahmedabad	Sabarmati
Patna	Ganga
Kota	Chambal
Jabalpur	Narmada
Panji	Mandavi
Ujjain	Kshipra
Guwahati	Brahmaputra
Kolkata	Hooghly
Cuttack	Mahanadi
Hyderabad	Musi
Nasik	Godavari
Lucknow	Gomti

Some of the Important Waterfalls of India

Waterfall	*Height* (km)	*River*	*State*
Kunchikal	455	Varahi	Karnataka
Jog/Gersoppa	260	Sharavati	Karnataka
Rakim Kund	168	Gaighat	Bihar
Chachai	127	Bihad	Madhya Pradesh
Kevti	98	Mahana	Madhya Pradesh
Sivasamudram	90	Cauveri	Karnataka

Important Lakes of India

Name of Lake	*State/UTs*	*Important Fact*
Chilka Lake	Odisha	It is largest brackish water lake of India.
Kolleru Lake	Andhra Pradesh	It is a freshwater lake.
Loktak Lake	Manipur	It is a freshwater lake having inland drainage in Manipur.
Lonar Lake	Maharashtra	It is a meteorite crater lake in Buldhana area of Maharashtra. The water is highly charged with Sodium carbonates and Sodium chloride.
Pangong Lake	Jammu and Kashmir	It is a salty lake.
Pulicat Lake	Tamil Nadu & Andhra Pradesh border	It is a saline and lagoon lake.
Sambhar Lake	Rajasthan	It is a shallow lake which is saline, located near Jaipur.
Tso Moriri Lake	Jammu & Kashmir	It is a salty lake.
Vembanad Lake	Kerala	It is a lagoon lake and largest lake by surface area.
Wular & Dal Lakes	Jammu and Kashmir	Wular lake was created due to tectonic activities and is largest fresh water lake of India.

Important Rivers of India

Name	*Originates from*	*Falls into*
Ganges	Gangotri Glacier	Bay of Bengal
Sutlej	Mansarovar Rakas Lakes	Chenab
Indus	Near Mansarovar Lake	Arabian Sea
Ravi	Kullu Hills near Rohtang Pass	Chenab
Beas	Near Rohtang Pass	Sutlej
Jhelum	Verinag in Kashmir	Chenab
Yamuna	Yamunotri Glacier	Ganga
Chambal	Singar Chouri Peak, Vindhyan escarpment	Yamuna
Ghaghara	Matsatung Glacier	Ganga
Kosi	Near Gosain Dham Peak	Ganga
Betwa	Vindhyanchal	Yamuna
Son	Amarkantak	Ganga
Brahmaputra	Near Mansarovar Lake	Bay of Bengal
Narmada	Amarkantak	Gulf of Khambat
Tapti	Betul District in Madhya Pradesh	Gulf of Khambat
Mahanadi	Raipur District in Chhattisgarh	Bay of Bengal
Luni	Aravallis	Rann of Kachchh
Ghaggar	Himalayas	Near Fatehabad
Sabarmati	Mewar hill, Aravallis	Gulf of Khambat
Krishna	Western Ghats	Bay of Bengal
Godavari	Nasik district in Maharashtra	Bay of Bengal
Cauveri	Brahmagir Range of Western Ghats	Bay of Bengal
Tungabhadra	Western Ghats	Krishna

Important River Projects and their Beneficiary States

Project	*River*	*Purpose*	*Beneficiary States*
Bhakra Nangal Project	Sutlej	Power and irrigation	Punjab, Himachal Pradesh, Haryana and Rajasthan
Damodar Valley	Damodar	Power, irrigation and flood control	Jharkhand and West Bengal, shared by Madhya Pradesh
Hirakud	Mahanadi	Power and irrigation	Odisha
Tungabhadra Project	Tungabhadra	Power and irrigation	Andhra Pradesh and Karnataka
Nagarjunasagar Project	Krishna	Power and irrigation	Andhra Pradesh and Telangana
Gandak River Project	Gandak	Power and irrigation	Bihar, Uttar Pradesh, Nepal (joint venture of India and Nepal)
Kosi Project	Kosi	Flood control, Power and irrigation	Bihar
Farakka Project	Ganga, Bhagirathi	Power, irrigation, avoid accumulation of slit to improve navigation	West Bengal
Beas Project	Beas	Irrigation and power	Rajasthan, Haryana, Punjab and Himachal Pradesh
Indira Gandhi Canal Project (*Rajasthan Canal Project*)	Sutlej, Beas and Ravi	Irrigation	Rajasthan, Punjab and Haryana
Chambal Project	Chambal	Power and irrigation	Madhya Pradesh and Rajasthan
Kakrapara Project	Tapti	Irrigation	Gujarat
Ukai Project	Tapti	Power and irrigation	Gujarat
Tawa Project	Tawa (Narmada)	Irrigation	Madhya Pradesh
Poochampad Project	Godavari	Irrigation	Telangana
Malaprabha Project	Malaprabha	Irrigation	Karnataka
Durgapur Barrage	Damodar	Irrigation and navigation	West Bengal and Jharkhand
Mahanadi Delta Project	Mahanadi	Irrigation	Odisha
Iddukki Project	Periyar	Hydroelectricity	Kerala
Koyna Project	Koyna	Hydroelectricity	Maharashtra
Ramganga Multipurpose Project	Chisot stream near Kala	Power and irrigation	Uttar Pradesh and Uttarakhand
Matatila Project	Betwa	Multipurpose power and irrigation	Uttar Pradesh and Madhya Pradesh
Tehri Dam Project	Bhilangana, Bhagirathi	Hydroelectricity	Uttarakhand
Rihand Scheme	Rihand	Hydroelectricity	Uttar Pradesh
Kundah Project	Kundah/Bhavani	Hydroelectricity and irrigation	Tamil Nadu

Natural Vegetation of India

Name	Climatic Requirement	Feature	Important Species	Found in Area
Tropical Wet Evergreen	Rainfall > 250 cm Temperature 25-27°C Humidity 80% or more	Dense forest, tall trees	Mesa, Dhup, White cedar, Jamun, Bamboo, Agar and Hopea	Noth-East India, Western slopes of Western Ghats, Andaman and Nicobar Islands
Tropical Semi-Evergreen	Rainfall > 200-250 cm, Temperature 24-27°C Humidity 80%	Evergreen mixed with deciduous, Height 24-36 m	Semul, Rosewood, Indian Chestnut, Kusum, Mesua	Lower slopes of Eastern Himalayas, Odisha Coast
Tropical Dry Evergreen	Areas receive rain from North-East Monsoon, Temperature 28°C, Humidity 74%	Presence of canopy, low height, about 9-12 m	Khirni, Jamun, Tamarind, Neem, Cane	Coromandal Coast of Tamil Nadu
Tropical Moist Deciduous	Moderate rainfall of 150-200 cm, Temperature 26-27°C, Humidity 60-80%	Trees shed their leaves in the dry season	Sal, Teak, Sandalwood, Ebony, Mahua, Shisham	Western Ghats, Eastern coastal plains, Eastern Plateau
Tropical Dry Deciduous	Rainfall < 150 cm, Dry season	Undergrowth is shrubby and grassy, trees shed their leaves in the dry season	Sal, Teak, Khair, Palash, Tendu, Laurel	Uttar Pradesh, Tamil Nadu, Western Ghats, Rajasthan and West Bengal
Tropical Thorny	Rainfall 50-70 cm, Temperature 25-27°C, Humidity < 47%	Trees are stunted (6-9 m), trees have long roots, sharp spines and glossy leaves to conserve water	Babul, Acacia, Khair, Khejri	South-Western Punjab, Western Haryana and Uttar Pradesh, Western Madhya Pradesh, Kachchh and Saurashtra, Rajasthan
Tidal/Littoral Mangrove	Rainfall > 200 cm, high water salinity and areas are flooded regularly	Trees are evergreen, breathing roots called pneumatophores	Keora, Amur, Sundari, Agar, Bhendi, Nipa	Delta regions of Ganga, Mahanadi, Godavari and Krishna

Soils in India

Types	*States where Found (Occurrence)*	*Composition*	*Crops Grow*
Alluvial	Punjab, Haryana, Uttar Pradesh, Bihar and Jharkhand	Rich in potash and lime but deficient in nitrogen and phosphorus.	Large variety of rabi and kharif crops such as wheat, rice, sugarcane, cotton and jute etc.
Black soil (Regur soil)	Deccan Plateau, Valleys of Krishna and Godavari, Andhra Pradesh, Madhya Pradesh and Tamil Nadu.	Rich in iron, lime, aluminium, magnesium, calcium, but lacks in nitrogen, phosphorus and humus.	Cotton sugarcane, jowar, tobacco, wheat and rice.
Red	Eastern parts of Deccan Plateau, Tamil Nadu, Goa, Odisha and Meghalaya.	Rich in iron and potash, but deficient in lime, nitrogen, phosphorus and humus.	Wheat, rice, cotton, sugarcane and pulses.
Laterite	Summits of Eastern and Western Ghats, Assam hills, Andhra Pradesh, Karnataka, West Bengal and Odisha.	Rich in iron but poor in silica, lime, phosphorus, potash and humus.	Tea, coffee, rubber, cashew and millets.
Desert	West and North-West India, Rajasthan, North Gujarat and Southern Punjab.	Rich in soluble salts, but deficient in organic matter.	Generally unsuitable for cultivation, but with irrigation useful for cultivation of drought-resistant lime, millets, barley, cotton, maize and pulses.
Mountain	Hills of Jammu and Kashmir, Uttarakhand and Assam hills.	Rich in iron and humus, but deficient in lime.	with fertilisers, tea, fruits and medicinal plants can be grown.
Saline (Reh, Kallar, Usar, Thur, Rukar) and Alkaline	Drier parts of Bihar, Jharkhand, Uttar Pradesh, Haryana, Punjab, Rajasthan and Maharashtra.	Many salts such as sodium, magnesium and calcium.	Unfit for agriculture.
Peaty and Marshy	Kerala, coastal regions of Odisha, Tamil Nadu and Suderbans of West Bengal.	Contain large amount of soluble salts and organic matter, but lack in potash and phosphates.	Useful for rice and jute cultivation.

Forests of India

Forest Type	Distribution	Climatic Conditions	Characteristics	Species
Tropical Evergreen Forests	▪ Rainy slopes of Western Ghats. ▪ NE India except Arunachal Pradesh. ▪ Eastern part of West Bengal and Odisha. ▪ Andaman and Nicobar Islands.	▪ Rainfall > 200 cm ▪ Relative Humidity > 70% ▪ Average temperature is about 24°C. ▪ Hot and humid climate.	▪ Height of trees is 40 to 60 m. ▪ Leaves are dark green and broad.	Mahogany, Mahua, Bamboo, Cones, Ironwood, Kadam, Irul, Jamun, Hopea, Rubber tree, Toon, Telsur etc.
Tropical Moist Deciduous Forests	▪ Eastern parts of Sahyadris (Western Ghats). ▪ North Eastern part of Peninsula. ▪ Middle and lower Ganga valley. ▪ Foothills of Himalayas in Bhabar and Tarai region. ▪ These cover about 20% India's forest area.	▪ 100 to 200 cm rainfall per annum. ▪ Moderate temperature.	▪ 30 to 40 m high trees. ▪ Due to deficiency of water, they shed their leaves in spring (onset of summer).	Sal, Teak, Arjun, Mulberry, Kusum, Sandalwood, Siris, Haldi, Khair, Mango, Banyan tree etc.
Tropical Dry Deciduous Forests	▪ Large parts of Maharashtra and Andhra Pradesh. ▪ Parts of Punjab, Haryana and Eastern parts of Rajasthan. ▪ Northern and Western parts of Madhya Pradesh. ▪ Tamil Nadu. ▪ Southern parts of Uttar Pradesh.	▪ 50 to 100 cm rainfall. ▪ Moderate humidity.	▪ 6 to 15 m high. ▪ Roots are thick and long.	Teak, Sal, Bamboo, Mango, Acacia, Neem, Shisham etc.
Dry Forests or Arid Forests	▪ Rajasthan and adjoining areas of Haryana, Gujarat and Punjab. ▪ Rainshadow area of peninsular India.	▪ Low rainfall (less than 50 cm per annum). ▪ Relative humidity is less.	▪ Thorny vegetation. ▪ Roots are very long. ▪ Leaves are small.	Cactus, Thorny bushes, Kikar, Babool, Date palm, Acacia, Khair, Euphorbias etc.

CLIMATE

Monsoon

A type of wind system, in which there is almost complete reversal of prevailing wind direction.

Types

1. South West Monsoon *(June and July)*
2. North East Monsoon *(Sept. to Dec.)*

Seasons of India

- Winter Season Mid December to Mid March
- Summer Season Mid March to May
- Rainy Season June to September
- Season of Retreating Monsoon October to Mid December

Climatic Regions of India

Type	*Area*	*Characteristic*
Tropical Rain Forests	Western Ghats, West Coastal Plains, Parts of Assam	High temperature throughout the year, heavy seasonal rainfall, annual rainfall 200 cm annually (May to November)
Tropical Savana Climate	Most of Peninsular region (except leeward side of Western Ghats)	Dry winters, annual rainfall varies from 76 cm to 150 cm.
Tropical Semi-Arid- Steppe Climate	Rainshadow belt running Southward from Central Maharashtra to Tamil Nadu.	Low rainfall varies from 38 cm to 80 cm and temperature from 20° to 30°C.
Tropical and Sub-tropical Steppes	Punjab, Haryana and Kachchh region	Temperature varies from 12°-35°C.
Tropical Desert	Western parts of Barmer, Jaisalmer and Bikaner districts of Rajasthan and parts of Kachchh	Scanty rainfall (mostly in form of cloud burst), high temperature.
Humid Sub-tropical Climate with dry winters	South of Himalayas	Mild winters and extremely hot summers.
Mountain Climate	Mountainous region (above 6000 m or more)	Rainfall varies from 63.5 cm to 254 cm. (Mostly during South-West Monsoon)

AGRICULTURE

India is essentially an agricultural land. Two-thirds of its population still lives on agriculture. It includes farming, animal rearing and fishing.

Agricultural Seasons in India

There are three major crop seasons in India

Kharif

Sown in June/July, harvested in September/October, e.g., rice, jowar, bajra, ragi, maize, cotton and jute.

Rabi

Sown in October/December, harvested in April/May e.g., wheat, barley, peas, rapeseed, mustard, sesame.

Zaid

Sown in February/March harvested in May/June, e.g., urad, moong, melons etc.

Green Revolution

It is the phrase generally used to describe the spectacular increase that took place during 1968 and is continuing in the production of foodgrains in India.

The components of Green Revolution are

High Yield Variety Seeds, Irrigation, Use of Fertilisers, Use of Insecticide and Pesticide, Command Area Development, Programme Consolidation of Holdings etc.

It was introduced by MS Swaminathon, who is also known as Father of Green Revolution.

Chief Crops and Producing States

Type	*Name*	*Major Producers*
Cereals	Wheat	Uttar Pradesh, Punjab and Madhya Pradesh
	Rice	West Bengal and Uttar Pradesh
	Gram	Madhya Pradesh, Maharashtra and Rajasthan
	Barley	Maharashtra, Uttar Pradesh and Rajasthan
	Bajra	Rajasthan, Maharashtra and Gujarat
Cash Crops	Sugarcane	Uttar Pradesh and Maharashtra
	Poppy	Uttar Pradesh and Himachal Pradesh
Oil Seeds	Coconut	Kerala and Tamil Nadu
	Linseed	Rajasthan, Madhya Pradesh and Haryana
	Groundnut	Gujarat, Andhra Pradesh and Tamil Nadu
	Rape seed and mustard	Rajasthan, Madhya Pradesh and Haryana
	Sesame	Gujarat, West Bengal and Karnataka
	Sunflower	Karnataka, Andhra Pradesh and Maharashtra
Fibre Crops	Cotton	Maharashtra and Gujarat
	Jute	West Bengal and Bihar
	Silk	Karnataka and Kerala
	Hemp	Madhya Pradesh and Uttar Pradesh
Plantations	Coffee	Karnataka and Kerala
	Rubber	Kerala and Karnataka
	Tea	Assam and Kerala
	Tobacco	Gujarat, Maharashtra and Madhya Pradesh
Spices	Pepper	Kerala, Karnataka and Tamil Nadu
	Cashewnuts	Kerala, Tamil Nadu and Andhra Pradesh
	Ginger	Kerala and Uttar Pradesh
	Turmeric	Andhra Pradesh and Odisha

MINERAL RESOURCES

Types of Minerals

Metallic Iron ore, copper, aluminium, tin, lead, gold and silver.

Non-metallic Coal, mica, manganese, petroleum and sulphur.

Radioactive Uranium and thorium

Gondwana rocks (Chhotanagpur Plateau) are the richest mineral deposits in India.

Mineral Resources of India

Mineral	*States*
Coal	West Bengal, Jharkhand, Odisha, Madhya Pradesh and Chhattisgarh
Copper	Madhya Pradesh, Rajasthan, Jharkhand, Karnataka
Gold	Karnataka, Andhra Pradesh
Iron	Karnataka, Chhattisgarh and Jharkhand
Bauxite	Odisha, Jharkhand, Gujarat and Madhya Pradesh
Mica	Jharkhand, Andhra Pradesh and Rajasthan
Petroleum	Assam, Gujarat, Mumbai High, Bassein (South of Mumbai High)
Uranium	Jharkhand, Rajasthan, Andhra Pradesh and Karnataka
Thorium	Kerala Coast, Rocks of Aravalli in Rajasthan
Silver, Zinc and Lead	Rajasthan, Andhra Pradesh, Karnataka (Kolar mines)
Diamond	Panna (Madhya Pradesh), Banda (Uttar Pradesh)

TRANSPORTATION IN INDIA

Railways

- Indian Railway system is the second largest in Asia and the 3rd largest in the world.
- The longest railway platform in India and world is now **Hubli** with a stretch of around **1.5 km**.

Railway Zone	*Headquarters*
Central	Mumbai (CST)
Eastern	Kolkata
Northern	New Delhi
North-Eastern	Gorakhpur
North-East Frontier	Maligaon-Guwahati
Southern	Chennai
South Central	Secunderabad
South-Eastern	Kolkata
Western	Mumbai Churchgate
East Coast	Bhubaneshwar
East Central	Hajipur
North Central	Prayagraj
North-Western	Jaipur
South-Western	Hubli
West Central	Jabalpur
South- East Central	Bilaspur
Kolkata Metro	Kolkata
South Coast Railway	Visakhapatnam

- **The first train** ran in India between Bombay and Thane, a stretch of 34 km on 16th April, 1853.
- **The second train** ran between Howrah and Hooghly in 1854.
- The first electric train in India was **Deccan Queen**. It was introduced in 1929 between Bombay and Poona.
- **The longest train** route is 'Vivek Express' from Dibrugarh in Assam to Kanyakumari in Tamil Nadu. It covers a distance of 4273 km (2655 miles).
- The first Metro train was introduced in Kolkata (West Bengal) on **24th October, 1984**. The two stations connected were Dumdum and Belgachhia.
- In 1990, Konkan Railway has been started between Goa, Maharashtra and Karnataka.
- Delhi metro rail was started in 2002 on 25th December between Shahdra and Tees Hazari.
- Rapid metro train was started in Gurgaon (Haryana) on 14th November 2013.
- The newest metro opened is Kanpur Metro on December 2021.
- Vande Bharat Express also known as Train 18, is an Indian semi-high speed electric (India's fastest train) train made by Integral Coach Factory, Chennai, under make in India Programme.
- Delhi-Meerut Regional Rapid Transit System (RRTS) is an 82.15 km long, under-construction, semi-high speed rail corridor connecting Delhi, Ghaziabad and Meerut.
- The Lucknow-New Delhi Tejas Express is the first Indian train operated by private operators, IRCTC, a subsidiary of Indian Railway.
- As of December, 2022 there are 16 operational rapid transit (Metro rail) in India. Delhi Metro is the largest and busiest metro in India.
- The Indian Railways operate in three different gauges i.e. Broad Gauge (distance between rails is 1.676 m), Metre Gauge (distance between rail is 1.00 mm) and Narrow Gauge (distance between rails is 0.762 or 0.610 m).

Road Transport

- India has one of the largest road networks in the world (48 lakh km approx). It consists of National highways, State highways; major/other district roads and rural roads.
- **NH 44** (3745 km) is the longest highway of India (Srinagar to Kanyakumari).
- **NH 548** is the shortest National Highways with the length of 5 km.
- The **North-South** and **East-West Corridor** (NS-EW) is the largest ongoing expressway project in India. It is the **second phase** of the National Highways Development Project (NHDP) and involves building **7300 km** of six lane expressway connecting Srinagar, Kanyakumari, Porbandar and Silchar.
- **Maharashtra** has the maximum length of surfaced roads in India.
- Eastern Peripheral Expressway or Kundli-Ghaziabad-Palwal Expressway is a 6-lane expressway passing through the states of Haryana and Uttar pradesh.
- India's longest greenfield 6 lane expressway, named as Agra-Lucknow expressway has been inaugurated in Uttar Pradesh.

Bharat Mala

It is a major highway, economic corridor and expressway development scheme of Government in India, launched in 2015, it is the biggest road Construction Plan in the country (approximately 83,677 km). Government of India has decided to construct a greenfield major port at Vadhavan in Gujarat under Sugarmala Project.

Important National Highways (New numbering)

NH	*Connects*
NH *1*	Uri-Baramula-Srinagar-Kargil-Leh
NH *4*	Mayabandar-Port Blair-Chiriyatapu
NH *7*	Fazilka-Patiala-Rudraprayag-Mana
NH *10*	Siliguri-Gangtok
NH *21*	Jaipur to Bareilly
NH *32*	Chennai-Puducherry-Tutticorn
NH *40*	Kurnool-Chittoor-Ranipettai
NH *44*	Srinagar-Ludhiana-Agra-Sagar-Hyderabad-Kanyakumari

Water Transport

As per the National Waterways Act, 2016, 111 Waterways have been declared as National Waterways including the 6 existing NWs given below:

NW*1*	Allahabad to Haldia on Ganga river	1620 km
NW2	Sadia to Dhubri on Brahmaputra river	891km
NW3	Kollam to Kottapuram (along Champakara and Udyogmandal Canal)	168 km
NW4	Kakinada to Marak-kanam along Godavari and Krishna river	1095 km
NW5	Mangalgarhi to Paradeep and Talcher to Dhamara along Mahanadi and Brahmini	623 km
NW6	Lakhipur to Bhanga on Barak river	121 km

13 Major Ports in India

Western Coast	*Eastern Coast*
Kandla (*child of partition*) Gujarat	**Paradip** (*exports raw iron to Japan*) Odisha
Mumbai (*busiest and biggest*) Maharashtra	**Vishakhapatnam** (*deepest port*) Andhra Pradesh
JL Nehru (*fastest growing*) Maharashtra	**Chennai** (*oldest and artificial*) Tamil Nadu
Marmugao (*naval base also*) Goa	**Ennore** (*most modern in private hands*) Tamil Nadu
Mangalore (*exports Kudremukh iron-ore*) Karnataka	**Tuticorin** (*Southernmost*) Tamil Nadu
Cochin (*natural harbour*) Kerala	**Port Blair** (*strategically important*) Andaman and Nicobar Islands
	Enayam Port (Tamil Nadu)

Note Kandla port was renamed as Pt. Deen Dayal Upadhyay port in 2017.

Air Transport

- In 1935, the 'Tata Air Lines' started its operation between Mumbai and Thiruvananthapuram and in 1937 between Mumbai and Delhi.
- In 1953, all the private airline companies were nationalised and Indian Airlines and Air India came into existence.
- Vayudoot Limited started in 1981 as a private air carrier and later on it merged with Indian Airlines.
- International Airports Authority of India and National Airports Authority were merged on 1995 to form Airports Authority of India.
- The Authority manages the Civil Aviation Training College at Allahabad and National Institute of Aviation Management and Research at Delhi.
- On January 2022, Government of India handed over Air India (AI) to the Tata Group.

Major International Airports in India

International Airports	*City*
Rajiv Gandhi International Airport	Hyderabad
Calicut International Airport	Calicut
Chhatrapati Shivaji International Airport	Mumbai
Kempe Gowda International Airport	Bengaluru
Goa Airport in Vasco di Gama City	Goa
Netaji Subhash Chandra Bose International Airport	Kolkata
Thiruvananthapuram International Airport	Thiruvanan-thapuram
Lokpriya Gopinath Bordoloi International Airport	Guwahati
Sardar Vallabhbhai Patel International Airport	Ahmedabad
Indira Gandhi International Airport	Delhi
Chennai International Airport	Chennai
Shri Guru Ram Dass Jee International Airport	Amritsar
Pakyong Airport (First green field airport in Northeast region)	Sikkim

ENVIRONMENT AND ECOLOGY

Environment All external conditions, factors, matter and energy living and non-living that affect any living organism or other specified system.

Ecology Biological science that studies the relationships between living organisms and their environment; study of the structure and functions of nature.

Ecosystem It is defined as a unit which include all the organisms (biological components) in a given area interacting with the enviornment (physical component), so that the flow energy leads to a clearly defined trophic structure, biotic diversity and material cycles.

Biome Terrestrial regions characterised by certain types of vegetation and other forms of life. Examples include various types of deserts, grasslands and forests.

Wetland Land that is covered all part of the time with saltwater or freshwater, excluding streams, lakes and the open ocean.

Biodiversity Variety of different species (species diversity), genetic variability among individuals within each species (genetic diversity), variety of ecosystems (ecological diversity) and functions such as energy flow and matter cycling needed for the survival of species and biological communities (functional diversity).

Biosphere Zone of the Earth where life is found. It consists of parts of the atmosphere (the troposphere), hydrosphere (mostly surface water and groundwater) and lithosphere (mostly soil and surface rocks and sediments on the bottoms of oceans and other bodies of water) where life is found.

Wildlife All free, undomesticated species. Sometimes the term is used to describe animals only.

Threatened Species Wild species that is still abundant in its natural range but is likely to become endangered because of a decline in numbers.

Ozone (O_3) Colourless and highly reactive gas and a major component of photochemical smog. Also found in the ozone layer in the stratosphere and protect us from ultra violet rays.

Smog Originally, a combination of smoke and fog but now used to describe other mixtures of pollutants in the atmosphere.

Acid Rain When fossil fuel is burnt, oxides are formed in the atmosphere. The oxides formed of sulphur and nitrogen get dissolve in water and cause acid rain.

Global Warming Warming of the Earth's lower atmosphere (troposphere) because of increases in the concentrations of one or more greenhouse gases. It can result in irreversible climate change that can last for decades to thousands of years.

Ecomarks The Ministry of Environment Forest and Climate change, Government of India instituted a scheme, that is operating on a national basis and provides accreditation and labelling for household and other consumer products which meet certain environmental criteria.

Coral Bleaching Coral bleaching occurs when the relations between the coral host and zooxanthallae, which give coral much of their colour, breaks down. Without the zooxanthallae, the tissue of the coral animal appears transparent and the coral's bright white skelton is revealed.

Sustainability Ability of Earth's various systems, including human cultural systems and economies, to survive and adapt to changing environmental conditions indefinitely.

Important Sanctuaries and National Parks

Name	*Location*	*Reserve For*
Kaziranga National Park	Assam	One-horned rhinoceros, gaur, elephant, leopard and wild buffalo
Sonai Rupai Wildlife Sanctuary	Assam	Elephant, sambhar, wild boar and one-horned rhinoceros
Namdapha National Park	Arunachal Pradesh	Elephant, panther, sambhar, tiger, cheetal and king cobra
Gautam Buddha Sanctuary	Bihar	Tiger, leopard, sambhar, cheetal and barking deer (Indian Muntgac)
Achanakmar Sanctuary	Chhattisgarh	Tiger, boar, cheetal, sambhar and bison
Velvadore National Park	Gujarat	Wolf and black buck
Wild Ass Sanctuary	Gujarat	Wild ass, wolf, nilgai and chinkara
Gir Forest	Gujarat	India's biggest wildlife sanctuary famous for Gir lions
Dachigam National Park	Jammu and Kashmir	Kashmiri stag, Long tailed marmot, Himalayan serow
Banerghatta National Park	Karnataka	Elephant, cheetal, deer and grey partridge and green pigeon
Bhadra Sanctuary	Karnataka	Elephant, cheetal, panther, sambhar and wild boar
Bandipur National Park Dandeli Sanctuary	Karnataka and Tamil Nadu	Elephant, tiger, panther, sambhar, deer and birds
Tungabhadra Sanctuary	Karnataka	Tiger, panther, elephant, cheetal, sambhar and wild boar
Nagarhole National Park	Karnataka	Panther, cheetal, sloth bear and four-horned antelope
Pachmarhi Sanctuary	Madhya Pradesh	Tiger, leopard, wild bear, cheetal, sambhar reshus maccaque
Gandhi Sagar Sanctuary	Madhya Pradesh	Tiger, panther, boar, sambar, nilgai and barking deer
Bandhavgarh National Park	Madhya Pradesh	Cheetal, sambhar, chinkara and wild birds
Simlipal Sanctuary	Odisha	Tiger, panther, cheetal, nilgai and wild boar
Ghana Bird Sanctuary	Rajasthan	Water birds, black buck, cheetal and sambar
Khangchendzonga National Park	Sikkim	Snow leopard, musk deer and Himalayan boar
Vedanthangal Bird Sanctuary	Tamil Nadu	Important bird sanctuary
Chandraprabha Sanctuary	Uttar Pradesh	Gir lions, cheetal and sambhar
Dudhwa National Park	Uttar Pradesh	Tiger, panther, sambar, cheetal, nilgai and barking deer
Corbett National Park	Uttarakhand	Tiger, leopard, elephant and sambhar (named in memory of Jim Corbett)
Jaldapara Sanctuary	West Bengal	Rhinoceros, Elephant
Sunderban Tiger Reserve	West Bengal	Tiger, deer, wild boar, crocodile and Gangetic dolphin

Biosphere Reserves of India

Name	*States*	*Type*	*Area (km^2)*
Manas	Assam	East Himalayas	2837
Dibru-Saikhowa	Assam	East Himalayas	765
Seshchalam Hills	Andhra Pradesh	Eastern Ghats	4755.997
Great Nicobar (UNESCO)	Andaman and Nicobar Islands	Islands	885
Dihang-Dibang	Arunachal Pradesh	East Himalayas	5112
Great Rann of Kachchh	Gujarat	Desert	12454
Cold Desert	Himachal Pradesh	Western Himalayas	7770
Agasthyamalai (UNESCO)	Kerala, Tamil Nadu	Western Ghats	1828
Pachmarhi (UNESCO)	Madhya Pradesh	Semi-Arid	4926
Achanakamar- Amarkantak (UNESCO)	Madhya Pradesh, Chhattisgarh	Maikala Range	3835
Nokrek (UNESCO)	Meghalaya	East Himalayas	820
Simlipal (UNESCO)	Odisha	Deccan Peninsula	4374
Khangchendzonga (UNESCO)	Sikkim	East Himalayas	2620
Nilgiri (UNESCO)	Tamil Nadu, Kerala and Karnataka	Western Ghats	5520
Gulf of Mannar (UNESCO)	Tamil Nadu	Coasts	10500
Nanda Devi (UNESCO)	Uttarakhand	West Himalayas	5860
Sunderbans (UNESCO)	West Bengal	Gangetic Delta	9630
Panna (UNESCO)	Madhya Pradesh	Semi-Arid	2998

Environment Related Important International Agreement/Conference

UN Conference on the Human Environment	Stockholm (1972)
Convention on Migratory Species	Bonn (1979)
Convention for the Protection of the Ozone Layer	Vienna (1985)
Pototocol on Substances that Deplete the Ozone Layer	Montreal (1987)
Convention on the Transboundary Movement of Hazardous Wastes	Basel (1989)
Earth Summit (UN Conference on Environment and Development)	Rio-de-Janeiro (1992)
Convention on Prior Informed Consent	Rotterdam (1998)
UN Conference on Sustainable Development	Rio-de-Janeiro (2012)
Nagoya Protocol on Genetic Resources (Nagoya Protocol)	Nagoya (2010)
Convention on Biological Diversity (CBD-CoP-11)	Hyderabad (2012)
Lima Climate Change Conference (CoP-20)	Lima (2014)
Paris Agreement (CoP-21)	Paris (2015)
Marrakech Conference (CoP-22)	Marrakech, Morocco (2016)
Bonn Conference (CoP-23)	Bonn (2017)
Katowice Conference (CoP-24)	Katowice, Poland (2018)
Madrid Conference (CoP-25)	Madrid, Spain (2019)
CoP-26	Glasgow (2021)
CoP-27	Sharm el-Sheikh (Egypt) (2022)
CoP-28	Dubai (Scheduled)

Wildlife Conservation in India

Project	*Year*
Project Hangul	1970
Project Gir	1972
Project Tiger	1973
Project Olive Ridley Turtles	1975
Crocodile Breeding Scheme	1975
Project Manipur Thamin	1977
Project Rhino	1987
Project Elephant	1992
Project Red Panda	1996
Project Sea Turtle	1999
Project Vulture	2006
Project Snow Leopard	2009
Project Dolphin	2020
Project Asiatic Lion	2020

Endangered Species of India

Birds	Great Indian Bustard, Forest Owlet, Vulture, Bengal Florican, Himalayan Quail, Siberian Crane
Mammals	Flying Squirrel, Red Panda, Pygmy Hog, Kondana Rat, Snow Leopard, Asiatic Lion, One-Horned Rhinoceros
Reptiles	Gharial, Hawksbill Turtle, River Terrapin, Sispara Day Gecko
Amphibians	Flying Frog, Tiger Toad

INDIAN POLITY

CONSTITUTION

Framing of the Indian Constitution

- The idea to have a Constitution was first given by **MN Roy** (A pioneer of Communist Movement in India).
- The Constitution was framed by the **Constituent Assembly** of India, set-up on 16th May 1946, in accordance with the Cabinet Mission Plan, under the Chairmanship of Sachchidanand Sinha, initially. **Dr Rajendra Prasad** and HC Mukherjee were elected as the President and Vice-President respectively on 11th December 1946. BN Rau was appointed as the Constitutional Advisor.
- The total membership of the Constituent Assembly was 389, of these 292 were representatives of British States; 93 were representatives of Princely States and 4 were from the Chief Commissioners Provinces of Delhi, Ajmer-Merwara, Coorg and British Baluchistan.
- The Chairman of the Drafting Committee was **Dr BR Ambedkar**, also known as the Father of the Indian Constitution.

Enactment of the Constitution

- The Constituent Assembly took **2 years, 11 months** and **18 days** to complete the Constitution.
- Some of the provisions related to citizenship, elections, provisional Parliament etc were given immediate effect.
- The Constitution, is adopted on 26th November, 1949, contained a Preamble, **395** Articles divided into 22 Parts and **8** Schedules. Presently, it has 448 Articles divided into 25 Parts and **12** Schedules.
- The enforcement of Constitution was delayed till 26th January because, in 1929, on this day Indian National Congress demanded **Poorna Swaraj** in Lahore Session, Chaired by JL Nehru.
- The Constitution came into force on 26th January, 1950, known as Republic Day of India. The Constituent Assembly adopted our National Flag on 22nd July, 1947. It was designed by **Pingali Venkayya**.

Interim Government (1946)

Members	*Portfolios Held*
Jawaharlal Nehru	External Affairs & Commonwealth Relations
Sardar Vallabhbhai Patel	Home, Information & Broadcasting
Dr Rajendra Prasad	Food & Agriculture
Dr John Mathai	Industries & Supplies
Jagjivan Ram	Labour
Sardar Baldev Singh	Defence
CH Bhabha	Works, Mines & Power
Liaquat Ali Khan	Finance
Abdur Rab Nishtar	Posts & Air
Asaf Ali	Railways & Transport
C Rajagopalachari	Education & Arts
II Chundrigar	Commerce
Ghaznafar Ali Khan	Health
Joginder Nath Mandal	Law

Note *Interim government was formed from the newly elected Constituent Assembly.*

Preamble

- It is the preface or the introduction of the Constitution. It is an integral part of the Constitution. The interpretation of the Constitution is based on the spirit of the Preamble.
- The **Objective Resolution,** drafted and moved by Pandit Jawaharlal Nehru and adopted by the Constituent Assembly, ultimately became the Preamble.

- The idea of the Preamble was borrowed from the Constitution of USA.
- The words, **Socialist**, **Secular** and **Integrity** were added by the 42nd Constitutional Amendment Act in 1976.

The Preamble

"WE, THE PEOPLE OF INDIA, having solemnly resolved to constitute India into a SOVEREIGN, SOCIALIST, SECULAR, DEMOCRATIC REPUBLIC and to secure to all its citizens:

JUSTICE, Social, Economic and Political

LIBERTY of thought, expression, belief, faith and worship;

EQUALITY of status and of opportunity; and to promote among them all

FRATERNITY assuring the dignity of the individual and the unity and integrity of the Nation; IN OUR CONSTITUENT ASSEMBLY this twenty-sixth day of November, 1949 do HEREBY ADOPT, ENACT AND GIVE TO OURSELVES THIS CONSTITUTION.

Sources of the Indian Constitution

Country	Features
UK	▪ Rule of Law ▪ Cabinet System ▪ Prerogative Writs ▪ Parliamentary Government ▪ Bicameral Parliament ▪ CAG Office ▪ Single Citizenship ▪ Law making procedures
USA	▪ Written Constitution ▪ Vice-President as the Ex-officio Chairman of Upper House ▪ Fundamental Rights ▪ Supreme Court ▪ Independence of Judiciary and Judicial Review ▪ Preamble
Erstwhile USSR	▪ Fundamental Duties
Australia	▪ Concurrent List ▪ Joint sitting of Parliament
Japan	▪ Procedure established by law
Germany	▪ Suspension of Fundamental Rights during the Emergency
Canada	▪ Scheme of federation with a strong Centre ▪ Distribution of powers between the Centre and the States and placing Residuary Powers with the Centre
Ireland	▪ Concept of Directive Principles of State Policy. Method of election of the President
South Africa	▪ Procedure for amendment of the constitution and election of member of Rajya Sabha
France	▪ Republic and the ideals of Liberty equality and fraternity in the Preamble.

Main Features

- Bulkiest written Constitution in the World.
- Combination of Rigidity and Flexibility
- Parliamentary System of Government
- Federal System with a Unitary bias
- Fundamental Rights and Duties
- Directive Principles of State Policy
- Integrated and Independent Judiciary
- Single Citizenship
- Emergency Powers
- Universal Adult Franchise

Important Articles

Part I

Union and its Territories (Article 1-4)

1. The Constitution says, "India, that is Bharat, shall be a Union of States".
2. Admission or establishment of new States.
3. The Constitution empowers the Parliament to form new States and to alter the areas, boundaries or names of existing States.

Note *Through J & K Reorganisation Act of 2019, the state of Jammu and Kashmir was divided into two Union Territories i.e. Union Territory of Ladakh and the Union Territory of Jammu and Kashmir.*

Part II

Citizenship (Article 5-11)

The Citizenship Act of 1955 prescribes five ways to acquire citizenship of India

1. By birth
2. By descent
3. By registration
4. By naturalisation
5. By incorporation

Three modes of losing citizenship

1. Renunciation
2. Termination
3. Deprivation

Through Citizenship (Amendment) Act 2019 members of Hindu, Sikh, Buddhist, Jain, Parsi and Christian religions minorities from Afghanistan, Bangladesh and Pakistan who entered India before 31st December, 2014 will be given Indian citizenship.

Part III

Fundamental Rights

(Article 12-35)

Rights to Equality (Article 14-18)

- Equality before Law (Article 14).
- Prohibition of discrimination on grounds of religion, race, caste, sex or place of birth.(Article 15)
- Equality of opportunity in matters of public employment. (Article 16)
- Abolition of untouchability (Article 17).
- Abolition of titles. (Article 18)

Rights to Freedom (Article 19-22)

- Protection of certain rights regarding; Speech and expression, assembly, association, movement, residence, and profession (Article 19)
- Protection in respect of conviction for offences. (Article 20)
- Protection of life and personal liberty (Article 21).
- Protection against arrest and detention in certain cases (Article 22).

Right to Education

Article 21A states that the state shall provide free and compulsory education to all children of the age of 6-14 years.

Rights against Exploitation (Article 23-24)

- Prohibition of human trafficking and forced labour (Article 23).
- Prohibition of employment of children in any factories, etc (Article 24).

Rights to Freedom of Religion (Article 25-28)

- Freedom of conscience and right to profess, practice and propagate one's religious beliefs. (Article 25)
- Freedom to manage religious affairs (Article 26).
- Freedom from taxation for promotion of any particular religion (Article 27).
- Freedom from attendance of religious instructions or religious worship in certain educational institutions (Article 28).

Cultural and Educational Rights

- Protection of interest of minorities (Article 29).
- Right of minorities to establish and administer educational institutions (Article 30).

Freedom of Press is implicit in the Article 19. Article 20 and 21 cannot be suspended even during National Emergency. (Article 352)

Right to Property under Article 19 (1) (f) was repealed by the 44th Amendment Act, 1978, and was made a legal right under Article 300A.

Rights to Constitutional Remedies

- Right to move to the Supreme Court (Article 32) and the High Courts (Article 226) in case of violation of the Fundamental Rights BR Ambedkar called Article 32 as the **Heart and Soul of the Constitution**.
- 5 Writs of habeas corpus, mandamus, prohibition, certiorari and quo-warranto can be issued under this.

Types of Writs

Writ	*Meaning*	*Intended Purpose*
Habeas Corpus	You may have the body	To release a person who has been detained unlawfully whether in prison or in private custody.
Mandamus	We Command	To secure the performance of public duties by lower court, tribunal or public authority.
Certiorari	To be certified	To quash the order already passed by an interior court, tribunal or quasi judicial authority.
Prohibition	The act of stopping something	To prohibit an inferior court from continuing the proceedings in a particular case where it has no jurisdiction to try.
Quo Warranto	What is your authority	To restrain a person from holding a public office to which he is not entitled.

Part IV

Directive Principles of State Policy (Article 36-51)

Directive principles are broad guiding principles that state shall keep in mind while formulating policies and enacting laws. *These are non-justiciable in nature*

Articles 36-37 Definition and application of the principles contained in this part.

Article 38 To secure and protect a social order, which stands for the welfare of the people.

Article 39 Certain principles of policy to be followed by the State.

Article 40 To organise village Panchayats as units of self- government.

Article 41 Right to work, to education and to public assistance in certain cases.

Article 42 To secure just and humane conditions of work and maternity relief.

Article 43 Living wage etc for workers, to promote cottage industries.

Article 44 Uniform Civil Code for the citizens.

Article 45 Provision of early childhood care and education to children below the age of 6 years.

Article 46 To promote the educational and economic interests of the weaker sections of the people, especially the Scheduled Castes and Scheduled Tribes.

Article 47 Improvement of public health and the prohibition of intoxicating drinks and drugs.

Article 48 Organisation of agriculture and animal husbandry on modern lines.

Article 49 To protect all monuments of historic interest and national importance.

Article 50 To bring about the separation of the judiciary from the executive.

Article 51 Promotion of international peace and security.

Part IV (A)

Fundamental Duties (Article 51A)

It was inserted by the **42nd Amendment Act** in 1976 on the recommendations of Swaran Singh Committee it was inspired by the Constitution of erstwhile USSR.

It shall be the duty of every citizen of India

(a) to abide by the Constitution and respect its ideals and institutions, the National Flag and the National Anthem.

(b) to cherish and follow the noble ideals which inspired our national struggle for freedom.

(c) to uphold and protect the sovereignty, unity and integrity of India.

(d) to defend the country and render national service, when called upon to do so.

(e) to promote harmony and the spirit of common brotherhood amongst all the people of India, transcending religious, linguistic and regional or sectional diversities; to renounce practices derogatory to the dignity of women.

(f) to value and preserve the rich heritage of our composite culture.

(g) to protect and improve the natural environment including forests, lakes, rivers and wildlife and to have compassion for living creatures.

(h) to develop scientific temper, humanism and the spirit of enquiry and reform.

(i) to safeguard public property and to abjure violence.

(j) to strive towards excellence in all spheres of individual and collective activity, so that the nation constantly rises to higher levels of endeavour and achievement.

The **86th Amendment Act, 2002** inserted Article 51A (K), "each parent or guardian to provide opportunities for education to his child or ward between the age of 6 and 14 years."

Part V

Union (Article 52-151)

THE PRESIDENT

- Executive Head of the State and the first citizen of India.

- The 42nd Amendment of the Constitution has made it obligatory on the part of the President to accept the advice of the Council of Ministers. However, 44th Amendment Act amended the word 'obligatory' and added that '*President can send the advice for reconsideration*'.

Qualifications Must be a citizen of India; of 35 years in age; eligible to be a member of the Lok Sabha and must not hold any office of profit.

Election Indirectly elected through Electoral College consisting of elected members of both the Houses of the Parliament and elected members of the Legislative Assemblies of the States and elected members of the Legislative Assemblies of Union Territories of Delhi and Puducherry.

- Members of the Legislative Councils have no right to vote in the Presidential election.
- Supreme Court decides all disputes regarding President's election.

Tenure The term is 5 years though there is no upper limit on the number of times a person can become the President (Article 57). He can give resignation to the Vice-President before the full-term.

- The salary of the President is ₹ 5,00,000 per month.
- In case, the office of the President falls vacant due to death, resignation or removal, the Vice- President acts as the President.
- If he is not available then Chief Justice of India, if not then the senior most Judge of the Supreme Court shall act as the President of India.
- The first President who died in the office, was Dr Zakir Hussain. Fakhruddin Ali Ahmed was the second president to die in office.
- Justice M Hidayatullah was the first Chief Justice of India to be appointed as the President (July 1969-August 1969).

Impeachment Procedure

- It is a quasi- judicial procedure. President can be impeached only on the grounds of violation of the Constitution. *(Article 61)*
- The impeachment procedure can be initiated in either House of the Parliament.

Powers of President

- He is the formal head of the administration.
- The President shall have the power to appoint and remove high authorities like the Prime Minister, other Ministers of the Union, Judges, Governors of States and appoints Chiefs of Army, Navy and Air Force.
- He nominates 12 members of the Rajya Sabha from persons of literature, art, science and social work and 2 members in the Lok Sabha of the Anglo-Indian Community.

  Note *Parliament has passed (126th) Amendment Bill in December 2019, doing away with the provision of Anglo-Indians to Lok Sabha and Some State Assemblies.*
- Declares wars and concludes peace subject to the approval of the Parliament.
- President has the **Veto** power.
- **Under Article 72**, the President has the power to grant pardons, reprieves, respites or remission of punishment or to suspend, remit or commute the sentence of any person convicted with death sentence.
- **Under Article 123**, President can promulgate Ordinances, when the Parliament is not in session.

Types of Vetoes

Absolute Veto Withholding the assent to the Bill.

Qualified Veto Can be overridden by the Legislature with a higher majority.

Suspensive Veto Can be overridden by the Legislature with an ordinary majority.

Pocket Veto Delay in giving assent to the Bill. *The Veto Power has been exercised only twice* (a) by Dr Rajendra Prasad and (b) by R.Venkata raman. President of India is vested with three vetos absolute veto, suspensive veto and pocket veto. There is no qualified veto in the case of Indian President.

Emergency Powers

- To declare National Emergency. (Article 352)
- To impose President Rule in a State. (Article 356)
- To declare Financial Emergency. (Article 360)

VICE-PRESIDENT

- **Article 63** of the Constitution stipulates a Vice-President for India.
- He is elected by both the Houses of Parliament.
- The Vice-President is the Ex-officio **Chairman** of the Council of States (Rajya Sabha) as mentioned in the **Article 64**.
- Present salary of the Vice-President is ₹ 4,00,000 per month.
- The first Vice-President of India was Dr S Radhakrishnan.
- The first and only Vice-President who died in the office, was Shri Krishna Kant (1997-2002).

COUNCIL OF MINISTERS

- Article 74 of the Constitution states that there shall be a Council of Ministers, with the **Prime Minister** at its head, to aid and advise the President.
- It is composed of all Union Ministers—the Prime Minister, Cabinet Ministers, Ministers of State and Deputy Ministers.
- The other Ministers shall be **appointed by the President** on the advice of the Prime Minister under Article 75(1).
- A Minister must be a member of either House of Parliament or be elected within 6 months of assuming office under Article 75(5).
- The Council of Ministers is **collectively responsible** to the Lok Sabha, It means the Lok Sabha can remove the Council of Ministers from office by passing a No-confidence Motion. [Article 75 (3)].
- Ministers are also responsible for their departments and can be removed from the office by the President on the advice of the Prime Minister. This is essentially an individual responsibility under Article 75 (2).

PRIME MINISTER

- The Prime Minister is the head of the Government and the head of the Council of Ministers.
- The Prime Minister is appointed by the President on the basis of his being the leader of the majority party in the Lok Sabha.
- If no party gets an **absolute majority** in the Lok Sabha or a Prime Minister resigns or dies, the President can use his own discretion in the choice of the Prime Minister.
- Article 78 stipulates that it is the duty of the Prime Minister (a) to communicate to the President all the decisions taken by the Cabinet and (b) to furnish such information relating to the administration of the Union or any Legislation as the President may call for. The Prime Minister serves in the office for five years though he can be re-appointed.
- When the Lok Sabha is dissolved, He can continue in office upon the request of the President until new government is formed.
- If the Government is defeated in the Lok Sabha, the Prime Minister and the entire cabinet must resign, however, if defeated in the Rajya Sabha, resignation is not obligatory.

Tit-Bits

- **Jawaharlal Nehru** was the first Prime Minister and the longest serving Prime Minister so far.
- The first and the 'only' acting Prime Minister was **Gulzarilal Nanda**.
- **Lal Bahadur Shastri** was the first PM who died abroad, while in office at Takshent. Gulzarilal Nanda has acted twice as the acting Prime Minister.
- **Chaudhary Charan Singh** was the only PM who did not face Parliament, while being in office.
- The youngest Prime Minister was **Rajeev Gandhi** and the oldest Prime Minister was **Morarji Desai**.
- **AB Vajpayee** *(May 1996–June 1996)* government had the shortest tenure *(13 days)*.

UNION LEGISLATURE

- Legislature of the Union is called the Parliament and consists of the Rajya Sabha (Council of States), the Lok Sabha (House of the People) and the President (Article 79).

- The business of Parliament is transacted either in Hindi or in English. However, the Presiding Officers of the two Houses may permit any member to address the House in his/her mother tongue too.

Rajya Sabha (Council of States)

- Rajya Sabha is the Upper House of the Parliament. First sitting of the Rajya Sabha was held on 3rd April, 1952.
- The maximum permissible strength of the Rajya Sabha is 250. Of these, 238 members are elected indirectly from the States and Union Territories, and 12 are nominated by the President for their expertise in art, literature, science, sports and social services (Article 80).
- Currently, the strength of the Rajya Sabha is 245. Of these, 229 members are elected from States and 4 members represent Union Territories while 12 members are nominated by the President.
- The Rajya Sabha is a **Permanent House** and is not subject to dissolution and members enjoy a tenure of six years. However, one-third of the members retire every second years (Article 83).
- It shares legislative powers with the Lok Sabha, except in the case of Money Bill where the Lok Sabha has overriding powers.

Lok Sabha (People's House)

- The Lok Sabha is the Lower House of the Parliament and its first sitting took place on 13th May, 1952. The current Lok Sabha is the 17th constituted Lok Sabha.
- Three Sessions of the Lok Sabha are held every year, namely Budget Session (February to May); Monsoon Session (July to September); and Winter Session (November to December).

Members 530 from States, **20** from Union Territories and **2** nominated by the President, from the Anglo Indian Community (now abolished).

Election The representatives of the states are directly elected by the people of the states on the basis of adult suffrage.

Qualifications Article 84 provides for the eligibility for membership of the Parliament. *The conditions are*

(*a*) citizen of India;

(*b*) Not less than 25 years of age for the Lok Sabha and 30 years of age for the Rajya Sabha; and

(*c*) possess such other qualifications as may be prescribed by the Parliament.

Bills It may be classified as Ordinary, Money, Financial and Constitutional Amendments.

- **The Ordinary Bills** can be introduced in either House of the Parliament, but **Money Bill** can be initiated only in the House of the People i.e. Lok Sabha.
- After a Money Bill has been passed by the Lok Sabha, it is sent to the Rajya Sabha for deliberations. The Rajya Sabha is given 14 days to make recommendations, which can be accepted or not by the Lok Sabha.
- Article 111 stipulates that a Money Bill cannot be returned to the House by the President for reconsideration.

Speaker of the Lok Sabha

- As soon as a new Lok Sabha is constituted, the President appoints a Speaker pro-tem, who is generally the senior most member of the House. (It is a temporary office that ceases to exist after new speaker is elected by the house.)
- **Speaker** is the head of Lok Sabha. He/She is elected from amongst the members of Lok Sabha. The Speaker of the Lok Sabha conducts the business in the House. A Deputy Speaker is also elected to officiate in the absence of the Speaker.

Facts about Speaker

- **GV Mavlankar** was the first Speaker of the Lok Sabha (1952-1956).
- **MA Ayyangar** was the first Deputy Speaker (1952-1956).
- **Dr Balram Jakhar** was the longest serving Speaker (1980-1989).
- **GMC Balyogi** is the first Speaker to die in the office (1998-2002).
- **Meira Kumar** is the first woman speaker of the Lok Sabha (2009-2013).

SUPREME COURT

The Supreme Court of India was inaugurated on 28 January, 1950. Presently, Supreme Court is functioning at full strength (sanctioned strength 34). A small Bench, with two to three Justices, is called a Division Bench. A large Bench, with five or more Justices, is called a Constitutional Bench.

Tenure and Qualification

- Judges of the Supreme Court are appointed by the President and retire at the age of 65.
- The **qualifications** are (a) must be a citizen of India; (b) a Judge of a High Court for at least 5 years; or (c) an advocate of a High Court for at least 10 years; or he should be a distinguished jurist in the opinion of the President.
- The Constitution has not prescribed a minimum age for appointment as a judge of the Supreme Court.

Independence of Judges (Article 125) The salaries and allowances of Judges are charged upon the Consolidated Fund of India (Present salary of the CJI is ₹ 2.8 Lakh and of other Judges is ₹ 2.5 Lakh).

Removal of Judges Judges can be removed only on the grounds of proved **misbehaviour** or **incapacity**.

Judges can be removed only by a resolution of both Houses of Parliament supported by a majority of total membership of both the Houses and 2/3 of members present and voting. The first Judge against whom the proceedings were initiated was **V Ramaswami** (1993) and the second one was **Soumitra Sen** (2011).

Jurisdiction

The Supreme Court has original, appellate, advisory and writ jurisdictions.

- Original Jurisdiction means that certain types of cases can originate with the Supreme Court only. The Supreme Court has original jurisdiction in (a) disputes between the centre and one or more States; (b) disputes between the Centre and any State(s) on one side and one or more States on the other side; (c) disputes between two or more States; and (Article 131).
- Appellate Jurisdiction means that appeals against judgements of lower courts can be referred to it. The Supreme Court is the highest court of appeal in the country. Four types of cases fall within its appellate jurisdiction, namely, constitutional cases, civil cases, criminal cases and appeals by special leave.

- The first Chief Justice of India was **HJ Kania** (1950–51).
- The shortest tenure so far is of **KN Singh** (25th November, 1991—12th December, 1991).
- The longest tenure, so far is of **YV Chandrachud** (1978–85).
- The first woman Judge of the Supreme Court was Justice **Fatima Beevi** in 1987 and the second woman Justice was **Gyan Sudha Mishra** in 2010.

- Advisory Jurisdiction refers to the process where the President seeks the court's advice on legal matters (Article 143). The Supreme Court is a court of record (Article 129).
- Under Article 139 (A) (inserted by the 44th Amendment), the Supreme Court may transfer to itself, cases from one or more High Court if these questions involve a significant question of law.

Comptroller and Auditor General (CAG) (Article 148-151)

- The Comptroller and Auditor General is appointed by the President under **Article 148** of the Constitution.
- The CAG audits all receipts and expenditures of the Union and State Governments.
- The CAG also acts as the external auditor for the government-owned companies.
- The CAG submits its reports to the President (in case of accounts relating to the Union Government) or to the concerned State Governors (for State Government Accounts).
- The CAG is also the head of the Indian Audits and Accounts Service (IA & AS). The office of the CAG was established in 1860.

- The first CAG of India was **V Narahari Rao** (1948-1954).
- The CAG can only be removed from office in manner similar to a Judge of the Supreme Court.
- The salary and benefits of the CAG cannot be changed to his disadvantage during his tenure.
- The CAG is not eligible for further office under the Union or State Governments. The expenses of the office of the CAG is charged upon the Consolidated Fund of India.

Attorney General of India

- The Attorney General is the **highest law officer** in the country appointed by the President under **Article 76** of the Constitution.
- The first Attorney General of Independent India was **MC Setalvad** (1950-1963). The 15th and Current Attorney General of India is **KK Venugopal**.
- To be appointed as Attorney General, a candidate must be qualified to be appointed as a Judge of the Supreme **Court**.
- The Attorney General can participate in proceedings of the Parliament without the Right to Vote (Article 88).

Part VI

The States (Article 152-237)

THE GOVERNOR

- The Governor is the **Constitutional Head** of the State and the same Governor can act as Governor of more than one State (Article 153).
- The Governor is appointed by the **President** (Article 155) and Article 156 states that the Governor holds office during the pleasure of the President.
- **Article 161** gives the Governor the power to grant pardons, reprieves, remission of punishment to persons convicted under the state law.
- **Article 163** talks of **discretionary powers** of the Governor, which is not even provided to the President. Moreover, the courts cannot question his discretion.
- **Article 171** states that the States where Legislative Councils exists, the Governor can **nominate some members** from amongst those distinguished in literature, science, art, cooperative movement and social service.
- **Article 213** empowers the Governor to issue the **ordinances** during the recess of the State Legislature.

Qualifications

- Must be a citizen of India.
- Completed 35 years of age.
- Shouldn't be a member of either House of Parliament or State Legislature.
- Must not hold any office of profit.

STATES LEGISLATURE

Article 163 Council of Ministers to aid and advise the Governor.

Article 165 An Advocate General for each of the State.

Article 169 Abolition or creation of Legislative Councils in States.

Most of the states have unicameral system, only 6 states have legislative council. These states are Andhra Pradesh, Bihar, Karnataka, Maharashtra, Uttar Pradesh and Telangana.

Legislative Assembly Legislative Assembly consists of Representatives directly elected by the people. The strength of assembly varies from 60 to 500 members. However assembly of Sikkim, Goa, Mizoram, Arunachal Pradesh, Nagaland and Puducherry have less than 60 members.

Composition of Legislative Council Unlike the members of the Legislative Assembly, the members of Legislative Council are indirectly elected. The maximum strength of the Council is fixed at one-third of the total strength of assembly and the minimum strength is fixed at 40.

HIGH COURTS (ARTICLE 214-232)

There are **25** High Courts in India. The Calcutta High Court, established in 1862, is the oldest High Court in India. The Bombay and Madras High

Courts were also established in the same year. The newest High Courts are the Tripura, Meghalaya and Manipur High Courts, all were established in the year 2013. High Court of Andhra Pradesh (25th High Court of India) came into existence from January 1, 2019.

Part IX

The Panchayats (Article 243-243 O)

- Introduced by the 73rd Amendment Act, 1992 which envisaged a three tier system of local government.

  These are

  1. **Gram Panchayat at the village level**
  2. **Panchayat Samiti at the block level**
  3. **Zila Parishad at the district level**

- The Panchayat system exists in all states except Nagaland, Meghalaya and Mizoram. It also exists in all Union Territories except Delhi.
- Panchayat system is provided for all states having a population more than 2 million. Every Panchayat can continue for 5 years from the date of its first meeting.

Part IXA

The Municipalities (Article 243 P-243 ZG)

- Introduced by the 74th Amendment Act, 1992 which envisages three types of urban local bodies, namely, Nagar Panchayat, Municipal Council and Municipal Corporation.

Jurisdiction and Seats of High Courts

Court Name	*Estd. in the Year*	*Territorial Jurisdiction*	*Seat*
Mumbai	1862	Maharashtra, Dadra and Nagar Haveli, Goa, Daman and Diu	Mumbai *(Bench at Nagpur, Panaji and Aurangabad)*
Kolkata	1862	West Bengal, Andaman and Nicobar Islands	Calcutta *(Circuit Bench at Port Blair)*
Chennai	1862	Tamil Nadu and Puducherry	Chennai *(Bench at Madurai)*
Allahabad	1866	Uttar Pradesh	Prayagraj *(Bench at Lucknow)*
Karnataka	1884	Karnataka	Bangalore *(Circuit Benches at Hubli Dharwad and Gulbarga)*
Patna	1916	Bihar	Patna
Madhya Pradesh	1956	Madhya Pradesh	Jabalpur *(Benches at Gwalior and Indore)*
Jammu & Kashmir	1928	Jammu and Kashmir	Srinagar and Jammu
Punjab and Haryana	1875	Punjab, Haryana and Chandigarh	Chandigarh
Orissa	1948	Odisha	Cuttack
Guwahati	1948	Assam, Nagaland, Mizoram and Arunachal Pradesh	Guwahati (Bench at Kohima, Aizwal and Itanagar
Rajasthan	1949	Rajasthan	Jodhpur *(Bench at Jaipur)*
Kerala	1958	Kerala and Lakshadweep	Ernakulam
Gujarat	1960	Gujarat	Ahmedabad
Delhi	1966	National Capital Territory of Delhi	New Delhi
Himachal Pradesh	1971	Himachal Pradesh	Shimla
Sikkim	1975	Sikkim	Gangtok
Chhattisgarh	2000	Chhattisgarh	Bilaspur
Uttarakhand	2000	Uttarakhand	Nainital
Jharkhand	2000	Jharkhand	Ranchi
Tripura	2013	Tripura	Agartala
Manipur	2013	Manipur	Imphal
Meghalaya	2013	Meghalaya	Shillong
Andhra Pradesh	2019	Andhra Pradesh	Amaravati
Telangana	2019	Telangana	Hyderabad

Committees to Study Panchayat System

Name	Established	Recommendation
Balwantrai Mehta	1957	Establish local bodies, devolve power and authority, basic unit of decentralised government to be Block/Samiti. Conceptualised PRIs as 3-tier system.
K Santhanam	1963	Panchayats to have powers to levy tax on land revenue etc, Panchayati Raj Finance Corporation to be set-up.
Ashok Mehta	1978	District to be a viable administrative unit for planning, PRIs as two-tier system with Mandal Panchayat and Zila Parishad.
GVK Rao	1985	PRIs to be activated and supported, Block Development Office *(BDO)* to be central to rural development.
LM Singhvi	1986	Local self-governments to be constitutionally recognised, non-involvement of political parties.

- The first Municipal Corporation in India was introduced in Madras in 1688. The Madras Municipal Corporation is the first municipal body in the whole commonwealth outside the UK. The Bombay and Calcutta Corporations were established in 1726.
- Municipal Corporations are established in cities with population greater than 1 million.
- Nagar Panchayat administers urban areas having population greater than 30000 and less than 100000.
- A Municipal Council administers an urban area of population 200000 or less.

Part XI

Relations between the Union and the States (Article 245-263)

- Legislative Relations
- Administrative Relations
- Financial Relations

Article 262 Adjudication of disputes relating to waters of inter-state rivers or river valleys.

Article 263 Inter-state council.

Part XII

Finance, Property, Contracts and Suits (Article 264-300 A)

Article 266 Consolidated Fund of India.

Article 267 Contingency Fund of India.

Part XIV

Services Under the Union and the States (Article 308-323)

Article 312 All India Services.

Article 315 Public Service Commissions for the Union and for the States.

- The first Public Service Commission was set-up in 1926, on the recommendations of the Lee Commission.
- The Government of India Act, 1935 provided for the establishment of a Federal Public Service Commission and Provincial Public Service Commissions.

Union and State Public Service Commissions

- Constitution provides a Public Service Commission for the Union, a Public Service Commission for each state or a Joint Public Service Commission for a group of states.
- The appointment is done by the President in case of the Union or Joint Commission and by the Governor of the State in the case of a State Commission.
- At least half of the members of these commissions should be civil servants with at least 10 years experience in central or state services.
- Age of retirement for a member of UPSC is 65 years and for a member of PSC of a State or a Joint Commission is 62 years.

Functions

- To conduct exams for appointment to services under the Union and the States.
- Maintains continuity in administration.
- Members of the UPSC and State Commissions can be removed by the President on the charges of misbehaviour, if these charges are upheld by the Supreme Court.

Elections (Article 324-329)

Article 324 stipulates that the superintendence, direction and control of elections shall be vested in the Election Commission.

Article 325 provides for a single electoral roll for every constituency. Also stipulates that no person shall be eligible or ineligible for inclusion in electoral rolls on the basis of race, religion, caste or sex.

Article 326 stipulates that elections shall be held on the basis of adult suffrage. Every person, who is a citizen of India and is not less than 18 years of age shall be eligible for inclusion.

Political Parties

Registration of the People Act, 1951 provides for registration of political parties with the election commission.

There are eight (8) National Parties in India, namely BJP, Congress, BSP, NCP, CPI, CPM, Trinamool Congress and National People's Party.

A political party shall be eligible to be recognised as a **National party** if

(*i*) It secures at least 6% of the valid votes polled in any four or more states, at a general election to the House of the People or to the State Legislative Assembly; and

(*ii*) In addition, it wins at least four seats in the House of the People from any State or States.

or

(*iii*) It wins at least 2% seats in the House of the People (*i.e.*, 11 seats in the existing House having 543 members) and these members are elected from at least three different States.

Likewise, a political party shall be entitled to be recognised as a **State party**, if

(*i*) It secures at least 6% of the valid votes polled in the State at a general election, either to the House of the People or to be Legislative Assembly of the State concerned; and

(*ii*) In addition, it wins at least two seats in the Legislative Assembly of the State concerned.

or

It wins at least 3% of the total number of seats in the Legislative Assembly of the State or at least three seats in the Assembly, whichever is more.

For elections of President and Vice-President, election petitions can only be filed with the Supreme Court.

Election Commission

- The Election Commission is an autonomous, quasi-judiciary constitutional body. Its function is to conduct free and fair elections in India.
- The Election Commission was established on 25th January, 1950 under **Article 324** of the Constitution.
- The first Chief Election Commissioner was **Sukumar Sen**.

Planning Commission

- The Planning Commission was established in March, 1950 by an executive resolution of the Government of India (*i.e.*, Union Cabinet) on the recommendation of the Advisory Planning Board constituted in 1946 under the Chairmanship of KC Neogi.
- Now, the Planning Commission has been replaced by NITI Aayog.

NITI Aayog

- NITI Aayog or National institution for transforming India Aayog is a policy think-tank of Union Government of India that replaces Planning Commission of India and aims to involve the states in economic policy-making in India. It will be providing strategic and technical advice to the central and the State Governments.
- Prime Minister of India heads the Aayog as its Chairperson.

National Development Council (NDC)

- Functions of the NDC was to review the working of national plan. The NDC was formed in **1952**, to associate the states in the formulation of the plans.
- The PM is the ex-officio chairman of NDC.
- It is an extra-constitutional and extra legal body.
- Since establishment of NITI Aayog, NDC has been proposed to be abolished.

Finance Commission

- **Article 280** of the Constitution of India provides for a Finance Commission as a quasi-judicial body. It is constituted by the President of India every fifth year.
- It consists of Chairman and 4 other members.

Functions The Finance Commission is required to make recommendation to the President of India in the following matters: The distribution of the net proceeds of taxes to be shared between the centre and the states and the allocation between the states, the respective shares of such proceeds. The 15th Finance Commission was appointed on 2nd January, 2017 under the Chairmanship of **NK Singh**.

AMENDMENTS OF THE CONSTITUTION (ARTICLE 368)

There are two categories of Amendment under Article 368 which are:-

1. By special majority of Parliament that is (more than 50 percent) of the total membership of each House and a majority of two-thirds of the members of each House present and voting.
2. By special majority of Parliament and with the consent of half of the State Legislature by a simple majority. Provisions related to Federal structure can be amended through this procedure.

   There is a third category of the Amendment which is done by simple majority though these amendments do not come under ambit of **Article 368**.

It has been held by the Supreme Court in the **Keshavananda Bharati Case** (1973) that every provision of the Constitution is amendable under the meaning of Article 368 except the basic structure of the Constitution.

e-GOVERNANCE

The word **electronic** in the terms e-Governance implies technology driven governance.

The prespective of the e-governance is "the use of the technology that both governing and have to be governed.

Generally five basic models are given in e-Governance

- G2C (Government to Citizens)
- G2B (Government to Business)
- G2E (Government to Employees)
- G2G (Government to Governments)
- C2G (Citizens to Governments)

The National e-Governance Plan (NeGP) takes a holistic view of e-governance initiatives across the country, integrating them into a collective vision.

Impacts of e-Governance

e-Governance brings about two major impacts **firstly**, making the government offices work smart. **Secondly**, e-governance makes services available to the citizen at his doorstep through the internet.

Some of the most successfull citizen oriented e-governance projects are the Railways Reservation System, MCA 21 is the Ministry of Corporate Affairs and Bhoomi Project in Andhra Pradesh, etc.

E-districts

It is a mission mode under e-governance. Its objective under National E-Governance Policy is to computerisation of services. Under it, different programmes are conducted in following states

- Jandoot Project - Madhya Pradesh
- Compact 2020 - Andhra Pradesh
- Land Programme - Karnataka
- Friends - Kerala
- Disha - Haryana

PARLIAMENTARY TERMS

Quorum It is the minimum number of members required to transact the business of the House. **Article 100** of the Constitution specifies that the Quorum of either House shall be 10% of the strength of the House.

Question Hour The first hour of every sitting of Parliament is called the Question Hour. Questions usually need a 10 day notice before being answered by the concerned minister.

Starred Questions To be answered orally on the floor of the House. Supplementary questions can be asked.

Unstarred Questions To be answered in writing. No supplementary questions may be asked.

Zero Hour Does not formally exist in the Parliamentary procedure. The hour after Question Hour is popularly known as Zero Hour. Members raise matters which they feel urgent.

Adjournment Motion Motion to adjourn the proceedings of the House, so as to take up a matter of urgent public importance. It can be moved by any member. Requires support from at least 50 members.

Calling Attention Motion A member may call the attention of a Minister to an urgent matter and the Minister may make a statement regarding it.

No Confidence Motion A No Confidence Motion indicates lack of confidence of the Lok Sabha in the Council of Ministers. It can be introduced in the Lok Sabha only. If the Motion is passed, the government must resign.

CONSTITUTIONAL AMENDMENTS

First Amendment Act, 1951 Added Ninth Schedule.

Seventh Amendment Act, 1956 Necessitated on account of reorganisation of States on a linguistic basis.

Fifteenth Amendment Act, 1963 Age of retirement of the Judges of High Court has been extended from 60 to 65 years.

Twenty Sixth Amendment Act, 1971 Abolished the titles and special privileges of former rulers of princely states.

Thirty Sixth Amendment Act, 1975 Made Sikkim a State.

Forty Fourth Amendment Act, 1978 The Right to Property was deleted from Part III. Article 352 was amended to provide 'Armed Rebellion' as one of the circumstances for declaration of emergency.

Seventy Third Amendment Act, 1992 The institution of Panchayati Raj receive constitutional guarantee, status and legitimacy. XIth Schedule was added to deal with it. It also inserted Part IX, containing Articles, 243, 243 A to 243 O.

Eighty Ninth Amendment Act, 2003 The Act adds Article 338 A and provides for the creation of National Commission for Scheduled Tribes.

Ninety First Amendment Act, 2003 Amended the Anti-Defection Law and also made a provision that the number of ministers in the Centre and State Government, cannot be more than 15% of the strength of Lok Sabha and the respective Vidhan Sabha.

Ninety Third Amendment Act, 2005 To reserve seats for socially and educationally backward classes, besides the Scheduled Castes and the Scheduled Tribes, in private unaided institutions other than those run by minorities.

Ninety Seventh Amendment, 2011 Amendment of Article 19(1)(i), Insertion of Article 43B, Insertion of Part IXB. This amendment gives constitutional status to cooperatives.

Ninety-Ninth Amendment Act, 2014 deals with replacing the collegium system for the appointments of the Judges of the Supreme Court and the 24 High Courts. But Supreme Court of India has declared this unconstitutional and void.

One Hundredth Amendment Act, 2015 to give effect to the acquring of territories by India and transfer of certain territories to Bangladesh in pursuance of the agreements and its protocol.

One Hundredth One Amendment Act, 2016 with deals Goods and Services Tax (GST)

One Hundredth Two Amendment Act, 2018 provides the Constitutional status to National Commission for Backward Classes.

One Hundredth Three Amendment Act, 2019 provides 10% reservation to the economically backward classes of society.

One Hundredth Fourth Amendment Act, 2020 extended the reservation of seats for SCs and STs in Lok Sabha and State Assemblies from seventy years to eighty years and removed the reserved seats for Anglo-Indian community in Lok Sabha and State Assemblies.

105th Amendment-2021 To restore the power of State govt and U.T to identify and specify socially and economically backward classes.

INDIAN ECONOMY

OUTLINE OF INDIAN ECONOMY

The economy of India is the 5th largest in the world by nominal GDP and 3rd largest by Purchasing Power Pariety (PPP).

Nature of the Indian Economy

(*i*) **Mixed Economy** Existence of both public and private sectors. This term was coined by Pat Mullins and Supported by JM Keynes.

(*ii*) **Agrarian Economy** Even after six-decades of independence 58% of the workforce of India is still agriculturist and its contribution to **GDP** is around 17% at current prices.

Features

Following are the features of Indian economy

(*i*) Slow growth of national and per capita income. (*ii*) Capital deficiency and low rate of capital formation, hence low rate of investment, low production, etc; poor quality of human capital. (*iii*) Over- dependence on agriculture alongwith low productivity in agriculture; heavy population pressure. (*iv*) Unequal distribution of income and wealth. (*v*) Mass poverty, chronic inflation and chronic unemployment.

Broad Sectors of Indian Economy

Primary Sector Agriculture, forestry and fishing, mining etc.

Secondary Sector manufacturing, electricity, gas and water supply and construction.

Tertiary Sector (also called service sector) business, transport, telecomm- unication, banking, insurance, real estate, community and personnel services.

Economic Planning in India

Planning Commission (1950) was set-up under the Chairmanship of Pandit Jawaharlal Nehru (Gulzarilal Nanda was the first Deputy Chairman).

Basic aim of Economic Planning is to bring rapid economic growth through agriculture, industry, power and all other sectors of the economy.

NITI Aayog

NITI Aayog or *National Institution for Transforming India Aayog* came into existence on 1st January, 2015; policy-making think-tank of government that replaces Planning Commission and aims to involve states in economic policy making. It will provide strategic and technical advice to the Central and the State Governments.

The Prime Minister heads the Aayog as its chairperson. Rajiv Kumar is the Vice-Chairperson of NITI Aayog of India.

Historical Milestones

Planned Economy for India (1934) M Visvesvaraya

National Planning Committee (1938) Jawaharlal Nehru

Bombay Plan (1944)

Gandhian Plan (1944) SN Agarwal

People's Plan (1945) MN Roy

Sarvodaya Plan (1950) JP Narayan

Five Year Plans At a Glance

Plan	*Growth Rate*		*Important Sector*
	Target	*Achieved*	
First Plan (1951-56) (*Based on Harrod Domar Model*)	2.1%	3.6%	Agriculture, irrigation, electricity
Second Plan (1956-61) (*Based on PC Mahalanobis two sector model*)	4.5%	4.2%	Heavy industries
Third Plan (1961-66)	5.6%	2.8%	Foodgrains, heavy industries
Plan Holiday (1966-69)			
Fourth Plan (1969-74)	5.7%	3.3%	Agriculture
Fifth Plan (1974-78)	4.4%	4.8%	Removal of poverty
Rolling Plan (1978-80)			
Sixth Plan (1980-85)	5.2%	5.4%	Agriculture, industries
Seventh Plan (1985-90)	5.0%	6.0%	Energy, foodgrains
Two Annual Plans (1990-92)			
Eighth Plan (1992-97)	5.6%	6.6%	Human resource education
Ninth Plan (1997-2002)	6.5%	5.4%	Social justice
Tenth Plan (2002-07)	8.1%	7.5%	Income, energy
Eleventh Plan (2007-2012)	8.0%	7.9%	Inclusive growth
Twelfth Plan (2012-2017)	8%	—	Faster, sustainable and more inclusive growth

National Income in India

National Income refers to the aggregate value of goods and services produced in an economy in one year. Following are the measures of National Income in India

- Gross Domestic Product (GDP) is the final value of the goods and services produced within the geographical boundaries of a country during a year.
- Net Domestic Product (NDP) equals to the GDP minus depreciation (value loss of an asset) on country capital goods.
- Gross National Product (GNP) is an estimate of the total value of all the final products and services produced in a given period (usually a year) by the nationals of a country.
- The Net National Product (NNP) is obtained by subtracting depreciation value from GNP.
- When NNP is obtained at factor cost it is called National Income. It is calculated by deducting indirect taxes and adding subsidies in NNP at market price.

Indian Tax Structure

Direct Tax The term direct tax generally means a tax paid directly to the government by the persons on whom it is imposed. *e.g.* income tax, Corporate income tax, capital gain tax, stamp duty, land tax, estate duty, wealth tax, petroleum revenue tax. The government earns maximum from corporate income tax.

Indirect Tax An indirect tax is a tax collected by an intermediary from the person who bears the ultimate economic burden of the tax. e.g. sales tax or VAT, customs duty, insurance premium tax, excise duties, landfill tax, electricity duty, climate change levy.

Goods and Service Tax (GST)

The GST as it is more commonly referred to is a system of taxation where there is a single tax in the economy for goods as well as services. Indian GST was first proposed in India in the Union Budget speech in 2006-07. This tax come into effect from 1 July, 2017.

The main feature of the GST is that there is a tax credit available at each stage of the value chain.

Inclusive Development

Human Development Index (HDI)

- HDI measure was given by Pakistani Nobel Prize Winner, Mehbub-ul-Haq
- Level of Human development is measured by Human Development Index (HDI), published by UNDP since, 1990.
- *Three dimensions*
  1. Life expectancy at birth;
  2. Education Index comprising means year of schooling and expected year of schooling;
  3. GNI per capita (PPP US $) Index.
- India has been ranked 132 out 191 countries on HDI-2022.

Programmes/Measures

- **NRHM** (National Rural Health Mission) was launched on 2nd April, 2005 to reduce Infant Mortality Rate and Maternal Mortality Rate.
- **NUHM** (National Urban Health Mission) launched on 2013. Education programmes like Sarva Shiksha Abhiyan, Mid-Day Meal Scheme etc were launched.
- Rural development programmes like **MGNREGA** and **Bharat Nirman**.

POVERTY

- **The erstwhile Planning Commission estimated poverty** rate based on data collected by National Sample Survey Organisation (NSSO).
- **Main Reasons for Rural Poverty** Rapid population growth, lack of capital, lack of alternate employment other than poor agriculture, illiteracy and lack of proper implementation of PDS.
- **Main Reasons for Urban Poverty** Migration from rural areas, lack of skilled labour, lack of housing facilities, limited job opportunities in cities.
- Based on **2400 calories** (rural) and **2100 calories** (urban) and monthly per capita consumption expenditure of ₹ 454 (rural) and ₹ 540 (urban), Planning Commission (Now NITI Aayog) estimated poverty ratio in India in 2004-05 was 27.5% and according to the Suresh Tendulkar Committee was 37.2%.
- The Tendulkar Committee stipulated a benchmark of daily per capita expenditure of ₹ 27 and ₹ 33 in rural and urban areas, respectively.

Socio-Economic Programmes

Programme/Measure	*Year of Launch*
Twenty Point Programme	1975
Indira Awaas Yojana	1985
Swarna Jayanti Shahri Rozgar Yojana	1997
Pradhan Mantri Gramodaya Yojana	2000
Pradhan Mantri Gram Sadak Yojana	2000
Sampoorna Grameen Rozgar Yojana	2001
Bharat Nirman	2005
Jawaharlal Nehru National Urban Renewal Mission	2005
Prime Minister Employment Generation Programme	2008
Mahatma Gandhi National Rural Employment Programme	2009
National Rural Livelihood Mission (NRLM)	2011
Nirmal Bharat Abhiyan	2012
Swachh Bharat Abhiyan	2014
Pradhan Mantri Jan Dhan Yojana	2015
Atal Pension Yojana	2015
Digital India Programme	2015
National Skill Development Mission	2015
HRIDAY (Heritage City Development and Augmentation Yojana)	2015
Smart City Mission	2015
AMRUT (Atal Mission for Rejuvenation and Urban Transformation)	2015
Pradhanmantri Jeevan Jyoti Beema Yojana	2015
Pradhanmantri Suraksha Beema Yojana	2015
Pradhan Mantri Krishi Sinchayee Yojana	2015
Start-up and Stand-up Yojana	2016
Pradhan Mantri Fasal Bima Yojana	2016
Ujala Yojana	2016
SWAYAM (Study Webs of Active-Learning for Young Aspiring Minds)	2016
Pradhan Mantri Garib Kalyan Yojana	2016
Pradhan Mantri Vaya Vandana Yojana	2017
Pradhan Mantri Matritva Vandana Yojana	2017
Pradhan Mantri Sahaj Bijli Har Ghar Yojana	2017
Rashtriya Vayoshri Yojana	2017
Saubhagya Yojana	2017

Programme/Measure	*Year of Launch*
UDAN Scheme	2017
Ayushman Bharat	2018
Pradhan Mantri Kisan Samman Nidhi	2019
Pradhan Mantri Shram Yogi Man-dhan Yojna	2019
SVAMITVA Scheme	2020
One Nation One Card Scheme	2020
Ghar Tak Fibre Scheme	2020
PM SVANidhi	2020
Atmanirbhar Bharat Scheme	2020
Kisan Suryodya Yojana	2020
Pradhan Mantri Matsya Sampada Yojana	2020
PM-WANI Scheme	2020
Ayushman Bharat CAPF Healthcare Scheme	2021
Gram Ujala Scheme	2021
PM Gatishakti	2021
Rail Kaushal Vikas Yojana	2021
PM Daksh Yojana	2021
RBI's Retail Direct Scheme Integrated Ombudsmen Scheme	2021
Govt. Scheme of 4G	2021
Ayushman Bharat Digital Mission	2021
Pradhanmantri Swasth Bharat Yojana	2021
AMRUT 2.0	2021
Integrated Pensioners Portal	2022
Smile-75 Initiative	2022
PM Aadi Adarsh Gram Yojana	2022
SVANidhi se Samriddhi	2022
Pradhan Mantri Garib Kalyan Ann Yojana	2023

UNEMPLOYMENT

It refers to a situation, when a person is able and willing to work at the prevailing wage rate, but does not get the opportunity to work.

Estimation of Unemployment

Since 1973 on the recommendation of **B Bhagwati Committee**, three estimates of unemployment have been brought about by Planning Commission, *viz*

1. **Usual Principal Status** Persons who remained unemployed for a major part of the year.
2. **Current Weekly Status** Persons who did not find even an hour of work in a week preciding the date of survey.
3. **Current Daily Status** Persons who did not find work even for 1 hour in a day.

Women Empowerment *and* Child Development

Programme/Measure	*Year*
Mid-Day Meal Scheme	1995
Swadhar	1995
Swayam Sidha	2001
SSA	2001
Support to Training and Employ-ment Programme for Women (STEP)	2003-04
Ujjwala	2007
Dhanlaxmi	2008
Integrated Child Protection Scheme	2009-10
Sabla Scheme	2010
National Mission for Empowerment of Women	2010
Bal Bandu Scheme	2011
Nai Roshni	2012
Beti Bachao, Beti Padhao	2015
PM Ujjwala Yojna	2016
PM Matri Vandana Yojna	2017
Suposhit Maa Abhiyan	2020
SheBox	2021
Mission Shakti	2022

AGRICULTURE

- Agriculture is the mainstay of Indian economy. It makes important contribution in GDP, National Income, employment, trade and industry.
- **Green Revolution** is associated with the use of **HYVS** (High Yielding Variety Seeds), chemical, fertilisers and new technology, which led to a revolutionary results in agricultural production.
- Dr. MS Swaminathan has been called the 'Father of Green Revolution' in India.

Major Agricultural Revolutions

Revolution	*Production*
Blue	Fish Production
Golden Fibre	Jute
Pink	Onion
Red	Meat
White	Milk
Yellow	Oilseed

Tricolour Revolutions

Tricolour revolution has 3 components

- Saffron revolution–Solar energy
- White revolution–Cattle welfare
- Blue revolution–fisherman's welfare

INDUSTRIES

Industrial Policies

- Industrial policies were launched in 1948, 1956, 1977, 1980 and 1991.
- Industrial Policy 1956 is called **Economic Constitution of India** and gave public sector the strategic edge.
- Industrial Policy 1991 opened up the economy. *Its main aims were*
  (a) to end license-permit raj;
  (b) to integrate Indian economy with the outer world;
  (c) to remove restrictions on FDI and
  (d) to reform public sectors.

Public Sector Enterprises (PSEs)

- Industries requiring **compulsory licensing** (a) distillation and brewing of alcoholic drinks; (b) cigar and cigarettes of tobacco; (c) electronic aerospace and defence equipment; (d) industrial explosives; (e) specific hazardous chemicals.
- Areas reserved for public sector are (a) atomic energy—production, separation and enrichment of fissionable materials and (b) railways.
- **Present Policy** on PSEs is to (a) not to privatise profit-making companies and to modernise and revive sick companies; (b) not to bring government stake in PSEs below 51%; (c) to adopt initial public offering route to disinvestment.

Maharatnas, Navratnas, and Miniratnas

- To impart greater managerial and commercial autonomy to the PSEs, the concept of Maharatna, Navratna and Miniratna was started.
- **Maharatnas** were started in 2009. Twelve Maharatnas are ONGC, SAIL, IOC, NTPC, Coal India Ltd, BHEL, GAIL (India) Ltd, BPCL, HPCI and Power Grid Corporation, PFC, RECL.
- **Navratnas** Bharat Electronics Ltd, HAL, MTNL, NALCO, National Mineral Development Corporation, Nevyeli Lignite Company Ltd, Oil India Ltd, Rashtriya Ispat Nigam Ltd, Shipping Corporation of India Ltd, CCIL, EIL and NBCCL.
- **Miniratnas** Public Sector Enterprises (PSEs) that have made profit continuously for the last three years and have positive net worth.

Industrial Committes

Hazari Committee on Industrial Policy.

Subimal Dutt Committee on Industrial licensing.

Abid Hussain Committee on Small Scale Industry.

C Rangarajan Committee on disinvestment.

Memorandum of Understandings (MoU) Arjun Sengupta.

Small Scale Industry

- A new thrust to Small Scale Industry, given in Industrial Policy of 1977.
- MSMED Act, was enacted in 2006.
- Contributes 8% to GDP, 45% to all manufactures and 42% to exports.
- According to the 4th census (2009) of SSIs, 67% of the MSME are in manufacturing and 33% are in services sector.

Classification of MSMEs

Category	*Annual turnover*
Micro	Between 1 and 5 crore
Small	Between ₹ 10 crores to ₹ 50 crores
Medium	₹ 50 to ₹ 250 crores

Major Industries in India

Iron and Steel

- First Steel Industry at Kulti, West Bengal—Bengal Iron Works Company was established in 1874.
- First large scale steel plant—TISCO at Jamshedpur (1907) was followed by IISCO at Burnpur (1919), West Bengal.
- The first public owned steel plant was Rourkela integrated steel plant. Presently, India is the 3rd largest producer of steel and comes 1st in the production of sponge iron.

Location (Plants)	*Assistance*
Rourkela *(Odisha)*	Germany
Bhilai *(Chhattisgarh)*	Russia
Durgapur *(West Bengal)*	Britain
Bokaro *(Jharkhand)*	Russia
Visakhapatnam *(Andhra Pradesh)*	Russia

Jute Industry

- India ranks no 1 in jute production and no 2 in raw jute exports after Bangladesh.
- More than two third jute industry is concentrated in West Bengal.

Cotton and Textile Industry

- Largest organised and broad-based industry accounting for 4% of GDP, 20% of manufacture value added and one third of total exports earning.

Cement Industry

- First cement producing unit was set-up at Chennai in 1904 but modern manufacturing unit of cement started at Porbandar (Gujarat) in 1914.
- India is the second largest producer of cement in the world.

Sugar Industry

- India is the second largest producer of sugar in the world with a 22% share. It is the second largest agro-based industry in the country.

Committees on Various Sectors of Indian Economy

AC Shah Committee	Non-Banking Financial Company
Bimal Jalan Committee	Market Infrastructure Instruments
Malegam Committee	Functioning of Micro Finance Institutions
Birla Committee	Corporate Governance
Kirit Parikh Committee	Rationalisation of Petroleum Product Prices
Chaturvedi Committee	Improving National Highways in India
SR Hashim Committee	Urban Poverty
Abhijit Sen	Wholesale Price Index
Abid Hussain Committee	Development of Capital Markets
Damodaran Committee	Customer Service in Banks
Khandelwal Committee	Human Resource in Commercial Banks
Patil Committee	Corporate Debt
VK Sharma Committee	Credit to Marginal Farmers
Sarangi Committee	Non-Performing Assets
Khanna Committee	Regional Rural Banks
Dantawala Committee	Lead Bank Scheme
Gadgil Committee	Financial Inclusion

BANKING AND FINANCE

- **Bank of Hindustan** was the first bank, established in India in 1770.
- First bank with limited liability managed by an Indian Board was the **Oudh Commercial Bank** in 1881.
- First purely Indian bank was **Punjab National Bank** (1894).

Nationalisation of Bank

- A step towards **social banking** was taken with the nationalisation of **14 commercial banks** on 19th July, 1969. Six more banks were nationalised on 1980, total number of public sector banks are 27.
- Later on, in the year 1993, the government merged New Bank of India with Punjab National Bank.
- **Bhartiya Mahila Bank**, India's first bank exclusively for women, headquarters in New Delhi was Inaugurated on 19th November, 2013. It has been merged with SBI in 2017.
- **IDBI Bank** is an Indian financial service company, formerly known as Industries Development Bank of India, head quartered in Mumbai, India.
- In September, 2004, the RBI incorporated IDBI as a scheduled bank under the RBI Act, 1934.

- In 2019, Oriental Bank of Commerce and United Bank got merged with Punjab National Bank. Syndicate Bank is merged with Canara Bank while Union Bank of India, Andhra Bank and Corporation Bank got merged. Similarly Indian Bank got merged with Allahabad Bank.

Reserve Bank of India (RBI)

RBI was established in 1935, under RBI Act, 1934. RBI is the Central Bank of India. The main purpose of creating RBI was to regulate money supply and credit in the country. RBI was nationalised in 1949 and its first Indian Governor was **CD Deshmukh**. Its headquarter is in Mumbai.

Functions of the RBI

- Monetary policy, regulation and supervision of the banking and non-banking financial institutions.
- Debt and cash management for Centre and State Governments.
- Foreign exchange management, current and capital account management.
- Management of foreign exchange reserves.
- Currency management; oversight of the payment and settlement systems.
- Development role.
- Research and statistics.

The RBI and Credit Control

Quantitative Credit Control

It is used to control the volume of credit and indirectly to control the inflationary and deflationary pressures. *The quantitative credit control consists of*

- **Bank Rate** It is the rate, at which the RBI gives finance to Commercial Banks.
- **Cash Reserve Ratio** (CRR) Cash that banks deposits with the RBI without any floor rate or ceiling rate.
- **Statutory Liquidity Ratio** (SLR) It is the ratio of liquid asset, which all Commercial Banks have to keep in the form of cash, gold and government approved securities with itself.
- **Repo Rate** It is the rate, at which RBI lends short-term money to the banks against securities.
- **Reverse Repo Rate** It is the rate, at which banks park short-term excess liquidity with the RBI. This is always 100 base point, 1% less than Repo rate.

Qualitative/Selective/Direct Credit Control

Qualitative measures are used to make sure that purpose, for which loan is given is not misused. It is done through

- credit rationing
- regulating loan to consumption etc.

New Bank Licence

In April 2015, Reserve Bank of India provided licence for operation to two new private banks namely Bandhan Financial Services and Infrastructure Development Finance Company (IDFC).

MUDRA Bank

Micro Units Development and Refinance Agency Bank (MUDRA Bank) was launched on 8th April, 2015. Bank set up under SIDBI (Small Industries Development Bank of India). Bank has launched 3 loan instruments

- Shishu–Cover loans upto ₹ 50,000
- Kishore–Cover loan above ₹ 50,000 and upto ₹ 5 lakh.
- Tarun–Cover loans above ₹ 5 lakh and upto ₹ 10 lakh.

Indradhanush Scheme 2015

This is for the banking reforms in India. The 7 key reforms of Indradhanush Mission includes. appointments de-stressing, capitalisation, empowerment, framework of accountability, governance reforms and bank board bureau.

15th Finance Commission

The 15th Finance Commission was constituted in accordance with the **Article 280** of the Indian Constitution.

The first finance commission was headed by **KC Neogi** and the 15th Finance Commission is headed by NK Singh.

Stock Exchange of India

- Capital market is the market for long-terms funds while money market is the market for short-term funds.
- Capital market of India is regulated by SEBI (Securities and Exchange Board of India, 1988).
- **A Stock Exchange** provides services for brokers and traders to trade stocks, bonds, and other securities.
- **The Bombay Stock Exchange** (BSE) is a stock exchange located on Dalal Street, Mumbai and is the oldest stock exchange in Asia. The BSE has the largest number of listed companies in the world established in 1875.
- **The National Stock Exchange** (NSE) is the 16th largest stock exchange in the world. It is situated in Mumbai.

Insurance

- Insurance industry includes two sectors, life Insurance and General Insurance.
- LIC was established on 1st September, 1956.
- **Insurance Regulatory and Development Authority of India** (IRDAI) was set-up on 19th April, 2000 to regulate the Insurance Sector IRDA has changed its name to Insurance Regulatory and Development Authority of India in December 2014.

Foreign Trade

Balance of Trade (BoT)

The difference between a nation's imports of goods and services and its exports of them is known as **Balance of Trade**. There are three possibilities in the Balance of Trade (BoT) *which are as follows*

1. Balance BoT *i.e.* Exports = Imports
2. Adverse BoT *i.e.* Exports < Imports
3. Favourable BoT *i.e.* Exports > Imports

Balance of Payment (BoP)

BoP records the transactions in goods, services and assets between residents of a country with the rest of the world for a specified time period typically a year. There are two main accounts in the BoP : the *current account* and the *capital account*. In addition to that BoP includes errors and omissions and change in foreign exchange reserves.

Foreign Direct Investment (FDI)

It is an investment in a foreign country through the acquisition of a local company or the establishment of an operation on a new greenfield site. Direct investment implies control and managerial and perhaps technical, input.

FDI Limits

Sector/Activity	*% of FDI/Equity*
Multi Brand Retail (food)	100%
Telecom Services	100%
Tea Plantation	100%
Asset Reconstruction Company	100%
Petroleum and Natural Gas	49%
Commodity Exchanges	49%
Insurance	74%
Power Exchanges	49%
Stock Exchanges/Clearing Corporations	49%
Credit Information Companies, Pharma	100% (Green Field), 74 % (Brown Field)
Courier Services	100%
Single Brand Product Retail Trading	100%
Defence Sector	100%
Airlines	100%

CENSUS 2011

Population Trend in India

1891-1921 Stagnant population
1921-1951 Steady growth
1951-1981 Rapid high growth (stage of population explosion)
1981-2001 High growth rate with definite signs of slowing down

Total Population	1210569573
Male	623121843 (51.47%)
Female	587447730 (48.53%)
Density	382 per sq km
Sex Ratio	943
Child Sex Ratio	914

Largest and the Smallest States/UTs (in Population)

Top States/UTs		*Bottom States/UTs*	
Uttar Pradesh	199281477	Lakshadweep	64,429
Maharashtra	112372972	Ladakh	2,74,000
Bihar	103804637	Andaman and Nicobar Islands	3,79,944
West Bengal	91347736	Dadra and Nagar Haveli and Daman and Diu	5,85,764
Andhra Pradesh	84665533	Sikkim	6,07,688

Effective Literacy Rate (2001-2011)

	2001 (%)	*2011 (%)*	*Difference*
Persons	64.83	74.04	10.21
Males	75.26	82.14	6.9
Females	53.67	65.46	11.8

States/UTs (according to Literacy)

Top States/Uts	(in %)	*Bottom States/Uts*	(in %)
Kerala	93.91	Bihar	63.82
Lakshadweep	92.28	Arunachal Pradesh	66.95
Mizoram	91.58	Rajasthan	67.06
Tripura	87.75	Jharkhand	67.63
Goa	87.40	Andhra Pradesh	67.66

Sex Ratio

	2001		*2011*	
	Population (in mn)	*Proportion* (in %)	*Population* (in mn)	*Proportion* (in %)
▪ Males	532.2	51.74	623.7	51.51
▪ Females	496.5	48.26	586.4	48.46
Adult Sex Ratio	**933**		**943**	
▪ Males	85.0	51.89	82.9	52.24
▪ Females	78.8	48.11	75.8	47.76
Child Sex Ratio	**927**		**914**	

ECONOMIC TERMS

Assets Property of any kind.

Balance of Trade (BoT) The difference between the exports and imports of two countries in trade with each other is called Balance of Trade.

Balance Sheet It is a statement of accounts, generally of a business concern, prepared at the end of a year.

Banker's Cheque A cheque by one bank to another.

Bank Rate It is the rate of interest charged by the Reserve Bank of India for lending money to commercial banks.

Barter To trade by exchanging one commodity for another.

Bearer This term on cheques and bills denotes that any person holding the same, has the same right in respect of it, as the person who issued it.

Black Money It means unaccounted money, concealed income and undisclosed wealth. The money which thus remains unaccounted for, is called the black money.

Bond A legal agreement to pay a certain sum of money (called principal) at some future date and carrying a fixed rate of interest.

Budget An estimate of expected revenues and expenditure for a given period, usually a year, item by item.

Budget Deficit When the expenditure of the government exceeds the revenue, the balance between the two is the budget deficit.

Bulls Speculators in the stock markets who buy goods, in some cases without money to pay with, anticipating that prices will go up.

Buyer's Market An area in which the supply of certain goods exceeds the demands so that purchasers can drive hard bargains.

Commercial Banks Financial institutions that create credit accept deposits, give loans and perform other financial functions.

Call Money Loan made for a very short period. It carries a low rate of interest.

Deflation It is a state in monetary market when money in circulation has decreased.

Depreciation Reduction in the value of fixed assets due to wear and tear.

Devaluation Official reduction in the foreign value of domestic currency. It is done to encourage the country's exports and discourage imports.

Dividend Earning of stock paid to shareholders.

Dumping Sale of a commodity at different prices in different markets, lower price being charged in a market where demand is relatively elastic.

Exchange Rate The rate at which Central Banks will exchange one country's currency for another.

Excise Duty Tax Imposed on the manufacture, sale and consumption of various commodities, such as taxes on textiles, cloth, liquor, etc.

Fiscal Policy Government's expenditure, tax policy and borrowing.

Gross Domestic Product (GDP) A measure of the total flow of goods and services produced by the economy over a specific time period, normally a year.

Repo Rate The rate at which banks borrow from RBI. It injects liquidity into the market.

Inflation A sustained and appreciable increase in the price level over a considerable period of time.

Monopoly Single seller selling single product.

Monopolistic Competition Existence of too many sellers selling differentiated products.

Bilateral Monopoly Existence of single buyer and single seller.

Monopsony Single buyer buying product being unique.

Oligopoly Existence of few sellers and few products. Price war is a common feature.

Reverse Repo Rate The rate at which RBI borrows from banks for a short-term. It withdraws liquidity into the market.

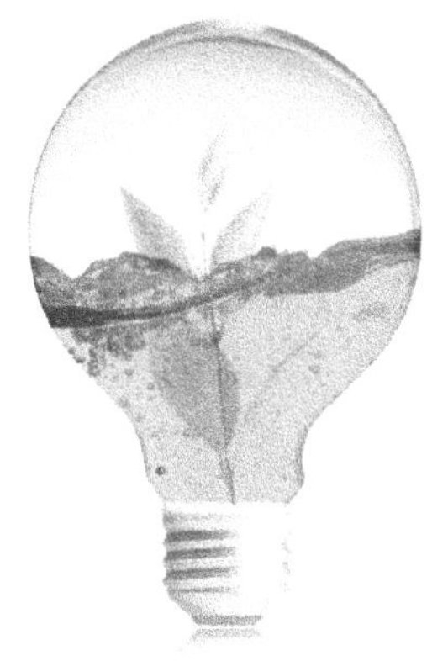

GENERAL SCIENCE

PHYSICS

In Physics, we study about a large number of physical quantities, which can be broadly classified into two categories : scalars and vectors.

Scalar Quantities Physical quantities which have magnitude only. e.g. Mass, speed, volume, work, time, distance, power, energy, etc. are scalar quantities.

Vector Quantities Physical quantities, which have magnitude and direction both, e.g., Displacement, velocity, acceleration, force, momentum, torque, etc.

For a quantity to be a vector, it is necessary that it follows the triangle rule of addition of two vectors.

NEWTON'S LAWS OF MOTION

First Law Every body maintains its initial state of rest or uniform motion on a straight line unless any external force acts on it. It is also called **Galileo's law of inertia.**

Example While jumping from a slowly moving train/bus one must run for a short distance, in the direction of motion.

Second Law The force acting on an object is directly proportional to the product of the mass of the object and the acceleration produced on it.

Third Law To every action, there is an equal and opposite reaction.

Example Bogies of the trains are provided with buffers to avoid severe jerks during shunting of trains.

Rocket moves up due to reaction of downward ejection of gas.

CIRCULAR MOTION

- When an object moves along a circular path, its motion is called circular motion.
- The direction of motion at any point in circular motion is given by the tangent to the circle at that point.
- The external force required to act radially inward over the circular motion of the body is called **centripetal force.**
- In the death well, the walls of well exert an inward force over the motorcycle and as a reaction, the motorcycle exert an outward force on the walls of the well.
- **Centrifugal force** is such a pseudo force that is equal and opposite to centripetal force.
- Cream separator, centrifugal dryer work on the principle of centrifugal force.

FRICTION

It is the opposing force that is set-up between the surfaces of contact of two bodies when one body slides or rolls or tends to do so on the surface of another body.

- Due to friction we are able to move on the surface of Earth.
- On applying brakes in automobiles, it stops only due to friction.

WORK

- Work is said to be done, if force acting on a body is able to actually move it through some distance in the direction of the force. Its SI unit is **joule.**

$$\text{Work} = Fs \cos \theta$$

where, F = force, s = displacement and θ is the angle between the direction of force and displacement.
- If $\theta > 90°$, then work will be negative.
- If $\theta < 90°$, then work will be positive.
- If $\theta = 90°$, then work will be zero.

> If a coolie carrying a load on his head is moving on a horizontal platform, then theoretically he is not doing any work because $\theta = 90°, W = FS \cos 90° = 0$

ENERGY

Capacity of doing work by a body is called its energy. Energy is a scalar quantity and its unit is **joule.** Mechanical energy is of two types.

- **Kinetic Energy** (K) Energy possessed by a body due to its motion.

$$K = \frac{1}{2} mv^2$$

where, m is mass and v is the velocity.
- **Potential Energy** (U) The capacity of doing work developed in a body due to its position or configuration.

$$U = mgh$$

where, m is mass, g is acceleration due to gravity and h is height.
- The sum of all kinds of energies in an isolated system remains constant at all times. This is the law of conservation of energy.

POWER

Rate of doing work is called power. Its unit is **watt.**

$$\text{Power} = \frac{\text{Work done}}{\text{Time taken}}$$

> - 1 watt hour = 3600 joule
> - 1 kilowatt hour = 3.6×10^6 joule
> - 1 HP = 746 watt

GRAVITATION

- Everybody in the universe attracts other body by a force called force of gravitation.
- The gravitational force of the earth is called **gravity.**
- The acceleration produced in a body due to force of gravity is called **acceleration** due to gravity (g) and its value is **9.8 m/s²**.
- Acceleration due to gravity is independent of shape, size and mass of the body.
- Escape velocity is the minimum velocity with which an object just crosses the Earth's gravitational field and never returns. Escape velocity at the Earth's surface is **11.2 km/s.**
- Escape velocity at the Moon's surface is **2.4 km/s.** Due to low escape velocity there is no atmosphere on the Moon.
- Value of g decreases with height or depth from Earth's surface.
- g is maximum at poles.
- g is minimum at equator.
- g decreases due to rotation of Earth.
- g decreases if angular speed of Earth increases and increases if angular speed of Earth decreases.
- The acceleration due to gravity at the **Moon** is one-sixth that of the Earth. So, the weight of a person on the surface of the Moon will be one-sixth of his actual weight on the Earth.

SATELLITES

- Satellites are natural or artificial bodies revolving around a planet under its gravitational force of attraction.
- **Moon** is a natural satellite, while INSAT-B is an artificial satellite of Earth.
- The period of revolution of satellite revolving near the surface of Earth is 1 hour 24 minutes (84 minutes).
- Geo-stationary satellite revolves around the Earth at a height of 36000 km (approx). The orbit of geo-stationary satellite is called parking orbit. Geo-stationary satellite revolves in equatorial plane from West to East. Time period of rotation of geo-stationary satellite is **24 h**.
- The **Earth** rotates on its axis from **West** to **East**. This rotation makes the Sun and the stars appears to be moving across the sky from East to West.

- Geo-stationary satellite is used to telecast TV programmes from one part of the world to another, in weather forecasting, in predictions of floods and droughts.
- **Polar satellite** revolves around the Earth in polar orbit at a height of **800 km** (approx). Time period of these satellites is **84 min**.
- These are used for weather forecasting, mapping, etc.

GENERAL PROPERTIES OF MATTER

Elasticity

Elasticity is the property of material of a body by virtue of which the body acquires its original shape and size after the removal of **deforming force**.

- A force, which changes the configuration of a body, is called a **deforming force.**
- Steel is more elastic than rubber.

Pressure

Pressure is defined as force acting normally on a unit area of the surface.

$$\text{Pressure} = \frac{\text{Force}}{\text{Area}}$$

Its unit is **N/m²**. It is a scalar quantity.

- Atmospheric pressure is measured by an instrument called the **barometer**.
- Sudden fall in barometric reading is the indication of storm.
- Slow fall in barometric reading is the indication of rain.
- Slow rise in the barometric reading is the indication of clear weather.
- The pressure exerted by liquid column at the surface given as p=hdg, where d is the density of liquid and h is height of liquid column. In a static liquid at same horizontal level, pressure is same at all points.

Atmospheric pressure decreases with altitude.

That is why

- It is difficult to cook on the mountain.
- The fountain pen of a passenger leaks in aeroplane.
- Bleeding occurs from the nose.
- It is difficult to breath on higher altitude due to less amount partial pressure of oxygen in air.
- Water starts to boil below 100°C.

Pascal's Law of Pressure

- If gravitational attraction is negligible in equilibrium condition, (approx) pressure is same at all points in a liquid.
- The pressure exerted anywhere at a point of confined liquid is transmitted equally and undiminished in all directions throughout the liquid.
- Hydraulic lift, hydraulic press and hydraulic brakes are based on the Pascal's law of pressure.

Archimedes' Principle

When a body is immersed partly or wholly in a liquid, there is an apparent loss in the weight of the body, which is equal to the weight of liquid displaced by the body.

- The weight of water displaced by an iron ball is less than its own weight whereas water displaced by the immersed portion of a ship is equal to its weight. So, small ball of iron ball sink in water, but large ship float.
- A fat person will quickly learn the swimming as compared to a slim person because he will displace more water. So, he will be more balanced.
- Hydrogen filled balloon float in air because hydrogen is lighter than air.
- A person can lift more weight in water.

Laws of Floatation

A body floats in a liquid if

- The density of material of the body is less than or equal to the density of liquid.
- When the density of material of the body is equal to density of liquid, the body floats fully submerged in liquid in neutral equilibrium.
- When body floats in neutral equilibrium, the weight of the body is equal to the weight of displaced liquid. The centre of gravity of the body and centre of gravity of the displaced liquid should be in one vertical line for this condition.

Density

- Density is defined as mass per unit volume.
- Relative density is measured by **hydrometer**.
- The density of sea water is more than that of normal water.
- When a ship enters in a sea from a river, it raises a bit because the density of saline water (salt water) is higher.
- The density of iron is more than that of water, but less than that of mercury. So, a solid chunk of iron sink in water but float in mercury.
- If ice floating in water in a vessel melts, the level of water in the vessel does not change.

Surface Tension

- It is the force (F) acting normally on unit length (l) of imaginary line drawn on the surface of liquid i.e., $T = \frac{F}{l}$, its unit is N/m.
- The property of a liquid by virtue of which it tries to minimise its free surface area is called the surface tension.
- Surface tension decreases with rise in temperature and becomes zero at the critical temperature.
- The surface tension of clean water is higher than that of a soap solution.
- Formation of lead shots, spraying result in coldness, floatation of needle on water, dancing of camphor on water, are based on surface tension.
- Rain drop form spherical shape due to surface tension.
- When kerosene oil is sprinkled on water, its surface tension decreases, due to which the excess of mosquitoes floating on the surface of water die due to sinking.

Cohesive and Adhesive Forces

Force of attraction applied between molecules of same substance is called **cohesive force** while attractive force between molecules of different substances is called **adhesive force**.

Capillarity

The phenomenon of rise or depression of liquids in a capillary tube is called capillarity.

- A piece of blotting paper soaks ink because the pores of the blotting paper serve as capillary tubes.
- The oil in the wick of a lamp rises due to capillary action of threads in the wick.
- The root hairs of plants draws water from the soil through capillary action.

Viscosity

Viscosity is the property of a fluid by virtue of which an internal frictional force acts between its layers, when it is in motion.

Bernoulli's Theorem

When an incompressible and non-viscous liquid (or gas) flows in streamlined motion from one place to another, then at every point of its path the total energy per unit volume (pressure energy + kinetic energy + potential energy) is constant.

Venturimeter, Atomizer, filter pump, motion of aeroplane are based upon the Bernoulli's theorem.

HEAT AND THERMODYNAMICS

Heat

- Heat is a form of energy, which measures the sensation or perception of warmness or coldness of a body or environment.
- Its units are calorie, kilocalorie or joule.
- 1 calorie = **4.18** joule.

Temperature

- Temperature is the measurement of hotness or coldness of a body.
- When two bodies are placed in contact, heat always flow from a body at higher temperature to the body at lower temperature.

- An instrument used to measure the temperature of a body is called a **thermometer**.
- The **normal temperature** of a **human body** is 37°C or 98.4°F.
- –40° is the temperature at which **Celsius** and **Fahrenheit** thermometers read same.
- The **clinical thermometer** reads from 96°F to 110°F.
- White roof keeps the house cooler in summer than black roof because white roof reflects more and absorbs less heat rays whereas black roof absorbs more and reflects less heat rays.
- Ice wrapped in a blanket does not melt away quicky because woollen blanket is a bad conductor of heat.
- Sliver is the best conductor of heat.
- Cooking utensils are made of aluminum, brass and steel because these substances have low specific heat and high conductivity.

Thermal Expansion

- Thermal expansion is the increase in size on heating.
- *A solid can undergo three types of expansions*
  (i) Linear expansion
  (ii) Superficial expansion
  (iii) Cubical expansion
- Telephone wires are kept loose to allow the wires for contraction in winter.
- A gap is provided between two iron tracks of the railway track, so that rails can easily expand during summer and do not bend.

Specific Heat

- The amount of heat required to raise the temperature of unit mass of a substance through 1°C, is called its specific heat.
- When temperature of water is increased from 0°C, then its volume decreases upto 4°C, becomes minimum at 4°C and then increases.
- This behaviour of water around 4°C is called anomalous expansion of water.

Latent Heat

- The heat energy absorbed or released at constant temperature per unit mass for change of state is called the latent heat.
- Latent heat of fusion of ice is **80 cal/g.**
- Latent heat of vaporisation of steam is **536 cal/g**.
- Hot water burns are less severe than that of steam burns because steam has high latent heat.

Evaporation

- It is the slow process of conversion of liquid into its vapour even below its boiling temperature.
- The amount of water vapour in air is called **humidity.**
- Relative humidity is measured by hygrometer.
- Relative humidity increases with the increase of temperature.

Transmission of Heat

- Transfer of heat from one place to other place is called transmission of heat.
- In solids, transmission of heat takes place by **conduction process**.
- In liquids and gases, transmission of heat takes place by **convection process**. In room, ventilators are provided to escape the hot air by convection.
- Heat from the Sun reaches the Earth by **radiation**.

Simple Pendulum

- Simple pendulum is a heavy point mass suspended from a rigid support by means of an elastic and inextensible string.
- The maximum time period of a simple pendulum is **84.6 min**.
- The time period of a simple pendulum does not depend upon the mass, shape and size of the bob and its amplitude of oscillation. A pendulum clock goes slow in summer and fast in winter.
- If a simple pendulum is suspended in a lift descending down with acceleration, then time period of pendulum will increase. If lift is ascending, then time period of pendulum will decrease.
- If a lift falling freely under gravity, then the time period of the pendulum is infinite.

WAVES

A wave is a disturbance, which propagates energy from one place to the other without the transportation of matter.

Waves are broadly of two types

(i) Mechanical wave (longitudinal wave and transverse wave)

(ii) Electromagnetic wave

Longitudinal Waves

In this wave, the particles of the medium vibrate in the direction of propagation of wave.

Waves on springs or sound waves in air are examples of longitudinal waves.

Transverse Waves

In this wave, the particles of the medium vibrate perpendicular to the direction of propagation of wave.

Waves on strings under tension, waves on the surface of water are the examples of transverse waves.

Electromagnetic Waves

- The waves, which do not require medium for their propagation i.e., which can propagate even through the vacuum are called electromagnetic waves.
- Light radio waves, X-rays, etc. are the examples of electromagnetic waves. These wave propagate with the velocity of light in vacuum.

Sound Waves

Sound waves are longitudinal mechanical waves. Based on their frequency range sound waves are divided into following categories.

- The sound waves which lie in the frequency range **20 Hz to 20000 Hz** are called audible waves.
- The sound waves having frequencies less than **20 Hz** are called infrasonic waves.
- The sound waves having frequencies greater than **20000 Hz** are called ultrasonic waves.
- Ultrasonic waves are used for sending signals, measuring the depth of sea, cleaning machinery parts located in hard to reach places, such as spiral tubes, etc.

Speed of Sound

- Speed of sound is maximum in solids and minimum in gases.
- When sound goes from one medium to another medium, its speed and wavelength changes, but frequency remains unchanged.
- The speed of sound remains unchanged by the increase or decrease of pressure.
- The speed of sound increases with the increase of temperature of the medium.
- The speed of sound is more in humid air than in dry air because the density of humid air is less than the density.

Echo The repetition of sound due to reflection of sound waves, is called **echo**.

Intensity It is defined as the amount of energy passing per unit time through a unit area that is perpendicular to the direction in which sound waves are travelling.

Pitch The sensation of a frequency is commonly referred to as the pitch of a sound.

SONAR It stands for sound navigation and ranging. It is used to measure the depth of a sea, to locate the enemy submarines and shipwrecks.

Doppler's Effect

- If there is a relative motion between source of sound and observer, the apparent frequency of sound heard by the observer is different from the actual frequency of sound emitted by the source. This phenomenon is called **Doppler's effect**.
- When the distance between the source and observer decreases, then apparent frequency increases and *vice-versa*.

LIGHT

- Light is a form of energy, which is propagated as electromagnetic wave.
- It is the radiation which makes our eyes able to see the object. Its speed is 3×10^8 m/s. It is the form of energy. It is a transverse wave. It takes 8 min 19 s to reach on the Earth from the Sun and the light reflected from Moon takes 1.28 s to reach Earth.

Reflection of Light

When a ray of light falls on a boundary separating two media comes back into the same medium, then this phenomenon is called reflection of light.

Laws of Reflection

- The incident ray, reflected ray and the normal to the reflecting surface at the incident point all lie in the same plane.
- The angle of reflection is equal to the angle of incidence.

Reflection from Plane Mirror

- The image is virtual and laterally inverted.
- The size of image is **equal** to that of object.
- If an object moves towards a plane mirror with speed v, relative to the object the image moves towards it with a speed $2v$.
- To see his full image in a plane mirror, a person requires a mirror of atleast half of his height.
- The number of images formed by two plane mirrors, inclined by an angle θ, $n = \left(\frac{360°}{\theta} - 1\right)$.

Spherical Mirror

- *Spherical mirrors are of two types*
  (i) Concave mirror (ii) Convex mirror
- Image formed by a convex mirror is always virtual, erect and diminished.
- Image formed by a concave mirror is generally real and inverted.

Uses of Concave Mirror

(i) As a shaving glass. (ii) As a reflector for the headlights of a vehicle, search light. (iii) In ophthalmoscope to examine eye, ear, nose by doctors. (iv) In solar cookers.

Uses of Convex Mirror

(i) As a rear view mirror in vehicle because it provides the maximum rear field of view and image formed is always erect. (ii) In sodium reflector lamp.

Refraction of Light

The bending of the ray of light passing from one medium to other medium is called refraction. When a ray of light enters from one medium to other medium, its frequency and phase do not change, but wavelength and velocity change. Due to refraction from Earth's atmosphere, the stars appear to twinkle.

$$\text{Refractive index } (\mu) = \frac{\text{Speed of light in vacuum}}{\text{Speed of light in the medium}}$$

Critical Angle

The angle of incidence in a denser medium for which the angle of refraciton in rarer medium becomes 90°, is called the critical angle.

Total Internal Reflection (TIR)

If light is travelling from denser medium to rarer medium and the angle of incidence is more than the critical angle, then the light is reflected back into the denser medium. This phenomenon is called total internal reflection.

Sparkling of diamond, mirage and looming, shinning of air bubble in water and optical fibre are examples of total internal reflection.

Optical Fibre

It works on the principle of TIR. It is used for telecommunication and various medical purposes like endoscopy.

Lens

- *Lens is generally of two types*
  (i) Convex lens (ii) Concave lens
- When lens is dipped in a liquid of higher refractive index, the focal length increases and convex lens behave as concave lens and *vice-versa*.
- An air bubble trapped in water or glass appears as convex, but behaves as concave lens.

Dispersion of Light

- When a ray of white light is passed through a prism, it gets splitted into its constituent colours. This phenomenon is called **dispersion of light.**

- The different colours appeared in the spectrum are in the following order, violet, indigo, blue, green, yellow, orange and red **(VIBGYOR)**.
- Rainbow is formed due to dispersion of sunlight by water droplets.
- Wavelength of red colour is maximum and for violet colour is minimum.
- Red, green and blue are **primary** colours. Green and magenta, blue and yellow, red and cyan are **complementary** colours.

Scattering of Light

- When light passes through a medium in which particles are suspended whose sizes are of the order of wavelength of light, then light striking on these particles deviated in different directions. Scattering of light is maximum in case of violet colour and minimum in case of red colour.
- Blue colour of sky is due to scattering of blue and violet light. The brilliant red colour of rising and setting sun is also due to scattering of light.

HUMAN EYE

- It is an optical instrument like camera. It forms the real image of the object on retina of the eye. Least distance of distinct vision is 25 cm.

Defects of Eye

Myopia *(Short sightedness)*	A short-sighted eye can see only nearer objects. Distant objects are not seen clearly. This defect can be removed by using concave lens of suitable focal length.
Hypermetropia *(Long sightedness)*	A long sighted eye can see distant objects clearly but nearer object are not clearly visible. This defect can be removed by using a convex lens.
Presbyopia	In this defect both near and far objects are not clearly visible. It can be removed by using bi-focal lens.
Astigmatism	In this defect eye cannot see horizontal and vertical lines clearly. This defect can be removed by using suitable cylindrical lenses.

Microscope

- **Simple** microscope is a convex lens of small focal length.
- **Compound microscope** is a combination of two convex lenses, called objective lens and eyepiece, separated by a distance.
- **Astronomical Telescope** is also a combination of two lenses in which objective lens is a convex lens of large aperture and large focal length while eye-piece is a convex lens of small aperture and small focal length.

ELECTRICITY AND MAGNETISM

Charge

Charge is the basic property associated with matter due to which it produces and experiences electric and magnetic effects. Similar charges repel each other and opposite charges attract each other. The SI unit of charge is **coulomb**.

Conductor	Conductors are those materials, which allow electricity to pass through themselves. Metals like silver, iron, copper and earth acts like a conductor. **Silver** is the best conductor.
Insulator	Insulator are those materials which do not allow electricity to flow through themselves. Wood, paper, mica, glass, ebonite are insulators.

Electric Current

- Electric current is defined as the rate of flow of charge or charge flowing per unit time. Its unit is **ampere**. It is a scalar quantity.
- A lightning conductor is fixed on tall buildings to protect them from the destructive effects of the lightning.
- An electric bulb produces a bang when it is broken because there is a vacuum inside the electric bulb, when the bulb is broken air rushes at great speed from all sides to fill the vacuum. The rushing of air produces a noise generally referred to as the **bang**.

Ohm's Law

At the constant physical conditions of any conductor, the current flowing through the conductor is directly proportional to the potential difference across it.

$I = \frac{V}{R}$, where R is the resistance.

- If a wire is stretched, its resistance will change but its specific resistance will remain unaffected.
- On increasing the temperature of the metal, its resistance increases.
- On increasing the temperature of semiconductor, its resistance decreases.
- On increasing the temperature of electrolytes, its resistance decreases.
- The reciprocal of resistivity of a conductor is called its **conductivity**. Its unit is **mho m^{-1}**.
- The heating effect of electric current is known as **Joule's law of heating**.
- Electric bulb, electric kettle, heater, etc devices work on the bases of heating effect of electric current.

Ammeter It is a device which is used to measure electrical current. It is connected in series. The resistance of an ideal ammeter is zero.

Voltmeter It is a device used to measure the potential difference between two points in a circuit. It is connected in parallel to the circuit. The resistance of an ideal voltmeter is infinite.

Fuse Wire It is a small conducting wire of alloy of copper, tin and lead having low melting point. So, it is protective device used in series.

MAGNETS

- Magnet is a piece of iron or other materials that can attract iron containing object and points toward North when suspended.
- When a magnet is freely suspended, its one pole always direct towards the North. This pole is called North pole. The other pole is called South pole.
- Like poles of a magnet repel each other and unlike poles attract each other.
- A current carrying coil containing a soft iron core, is called an electromagnet, which is utilised in electric bell, telegraph receiver, telephone, transformer, dynamo, etc.

ATOMIC AND NUCLEAR PHYSICS

Cathode Rays

Cathode ray was discovered by **Sir William Crooke** and its properties are

- These rays travel in straight lines.
- These rays produce fluorescence.
- These rays can penetrate through thin foils of metal and deflected by both electric and magnetic fields.
- These rays have velocity ranging **1/30th** to **1/10th** of the velocity of light.

Positive or Canal Rays

- These rays were discovered by **Goldstein.**
- The positive rays consists of positively charged particles.
- These rays travel in straight line.
- These rays are deflected by electric and magnetic fields.
- These rays are capable of producing physical and chemical changes.
- These rays can produce ionisation in gases.

X-Rays

- X-rays are electromagnetic waves with wavelength range 0.1 Å–100 Å. X-rays were discovered by **Roentgen**.
- X-rays travel in straight line. These rays show reflection, refraction, interference, diffraction and polarisation and do not deflected by electric and magnetic fields.
- Long exposers of X-rays is injurious to the human body.
- X-rays shows **photoelectric effect**.

Uses of X-Rays

- **In Medical Sciences** X-rays are used in surgery for the detection of fractures, diseased organs, foreign matter like bullet, stones, etc. They are used in treatment of cancer and in skin diseases.
- **In Engineering** X-rays are used in detecting faults, cracks, flaws and gas pockets in the finished metal products and in heavy metal sheets.
- **In Scientific Work** X-rays are used in studying crystal structure and complex molecules.
- **In Custom Department** X-rays are used in custom department for detection of banned materials kept hidden.

Radioactivity

- Radioactivity was discovered by **Henry Becquerel**, **Madame Curie** and **Pierre Curie** for which they jointly won Nobel Prize.
- The nucleus having protons 83 or more are unstable. They emit α, β and γ particles and become stable. The elements of such nucleus are called **radioactive** elements and the phenomenon of emission of α, β and γ particles is called **radioactivity.**
- **Robert Pierre** and his wife **Madame Curie** discovered a new radioactive element radium.
- The end product of all natural radioactive elements after emission of radioactive rays is lead.
- With the emission of an α-particle, atomic number is decreased by 2 and mass number is decreased by 4.
- With the emission of a β-particle, atomic number is increased by 1 and mass number does not change.

Nuclear Fission

- The nuclear reaction, in which a heavy nucleus splits into two nuclei of nearly equal mass is nuclear fission.

$$_{92}U^{235} + _0n^1 \rightarrow _{56}Ba^{141} + _{36}Kr^{92} + _{30}n^1 + \text{energy}$$

- **Atom Bomb** is based on nuclear fission. U^{235} and Pu^{239} are used as fissionable material.
- Nuclear fission was first demonstrated by **Hatin** and **Fritz Strassmann**.

Nuclear Fusion

- When two or more light nuclei combined together to form a heavier nucleus is called as nuclear fusion.
- For the nuclear fusion, a temperature of the order of $\mathbf{10^8}$ **K** is required.
- **Hydrogen Bomb** was made by the American Scientist in 1952. This is based on nuclear fusion. It is 1000 times more powerful than atom bomb.

Nuclear Reactor or Atomic Pile

- Nuclear reactor is an arrangement, in which controlled nuclear fission reaction takes place.
- First nuclear reactor was established in Chicago University under the supervision of Prof **Enrico Fermi**.
- Heavy water, graphite and beryllium oxide are used to slow down the fast moving neutrons. They are called **moderator**.
- The cold water, liquid oxygen, etc. are used as coolant to remove heat generated.
- Cadmium or boron rods are good absorber of neutrons and called the control rods.

Uses of Nuclear Reactor

(i) To produce electrical energy from the energy released during fission.

(ii) To produce different isotopes, which can be used in medical, physical and agriculture science.

There are several components of nuclear reactor which are as follows

- **Fissionable Fuel** U^{235} or U^{239} is used.
- **Moderator** Moderator decreases the energy of neutrons, so that they can be further used for fission reaction. **Heavy water** and **graphite** are used as moderator.
- **Control Rod** Rods of cadmium or boron are used to absorb the excess neutrons produced in fission of uranium nucleus, so that the chain reaction continues to be controlled.
- **Coolant** A large amount of heat is produced during fission. Coolant absorbs that heat and prevents excessive rise in the temperature. The coolant may be water, heavy water or a gas like He or CO_2.

LASER (Light Amplification by Stimulated Emission of Radiation)

It is a device that produces an intense, coherent and highly directional beam of the single frequency. It can be transmitted over a great distance without being spread.

LASER Technology in India

In 1964, the first laser as Gallium Arsenide (GaA) semi-conductor laser was designed and fabricated by Bhabha Atomic Research Centre (BARC).

Various Institutions as CAT (Centre for Advanced Technology), DRDO (Defence Research and Development Organisation) and Indian Institute of Science (IISc) work on the laser plasma, quantum optics, etc., are going to work with American collaboration.

MASER (Microwave Amplification by Stimulated Emission of Radiation)

It was invented by three American scientist **Gordon**, **Gieyer** and **H Townes** in 1952.

It uses microwaves in amplified form of longer wavelength of the light, while ordinary laser uses light.

Units of Measurement

Quantity	*Unit (SI)*	*Quantity*	*Unit* (SI)
Length	Metre	Viscosity	Newton.sec/m^2
Time	Second	Surface tension	Newton/metre
Mass	Kilogram	Heat	Joule
Area	Square metre	Temperature	Kelvin
Volume	Cubic metre	Absolute temperature	Kelvin
Velocity	Metre/second	Resistance	Ohm
Acceleration	Metre/$second^2$	Electric current	Ampere
Density	Kilogram/$metre^3$	Electromotive force	Volt
Momentum	Kilogram-metre/second	Electrical conductivity	mho/metre
Work	Joule	Electric energy	Kilowatt-hour
Energy	Joule	Electric power	Kilowatt or watt
Force	Newton	Magnetic intensity	Oersted
Pressure	Pascal or Newton/$metre^2$	Charge	Coulomb
Frequency	Hertz	Magnetic induction	Gauss
Power	Watt	Luminous flux	Candela
Weight	Newton or Kilogram	Intensity of sound	Decibel
Impulse	Newton-second	Power of lens	Dioptre
Angular velocity	Radian /second	Depth of sea	Fathom

CHEMISTRY

Chemistry, a branch of physical science, is the study of the composition, properties and behaviour of matter.

Physical and Chemical Changes

- Physical changes are the changes which only affect the physical properties like colour, hardness, density, melting point etc, of matter, but do not affect the composition and chemical properties of matter.
- A physical change is temporary, while a chemical change is permanent.
- Crystallisation, sublimation, boiling, melting, vaporisation, cutting of trees, dissolving sugar or salt in water etc are physical changes.
- Chemical changes affect the composition as well as chemical properties of matter and result in the formation of a new substance.
- Burning of fuel, burning of candle and paper, electrolysis of water, photosynthesis, ripening of fruits etc, are examples of chemical changes.

MATTER

- Anything which occupies space and has mass is called matter. In general, it exists in three states i.e., solid, liquid and gas.
- Now-a-days there is a discussion on two more states of matter i.e., Plasma (Ionised gases containing super energetic and super excited particles) and Bose-Einstein Condensates or BEC (a gas at super low temperature with extremely low density).

Boiling Point

- The temperature at which liquid converts into vapour is called its boiling point.
- Boiling point of water is 100°C.
- The boiling point increases in the presence of impurities that's why boiling point of sea water is more than the boiling point of pure water (as the former contains impurity).
- It usually decreases at high altitudes. That's why at high altitudes, the boiling point of water is less than 100°C and more time is required to cook a food.

Melting Point

- It is a temperature at which a substance converts from its solid state to liquid state. Melting point of ice is 0°C. It decrease in the presence of impurity.

ATOM, MOLECULE AND ELEMENT

- An atom is the smallest particle of the element that can exist independently and retain all its chemical properties.
- Atom is made up of electrons, protons and neutrons.
- Protons and neutrons reside in the nucleus (at the centre of atom) whereas electrons revolve around the nucleus.
- A molecule is the smallest part of an element or a compound cabable of independent existence under ordinary conditions.
- Element contains only one type of atoms. e.g. carbon (C), sulphur (S), diamond, graphite etc.
- Oganesson, with symbol Og and atomic number 118 is recent element synthesized.
- **Ununseptium** (a superheavy chemical element with atomic number 117) is a member of group-17 in the periodic table below the five halogens (fluorine, chlorine, bromine, iodine and astatine). Its synthesis was claimed in Dubna, Russia by a joint Russian-American collaboration.
- In 2014, the GSI Helmholtz Centre for Heavy Ion Research in Germany also claimed to have successfully repeated original experiment.

Isotopes and Isobars

- Isotopes have the same number of protons (i.e. atomic number), but different number of neutrons and mass number (atomic number + number of neutrons), e.g. ${}_1H^1, {}_1H^2, {}_1H^3$.
- Isobars have the same mass number but different atomic number. e.g. ${}_{18}Ar^{40}$, ${}_{19}K^{40}$ and ${}_{20}Ca^{40}$.

Dating Techniques

- Radiocarbon dating is used to determine the age of carbon bearing materials like wood, animal fossils etc.
- Uranium dating is used to determine the age of Earth, minerals and rocks.

Colloids

- These are heterogeneous solutions, containing two phases : dispersed phase and dispersion medium.
- These show Tyndall effect (i.e. scattering of light by colloidal particles) and Brownian motion (zig-zag motion).
- Colloids can be dispersion medium loving (i.e. lyophilic) or dispersion medium repelling (i.e. lyophobic).

Some Colloids and their Example

Dispersed Phase	*Dispersion Medium*	*Type of Colloid*	*Example*
Liquid	Gas	Aerosol	Fog, clouds, mist
Solid	Gas	Aerosol *(solid)*	Smoke, automobile exhaust
Gas	Liquid	Foam	Shaving cream
Liquid	Liquid	Emulsion	Milk, face cream
Solid	Liquid	Sol	Mud, milk of magnesia
Gas	Solid	Foam	Foam, rubber, sponge, pumice
Liquid	Solid	Gel	Jelly, cheese, butter
Solid	Solid	Solid sol	Milky glass, coloured gem stone

Battery

Battery is a device, used to convert chemical energy into electrical energy and is of two types :

- **Primary batteries** (non-rechargeable) act as galvanic cell, e.g. dry cell, mercury cell etc.
- **Secondary batteries** (rechargeable) act as galvanic as well as voltaic cell e.g. lead storage battery, nickel cadmium battery etc.

In electrolytic refining, anode is made by impure metal and a strip of pure metal acts as cathode.

Types of Batteries

Battery	*Anode*	*Cathode*	*Electrolyte*	*Used in*
Leclanche cell	Zinc	Graphite	Paste of ammonium chloride and zinc chloride	Transistors, clocks
Mercury cell	Zinc-mercury amalgam	Paste of HgO (Mercuric oxide) and carbon	Paste of KOH and ZnO	Hearing aids and camera
Lead storage battery	Lead	Lead packed in lead dioxide	38% solution of sulphuric acid	Automobiles, invertors

Corrosion

- The oxidative deterioration of a metal surface by the action of environment is called corrosion, it is an electrochemical process.
- When iron is exposed into air, iron surface turns red due to the formation of hydrated ferric oxide ($Fe_2O_3 \cdot xH_2O$) which is also called rust, silver surface turns black due to the formation of silver sulphide (Ag_2S) and copper or bronze surfaces turn green due to the formation of basic copper carbonate, $Cu(OH)_2 \cdot CuCO_3$.
- Corrosion of iron is called rusting and is accelerated by the presence of impurities, H^+, electrolyte such as NaCl and gases like CO_2, SO_2, NO_2 etc.
- Corrosion is prevented by electroplating, oiling, greasing, painting, varnishing and by galvanisation (i.e. deposition of zinc layer over iron articles).

- A sliced apple, when exposed to air, turns brown after sometime. This is because apple contains iron, which gets oxidised and gives a brownish colour to apple.

Renewable and Non-renewable Natural Resources

- Renewable resources are available in large excess, i.e. never ends, e.g. air, sunlight etc.
- Non-renewable resources are available in limited quantity and end, if used excessively, after a limited period of time. e.g. mineral, coal, petroleum, natural gas etc.

Coal

Coal is obtained by carbonisation of vegetable matter and is available in different varities : Peat (60% C), lignite or brown coal (70% C), bituminous coal (60% to 80% C), anthracite coal (90% C). Out of these, bituminous is the most common form.

Flame

Flame contains three parts

1. **Innermost part** which is black due to the presence of unburnt carbon particles and has lowest temperature.
2. **Middle part** is yellow due to incomplete combustion of fuel.
3. **Outermost part** is blue due to complete combustion of fuel, which is the hottest part and used by goldsmith to heat the gold.

Fire Extinguishers

- Water extinguishes fire because as it evaporates the vapours surround the burning substance, cutting off the oxygen supply, thus inhibiting burning process.
- In case of electrical or oil (petrol) fires, water cannot be used as extinguisher. This is because water is a conductor of electricity and heavier than oil. Thus, oil floats over it and continues to burn. Carbon dioxide, which is generated by the reaction of baking soda with acid, is used to extinguish electrical or oil fires.
- Quality of petrol is measured in terms of octane number and that of diesel in terms of cetane number. TEL (Tetra Ethyl Lead) is an antiknock compound. Higher the octane number better is the quality of fuel.

Fuels

- The substance, which produce heat and light on combustion are called fuels.
- A strong foul smelling substance, called ethyl mercaptan, C_2H_5SH, is added to LPG to detect its leakage as LPG is an odourless gas.
- The amount of heat obtained, when 1g of a fuel is burned in excess of oxygen is called **calorific value.**
- Vehicle carrying inflammable substances have metallic ropes, touching the ground during motion in order to provide earthing for lightning.
- Fuels used in rocket are called rocket propellants. A mixture of liquid hydrogen and liquid oxygen, is most common rocket propellant.

Some Important Fuels and their Compositions

Fuel	*Composition*	*Sources*
Water Gas	Carbon monoxide (CO) + Hydrogen (H_2)	By passing steam over red hot coke
Producer Gas	Nitrogen (N_2) + Carbon monoxide (CO) (2 : 1 ratio)	By passing insufficient air over red hot coke
Coal Gas	Hydrogen + Methane + Ethylene (C_2H_4) + Acetylene (C_2H_2) + CO + Nitrogen	By fractional distillation of wood
Natural Gas	Methane (83%) + Ethane (16%)	From petroleum
Liquified Petroleum Gas (LPG)	Butane (C_4H_8) + Propane (C_3H_6)	From oil wells
Compressed Natural Gas (CNG)	Methane (CH_4) 95%	From petroleum
Biogas or Gobar Gas	Methane (CH_4) + Carbon dioxide (CO_2) + Hydrogen (H_2) + Nitrogen (N_2)	From organic wastes

Calorific Value of Some Substances

Fuel	*Calorific Value* (kJ/g)
Coal	25-32
Kerosene oil	48
Petrol	50
Diesel	45
Biogas	35-40
LPG	50
Cow dung	6-8
Hydrogen	150
Natural gas	35-50

Safety Matches

In safety matches, the stick consists of a mixture of antimony trisulphide and potassium chlorate at its one end. The box side contains a mixture of powdered glass and red phosphorus.

ACIDS, BASES AND SALTS

Acids

- These are the substance, which have a sour taste and turn blue litmus red.
- These are good conductor of electricity in aqueous solution.
- Pickels are always kept in glass jar because acid present in them reacts with metal to produce hydrogen gas.

Bases

- These are the substances, which have bitter taste, soapy to touch and turn red litmus blue.
- Bases like NaOH, KOH, etc. are good conductors of electricity in their aqueous solution and in molten state.
- Base react with acid to form salt and water.

Salts

- These are the product of neutralisation reaction between an acid and a base.
- pH is the measure of acidity/basicity.

Some Important Compounds in Everyday Life

Carbon Dioxide

It is an acidic oxide of carbon and is used by green plants for photosynthesis. It does not help in burning.

Air and our breath contain carbon dioxide. Thus, when lime water is kept in air or we pass our breath into it, the lime water turns milky.

Carbon Monoxide

It is a neutral oxide of air and has more affinity towards haemoglobin than oxygen (about 200 times more). That's why in the environment of carbon monoxide (which is a non-poisonous gas) people die for the need of oxygen.

It is dangerous to sleep in an unventilated room with fire burning inside because the fire produce carbon monoxide and carbon dioxide gases.

Plaster of Paris

- It is chemically calcium sulphate hemihydrate ($CaSO_4 \cdot \frac{1}{2} H_2O$) and is prepared by heating gypsum which is calcium sulphate dihydrate ($CaSO_4 \cdot 2H_2O$) at 373 K.
- On mixing with water, Plaster of Paris further sets into a hard solid, called gypsum. Thus, it is used to plaster fractured bones, for making toys, materials for decoration and for making surfaces smooth.

Portland Cement

- It is a complex mixture of silicates and aluminates of calcium with small amount of gypsum. Raw material used for the manufacture of Portland cement are limestone and clay.
- The composition of Portland cement is calcium oxide (50-60%), alumina (5-10%), and magnesium oxide (2-3%) Gypsum is added to cement to decrease its rate of setting.
- In cement, if lime is in excess, cement cracks during setting and if lime is less, cement is of weak strength.
- Mortar a mixture of sand, cement and water is used for joining bricks and plastering walls.
- Concrete, a mixture of gravel, sand, cement and water is used for flooring and making roads.

- Reinforced Concrete Cement (RCC) which is concrete with steel bars and wires is used for constructing roofs, bridges and pillars.

Soaps

These are sodium and potassium salts of higher fatty acids, e.g. sodium palmitate, sodium stearate, etc.

Glass

- Glass, an amorphous solid or super-cooled liquid contains mainly silica (SiO_2).
- Different substances are added to obtain glass of different colours e.g.

Colour	*Substance Added*
Red	Copper oxide (CuO)
Green	Chromium oxide (Cr_2O_3)
Ruby Red	Goldchloride ($AuCl_3$)
Blue	Cobalt oxide (CoO)
Brown	Iron oxide (Fe_2O_3)

Pesticides

These chemicals are used to destroy the organisms that harm the crop.

These are of following types

Insecticides e.g. DDT, gammaxene, aluminium phosphate.

Fungicides e.g. Bordeaux mixture, organo-mercury compounds.

Herbicides e.g. Benzipram, sodium chlorate.

Rodenticides e.g. Aluminium phosphide.

Heavy Water

Heavy water is **deuterium oxide** (D_2O), molecular mass =20) which used as moderator in nuclear reactors. It is called heavy due to the presence of deuterium, the heavy hydrogen.

Hard Water

- The water in which soluble bicarbonates of calcium and magnesium are present, is called **temporary hard water** and in which soluble sulphates and chlorides of magnesium and calcium are present is called **permanent hard water**.
- The temporary hardness of water is removed by boiling or by adding calcium hydroxide, $Ca(OH)_2$—the **Clark's process**.
- The permanent hardness of water is removed by adding sodium carbonate (Na_2CO_3), or calgon (sodium hexametaphosphate, $Na_2[Na_4(PO_3)_6]$.

Hardening of Oil (Hydrogenation)

Oil, an unsaturated fat when heated with nickel catalyst and hydrogen, gets converted into a solid mass called ghee, a saturated fat. This process is called hardening of oil and is carried out through hydrogenation in the presence of nickel as a catalyst.

Medicines

These are the chemicals used for treating diseases and reducing suffering from pain.

Different Medicines and their Examples

Medicine	*Used to*	*Example*
Analgesics	Reduce pain	Aspirin, paracetamol, morphine, phenacetin
Tranquilizers	To treat stress, mild and severe mental diseases	Equanil, valium, chlorodiazoepoxide, serotonin and meprobamate
Antiseptic	Prevent the growth of micro-organisms or kill them *(applied to living tissues)*	Dettol (a mixture of chloroxylenol—the antiseptic and α-terpineol), savlon, iodine tincture (solution of I_2 in alcohol water mixture), boric acid (antiseptic for eyes), hydrogen peroxide, iodoform
Antibiotic	Destroy microorganisms *(These are obtained from microorganisms.)*	Penicillin *(discovered by* **A Fleming** *in 1929, ampicillin, amoxicillin,* ofloxacin, *chloramphenicol)*
Antimalarial	Cure malaria	Chloroquine
Sulphadrugs	Alternative for antibiotics	Sulphanilamide, sulphadiazine
Antacids	Reduce acidity	Baking soda, magnesium hydroxide

Polymers

- A polymer is a compound of high molecular weight formed by the combination of a larger number of molecules of one or two types of low molecular weight (known as monomers) and the process is called polymerisation.
- Polymers are the backbones of four major industries; plastics, fibres, paints and varnishes.

Some Fibres and their Monomers

Fibre	*Monomers*	*Uses*
Nylon-6,6	Adipic acid + hexamethylene diamine	In making bristles for brushes, synthetic fibres, parachutes, as a substitute for metal in bearings.
Nylon-6 or perlon	Caprolactum	In making fibres, plastic tyre cords and ropes.
Terylene	Ethylene glycol and terephthalic acid	For making wash and wear fabrics, tyre cords, safety belts, tents etc .
Kevlar	Terephthalic acid + 1,4-diamino benzene	For making bulletproof vests.
Lexan or polycarbonate	Diethyl carbonate + *bis*-phenol-A	In making bulletproof windows and safety helmets.
Polyurethanes	Toluene diisocyanate + ethylene glycol	For making washable and long lasting mattresses, cushions.

Some Important Industrial Compounds

Industrial Name	*Chemical Name*	*Chemical Formula*
Alum	Potassium aluminium sulphate	$KAl(SO_4)_2 \cdot 12H_2O$
Alcohol	Ethyl alcohol	C_2H_5OH
Baking soda	Sodium bicarbonate	$NaHCO_3$
Bleaching powder	Calcium oxychloride or calcium hypochlorite	$CaOCl_2$
Brine (or common salt)	Sodium chloride	$NaCl$
Borax	Sodium tetraborate decahydrate	$Na_2B_4O_7 \cdot 10H_2O$
Caustic potash	Potassium hydroxide	KOH
Caustic soda	Sodium hydroxide	$NaOH$
Chalk (marble) or pearl	Calcium carbonate	$CaCO_3$
Chilli salt petre	Sodium nitrate	$NaNO_3$
Chloroform	Trichloro methane	$CHCl_3$
Epsom salt	Magnesium sulphate	$MgSO_4 \cdot 7H_2O$
Glauber's salt	Sodium sulphate decahydrate	$Na_2SO_4 \cdot 10H_2O$
Gypsum	Calcium sulphate dihydrate	$CaSO_4 \cdot 2H_2O$
Hypo	Sodium thiosulphate pentahydrate	$Na_2S_2O_3 \cdot 5H_2O$
Laughing gas	Nitrous oxide	N_2O
Lunar caustic	Silver nitrate	$AgNO_3$
Marsh gas	Methane	CH_4
Quick lime	Calcium oxide	CaO
Sal ammonia (Nausadar)	Ammonium chloride	NH_4Cl
Sapphire (Ruby)	Aluminium oxide	Al_2O_3
Slaked lime	Calcium hydroxide	$Ca(OH)_2$
Soda ash	Sodium carbonate	Na_2CO_3
Spirit	Methyl alcohol	CH_3OH
Washing soda	Sodium carbonate decahydrate	$Na_2CO_3 \cdot 10H_2O$

BIOLOGY

Biology (coined by **Lamarck** and **Treviranus** 1802), is a branch of science which deals with study of living organisms. It mainly includes Botany (Study of plants) and Zoology (Study of animals).

The scientist who gave this thoughts for the first time about the life of plants and animals was **Aristotle**, that's why he is known as the father of Biology. He is also known as the father of Zoology.

LIVING WORLD

In 18th Century, **Carolus Linnaeus** developed **binomial nomenclature** for living organisms, i.e., scientific name consisting of **genus** and **species**.

- **Whittaker** (1969) classified living organisms into five kingdoms— Monera, Protista, Fungi, Plantae and Animalia.
- Monera includes bacteria and *Mycoplasma*, while Protista includes Protozoa (unicellular Eukaryotes).
- **Viruses** are sub-microscopic, obligate, intracellular parasite consisting of nucleoprotein. **WM Stanley** firstly crystallised TMV (Tobacco Mosaic Virus).
- **Viroids** are smallest infectious single stranded RNA molecules discovered by **TO Diener.**

THE CELL

- According to cell theory proposed by **Schleiden** and **Schwann** (1838) cell is the structural and functional unit of living organisms.
- An organism may be composed of single cell (unicellular) or many cells (multicellular).
- Cells are of two types i.e., **prokaryotic** (which lacks nucleus and membrane bound organelles) and **eukaryotic** (which have nucleus and membrane bound organelles).
- Prokaryotic cell is found in bacteria, mycoplasma and blue-green algae while eukaryotic cell in plants, animals and fungi.

Nucleic Acids

- These contain the genetic instructions used in the development and functioning of all known living organisms. These are of two types namely DNA and RNA. **Deoxyribo Nucleic Acid** (DNA) It is a long polymer made from repeating units called nucleotides. It has four bases i.e. adenine, guanine, cytosine and thymine.
- **Ribo Nucleic Acid** (RNA) It is also made up of a long chain of nucleotides. It contains uracil in place of thymine.

HUMAN SYSTEMS

The cells of human and other multicellular animals are organised into **tissues**. Two or more tissues grouped together to form organs. An organ system is a group of organs that function together to carry out the principal activities of the body.

Digestion

Digestion is the process by which complex food is converted into simple components with the help of digestive enzymes, i.e. hydrolysis process.

Respiratory System

Respiration in an oxidative process involving oxidation of food substances such as carbohydrate, fat and proteins to form CO_2, water and to release energy.

Respiration may be anaerobic, (i.e. without O_2) and aerobic (i.e. with O_2).

Respiratory Organs of Animals

Organ	*Animal*
Lungs	Reptiles and mammals
Skin	Frog, earthworm and leeches
Gills	Fishes, tadpoles and prawns
Tracheae	Insects, centipedes and millipedes
Body surface	Protozoans, porifera and coelenterates
Book lungs	Spider and scorpion
Book gills	King crab, prawn, cray fish and *Daphnia*
Mental	Mollusca (*Unio*)
Air bladdar	Long fish and bony fishes (e.g. *Labeo)*
Airsacs/lungs	Birds

Vitamins

Fat Soluble Vitamins

Vitamin (Name)	*Rich Food Source*	*Function*	*Deficiency Disease*
A *(Retinol)*	Fish liver oils, dairy products, liver, most leafy vegetables and carrots contain carotene that can be converted into retinol	Needed for healthy epithelial cells and regeneration of rhodopsin in rod cells of the eye	Dry skin and night blindness (Nyctalopia)
D *(Calciferol)*	Fish oils, egg yolk and butter. It can be made by the action of sunlight on skin	Promotes absorption of calcium from intestines. Necessary for formation of normal bone and reabsorption of phosphate from urine	Rickets in children *('soft' bones that bend easily)* *Osteomalacia (painful bones)* in adults
E *(Tocopherol)*	Vegetable oils, cereal products and many other foods	Formation of red blood cells, affects muscles and reproductive system.	Mild anaemia and sterility . Deficiency is rare in humans
K *(Phylloquinone)*	Fresh and dark green vegetables. Also made by gut bacteria	Formation of prothrombin *(involved in blood clotting)*	Delayed clotting time. May occur in new-born babies before their gut bacteria become established

Water Soluble Vitamin

Vitamin (Name)	*Rich Food Source*	*Function*	*Deficiency Disease*
B_1 *(Thiamine)*	Yeast, cereals, nuts, seeds and pork	Co-enzyme in cell respiration, necessary for complete release of energy from carbohydrates.	Beri-beri *(muscular dystrophy, stunted growth and nerve degeneration)*
B_2 *(Riboflavin)*	Liver, milk, eggs and green vegetables	Co-enzyme in cell respiration. Precursor of FAD	Cracked skin and blurred vision
B_3 *(Niacin)*	Liver, yeast, whole cereals and beans	Co-enzyme in cell respiration. Precursor of NAD/NADP	Pellagra *(severe skin problems, diarrhoea and dementia)*
B_5 *(Pentothenic acid)*	Animal tissue, whole grain cereals and legumes	Needed to manufacture adrenal hormone	Pellagra, Dermatitis and Diarrhoea
B_6 *(Pyridoxine)*	Meat, fish, eggs, cereals bran and some vegetables	Interconversion of amino acids.	Skin problems and nerve disorder
B_{10} *(Folic acid)*	Liver, raw green vegetables, yeast and gut bacteria	Formation of nucleic acids and red blood cells	Anaemia *(especially during pregnancy)*
B_{12} *(Cyanocobalamine)*	Liver, milk, fish and yeast. None in plant foods	Maturation of red blood cells in bone marrow. Maintenance of myelin sheath of nerves	Pernicious anaemia and nerve disorders
C *(Ascorbic acid)*	Blackcurrants, peppers, sprouts and citrus fruits	Formation of collagen and intercellular cement	Scurvy and poor wound healing

Major Enzymes of Digestion

Enzyme	*Source*	*Where Active*	*Substrate*	*Main Breakdown Product*
Carbohydrate Digestion				
Salivary amylase	Salivary glands	Mouth	Polysaccharides	Disaccharides
Pancreatic amylase	Pancreas	Small intestine	Polysaccharides	Disaccharides
Disaccharides	Small intestine	Small intestine	Disaccharides	Monosaccharides (e.g., glucose)
Protein Digestion				
Pepsin	Stomach mucosa	Stomach	Proteins	Peptide fragments
Trypsin and chymotrypsin	Pancreas	Small intestine	Proteins and polypeptide	Peptide fragments
Carboxypeptidase	Pancreas	Small intestine	Peptide fragments	Amino acids
Amino peptidase	Intestinal mucosa	Small intestine	Peptide fragments	Amino acids
Fat Digestion				
Lipase	Pancreas	Small intestine	Triglycerides	Free fatty acids and monoglycerides
Nucleic Acid Digestion				
Pancreatic nucleases	Pancreas	Small intestine	DNA and RNA	Nucleotides
Intestinal nucleases	Intestinal mucosa	Small intestine	Nucleotides	Nucleotides bases and monosaccharides

Blood (Lymphatic System)

- Fluid connective tissue composed of plasma and blood cells.
- An adult person has 5-6 litre blood.
- It is slightly alkaline having pH 7.3-7.4.
- Plasma is pale yellow transparent and constitute about 60% volume of blood.
- Plasma is composed of 90-92% water, 7% organic substances (albumin, globulin and fibrinogen protein) and 1% inorganic substances.
- Red blood corpuscles (Most abundant) are non-nucleated and contains haemoglobin (the respiratory pigment).
- White blood cells are colourless, nucleated and granular or agranular.
- **Eosinophils** are also called acidophils. (2-8%) are phagocytic granulocytes and play important role in hypersensitivity.
- **Basophils** (2%) are non-phagocytic granulocytes and increases during chickenpox.
- **Neutrophils** (65%) are phagocytic granulocytes and increase during bacterial infection.

Blood Groups, Genotypes and their Transfusion Possibility

Blood Group (phenotype)	*Antigen in Red Blood Cells*	*Antibodies in Plasma*	*Can Give Blood to Groups*	*Can Receive Blood from Group*	*Genotype*
O	None	Anti-*a*, Anti-*b*	O, A, B and AB	O	$I^o I^o$
A	A	Anti-*b*	A and AB	O and A	$I^A I^A$ or $I^A I^o$
B	B	Anti-*a*	B and AB	O and B	$I^B I^B$ or $I^B I^o$
AB	A and B	None	AB	O, A, B and AB	$I^A I^B$

- **Monocytes** (0.5%) are agranulocytes called policeman of blood and increase during tuberculosis.
- **Lymphocytes** (26%) are agranulocytes producing antibodies and increase during viral infection.
- **Platelets** (thrombocytes) are non-nucleated. Platelets have a life span of about 8 to 10 days.
- **Rh factor** discovered by **Landsteiner** and **Veiner** in **Rhesus** monkey, which is responsible for **erythroblastosis foetalis disease**.
- Important component of blood clotting are fibrinogen, prothrombin, thromboplastin, calcium ions and Vitamin-K.

Heart

- Human heart is **myogenic** *i.e.*, contraction is initiated by a pulse produced by **Sino-atrial node** (SA node) located in right atrium. It is also called **pacemaker**. First heart sound is **lub** and second heart sound is **dub**.
- Contraction of heart is called **systole**. 120 mm Hg, while relaxation is called **diastole** (80 mm Hg).

Excretion

- It is the process elimination of harmful waste products from the animal body to regulate the composition of the body fluids and tissues.
- Human excretory system is composed of two kidneys. **Nephron** is the structural and functional unit of kidneys.
- Colour of urine is pale yellow. It is due to pigment **urochrome.**
- Human urine contains about 95% water, 2% salts, 2.6% urea and 0.3% uric acid.

Main Excretory Organs

Excretory Organ	*Animal*
Contractile vacuole	Amoeba
Flame cells/solenocytes	Tapeworm
Renette cell	Ascaris
Nephridia	Earthworm
Malpighian tubules	Cockroach
Coxal glands	Scorpion
Green glands	Prawn

- pH of urine is about 6.0 (mildly acidic).
- The urine on standing gives a pungent smell. It is due to the conversion of urea into ammonia.
- Specific gravity of urine is 1.015-1.025.
- Volume of urine is 1 to 2 L per day.

Main Excretory Products

Product	*Animal*
Ammonia	Most invertebrates, fishes etc.
Urea	Ascaris, earthworm, cartilaginous fishes, amphibian and mammals
Uric acid	Insects, land reptiles and birds

Central Nervous System

The brain is the organising and processing centre of the body. It is the site of consciousness, sensation, memory and intelligence.

The brain receives impulses from the spinal cord and from 12 pairs of cranial nerves coming from it and extending to the senses and to other organs. In addition, the brain initiates activities without environmental stimuli.

Three major portions of the brain are recognised as the **hindbrain, midbrain** and the **forebrain**.

Important Functions of Brain

Forebrain	
Olfactory region	Smell
Cerebrum	Thinking, intelligence, memory, ability to learn from experience, will power, skilled work, reasoning knowledge, consciousness and speech.
Control	Laughing, weeping, micturition *(passing of urine)*, defecation voluntary forced breathing and voluntary muscular co-ordination.
Diencephalon (sensation of)	Heat, cold and pain control centre of autonomic nervous system, control hunger, thirst, sweating, sleeping and sex.
Hypothalamus	Regulated body temperature so 'thermostat' of body. Appetite and safety control emotions like love, anger, pleasure and satisfaction. Control metabolism of carbohydrate, fat and water.

Midbrain and Hindbrain	Reflex centre of visual and auditory sensation.
Cerebellum	Involuntary muscular co-ordination, maintain posture, orientation and equilibrium of the body.
Medulla oblongata	Regulate heart rate, involuntary breathing, respiratory centre, blood pressure, *(vasoconstriction and vasodilation)* gut peristalsis, food swallowing and vomiting gland secretion.

Some Human Diseases Caused by Viruses and Bacteria

Disease	*Pathogen*	*Incubation*	*Symptoms*	*Prevention/ Vaccine*
Chickenpox (Varicella)	Herpes zoster virus	12-20 days	Dark red coloured rash or pox changing into vesicles, crusts and falling	Varicella vaccine
Smallpox	Variola virus	12 days	Appearance of rash changing into pustules, scaps and falling pockmarks are left	Smallpox vaccine
Poliomyelitis	Polio virus	7-14 days	Damages motor neurons causing stiffness of neck, convulsion, paralysis of limbs generally legs	Salk vaccine and Oral Polio Vaccine (OPV)
Measles (Rubella disease)	Rubella virus	10 days	Rubella *(skin eruptions)*, coughing, sneezing, etc	Measles-mumps-rubella-Varicella Combo (MMRV vaccine)
Mumps	Mumps virus	12-26 days	Painful enlargement of parotid and salivary glands	Mumps-vaccine, isolation
Rabies (Hydrophobia)	Rabies virus	10 days to 1-3 months	Spasm in throat and chest muscles, fears from water, paralysis and death	Immunisation of dogs
Tuberculosis	*M tuberculosis*	2-10 weeks	Coughing, chest pain and bloody sputum with tuberculin	BCG vaccine
Diphtheria	*C diphtheriae*	2-6 days	Inflammation of mucosa of nasal chamber, throat, etc, respiratory tract blocked	DPT vaccine
Cholera	*Vibrio cholerae*	6 h to 2-3 days	Acute diarrhoea and dehydration	Sanitation, boiling of water and oral cholera vaccine
Leprosy	*Mycobacterium leprae*	2-5 years	Skin hypopigmentation, nodulated skin, deformity of fingers and toes.	BCG also offers variable amount of protection against leprosy. Lepromin skin tests
Tetanus (Lock jaw)	*Clostridium tetani*	3-21 days	Degeneration of motor neurons, rigid jaw muscles, spasm and paralysis	ATS and DPT vaccines
Typhoid	*Salmonella typhi*	1-3 weeks	Classic typhoid fever	TAB vaccine and screening of food and water
Plague	*Pasteurella pestis*	2-6 days	Bubonic plague affects, lymph nodes, pneumonic plague affects lungs and septicemic plague causes anaemia	Killing of rats and rat fleas, plague vaccine
Gonorrhoea	*Neisseria gonorrhoeae*	2-10 days	Inflammation of urinogenital tract	Avoid prostitution
Pneumonia	Streptococcus pneumoniae	1-3 days	Decrease in respiratory efficiency	PCV 13

Disease	Pathogen	Incubation	Symptoms	Prevention/ Vaccine
Salmonellosis	*Salmonella enteritidis*	48 h	Diarrhoea	RASV vaccine
Swine Flu	H1N1flu virus (Orthomy)	1-4 days	Fever with or without chill, sore throat, dyspneat, myalgia, diarrhea, vometing and dizziness	*Oseltamivir* (Tamiflu), Zonamivir (Relenza) are antiviral drugs vaccines are available against this disease.
Ebola Virus Disease (EVD)	*Ebola* virus (Filovirus)	2-21 days	Haemorrhagic fever, muscle pain, headache, sore throat, diarrhoea, kidney and liver dysfunction, internal and external bleeding.	No licensed vaccine available, immune therapies are done currently.
Dengue	RNA virus of genus Flavivirus	3-14 days	muscle pain, swollen lymph nodes, fever, headache and rash	No specific antiviral drug is available, however symptoms based treatment is done.
Chikunguniya	RNA virus of genus Alphavirus	1-12 days	Headache, fatigue, digestive complaints and conjunctivitis	No specific treatment, however supportive case through drugs like naproxen, paracetamol is done.
COVID-19	Novel Corona Virus	5-14 days	Fever, dry cough, tiredness, aches, pains, nasal congestion, headache, conjunctivitis, sore throat, diarrhoea, loss of taste or smell or a rash on skin or discoloration of fingers or toes.	—

Human Diseases Caused by Fungi

Disease	Fungus
Aspergillosis	*Aspergillus flavus, A fumigatus and A niger*
Blastomycosis	*Blastomyces dermatitidis*
Candidiasis	*Candida albicans*
Chromomycosis	*Cladosporium corrionii*
Coccidiomycosis	*Coccidiodes immitis*
Cryptococcosis	*Lipomyces neoformans*
Geotrichosis	*Geotrichum candidum*
Histoplasmosis	*Histoplasma capsulatum*
Neuritis	*Mucor pusillus*
Onychomycosis	*Trichophyton purpureum*

Animal/Human Diseases Caused by Fungi

Disease	Fungus
Athelete foot	Trichophyton
Ringworm	*Trichophyton, Microsporum and Epidermophyton*
Mucormycosis	*Mucor and Rhizopus*
Penicilliosis	*Penicillium*

Important Vaccines Discoverer

Vaccine	Discovered By
Small pox	Edward Jenner (1786)
Cholera	Louis Pasteur (1880)
Diphtheria and Tetanus	Emil Adolf Von Behring and Shibasaburo Kitasato
Tuberculosis	Leon Calmette and Camille Guerin (1992)
Polio	Jonas E Salk (1954)
Oral polio	Albert Bruce Sabin (1995)
Measles	John F Enders (1960)
Rabies	Charles Nicolle (1909)

Some Antibiotics Developed through Biotechnology

Antibiotic	Microbial Source
Penicillin	*Penicillium notatum and P chrysogenum*
Bacitracin	*Bacillus subtilis*
Cephalosporin	*Cephalosporium acremonium*
Griseofulvin	*Penicillium griseofulvum*
Streptomycin	*Streptomyces griseus*
Tetracycline	*S erythraeus*
Erythromycin	*S aureofaciens*
Chloramphenicol	*S venezuelae*

Ebola Virus

According to World Health Organisation WHO's **19th August, 2015 Situation Report**, there were three confirmed cases of Ebola reported in the week up to 16th August all of which were reported from **Guinea**. For the first time since the beginning of the outbreak in **Sierra Leone**, a full epidemiological week has passed with no confirmed cases reported. A total of 72 cases remain under monitoring in Sierra Leone.

On 29th, June 2015, a confirmed case of Ebola was reported in a 17 year old male who had died in **Liberia**.

Apart from Africa, ebola virus has spread to USA, Spain, Mali and to an extent in Italy and UK.

ECOLOGY

- **Ecology** (term used by **Reiter**) deals with various principles which govern the relationship between organisms and their environment. **Pyramid of number** is upright in grassland and pond ecosystem, while inverted in tree ecosystem.
- **Pyramid of biomass** is upright in grassland and forest ecosystem whereas, inverted in pond ecosystem.
- **Pyramid of energy** is always upright.

Pollution

- Motor vehicle contribute 60% of air pollution in major cities. Photochemical smog comprising of O_3, H_2O_2, PAN, etc.
- CO has 250 times more binding affinity with haemoglobin as compared to O_2.
- **Acid rain** is composed of H_2SO_4 and HNO_3.
- Chlorofluorocarbons released into stratosphere release free chlorine atom that causes **depletion of ozone**.
- **Sewage** is major source of water pollution.
- **Bioremediation** is the process of using micro-organisms to remove environmental pollutant, e.g. using oil-zapper developed by TERI to prevent oil spills.
- **Biomagnification** The increase in concentration of persistent chemicals in organisms in successive trophic levels.
- Endosulfan is an organic pollutant used as a pesticide in Southern states for cashew crops, which is now banned world over.
- **Chernobyl disaster** occurred in Ukraine (USSR) 26th April, 1986 due to explosion of nuclear power station.
- Nitrate fertilisers cause **blue baby syndrome** or **methemoglobinemia**.
- Noise pollution is measured in decibels (Generally sound beyond 80 dB is termed as noise).

BIOTECHNOLOGY

- **Biotechnology** is a field of applied biology that involves the use of living things in engineering, technology, medicine and other useful applications.
- **Genetic Engineering** Insertion of a foreign gene fragment into another DNA molecule to produce DNA clones.
- **Gene Therapy** It is the insertion of genes into an individual cells and tissue to treat diseases especially hereditary diseases.

Test Tube Baby

- Test tube baby is a fusion of ovum and sperm outside body followed by implantation in uterus at 32 celled stage and further normal development to birth.
- The IVF (In Vitro Fertilisation) technology is a boon to childless couples.
- First attempt to produce a test tube baby was made by an Italian scientist Dr. Petrucci in 1959.
- But this human embryo survived for only 29 days.
- The **World's first test tube baby** (a baby girl) named as Louise Joy Brown was born on 25th July, 1978 in Great Britain.
- **India's first test tube baby** was born in Mumbai on 6th August 1986. Her name is Kanupriya.

Cloning

- Cloning in biology is the process of producing similar populations of genetically identical individuals that occurs in nature when organisms

such as bacteria, insects or plants reproduce asexually.

- **Dolly** a sheep, the first mammal clone was developed by Dr Ian Wilmut, UK.

Bt Crops

- Crop plants that contain genes for *Bt* toxins. *Bt* toxin gene has been cloned from the bacteria (*Bacillus thuringiensis*) and been expressed in plants to provide resistance from insects without the need of insectisides e.g. *Bt*-cotton (first GM crop), *Bt*-corn, golden rice, etc.

Seed Village Concept

It is the starting point of agriculture and dictates ultimate productivity of other inputs. It was organised by **Dr Swaminathan** in the Jounti village of Delhi state in 1965, which was designed to convert the entire village into a high quality seed producing centre.

Over the years, this concept have grown and been refined which aims to import **techniracy** (technical literacy or imparting the latest skills to farmers solely) for quality seed production and thereby to make available quality seed to others at appropriate time and affordable cost.

Some smallest in their categories

Bacteria	*Dialister* Pneumosintes	Flower	*Wolffia microscopica* (Angiosperm)
Bird	Humming bird *(Cuba)*	Mammal	Shrew (*Suncus etruscus*)
Bone	Stapes	Muscles	Stapedius or arrector pili
Endocrine gland	Pituitary	Virus	Foot and mouth disease virus

Some largest in their categories

Mammal *(on land)*	African elephant (*Loxodonta africana*)
Mammal *(in the biosphere)*	Blue whale
Flower	*Rafflesia*
Flower in India	*Sapria*
Vertebral	Lumbar vertebrae
Bone	Femur
Bone *(in frog)*	Tibia-fibula
Muscles	Gluteus maximus *(buttock muscle of hip)*
Tooth	Tusk of elephant *(upper incisor modification)*
Tallest angiosperm	*Eucalyptus*
Tallest gymnosperm	*Sequoia sempervirens* (*Sequoia gigantea*)
Coral reef	In Australia, great barrier reef
Egg or cell	Ostrich
Vein	Inferior vena cava
Artery	Abdominal aorta
Cell of the body	Neuron or nerve cell
Virus	Parrot fever virus

Some Important Branches of Biology

Branch	*Concerned Field*
Agriculture	Study of producing crops from the land
Anatomy	Study of the animal forms with an emphasis on human bodies.
Anthology	Study of flowers.
Anthropology	Study of apes and man.
Apiculture	Honey industry *(Bee keeping).*
Biochemistry	Deals with the study of chemical reactions in relation to life activities.
Cardiology	Study of heart.
Cryogenics	Study concerning with the application and uses of very low temperature.
Cytology	Study of cells.
Dermatology	Study of skin.
Floriculture	Study of flower yielding plants.
Genetics	Study of horodity and variations.
Gerontology	Study of growing old.
Horticulture	Study of garden cultivation.
Myology	Study of muscles.
Nephrology	Study of kidneys
Obstetrics	Branch of medicine dealing with pregnancy.
Ornithology	Study of birds
Phycology	Study of algae.

Branch	Concerned Field
Pedology	Study of soils
Pathology	Study of disease causing organisms.
Physiology	Science dealing with the study of functions of various parts of organisms.
Pisciculture	Study of fish.
Sericulture	Silk industry *(culture of silk moth and pupa).*
Serpentology	Study of snakes.
Taxonomy	Study of classification of organisms.
Virology	Study of virus.

Some Important Discoveries

Discovery	*Made by*	*Country*
Antibiotic	Alexender Flemming (1928)	Scotland
Antiseptic	Joseph Lister (1867)	Scotland
Blood circulation	William Harvey (1628)	Britain
Blood transfusion	Jean-Baptiste Denys (1625)	France
Cholera and TB germs	Robert Kock (1883)	Germany
Electrocardiogram (ECG)	William Einthoven (1903)	Dutch
CT Scan	Godfrey Hounsfield (1973)	England
Sphygmomanometer	Scipione Riva-Rocci (1898)	Italy
Stethoscope	Rene Laennee (1819)	France
Thermometer	Sir Thomas Aelburt (1867)	England
Ultrasound	Ian Donald (1950)	Ireland
X-ray	WC Roentgen *(1895)*	Germany
Electroencephalogram (EEG)	Hans Berger *(1929)*	Germany

Some Important Antibiotics

Antibiotics	*Source*	*Action*
Penicillin	*Penicillium chrysogenum, P. notatum + Phenyl Acetic Acid*	Tonsilitis, Sore Throat, Gonorrhea, Rheumatic Fever, some Pneumonia types
Griseofulvin	*Penicillium griseofulvum*	Antifungal, especially for Ringworm
Nystatin	*Streptomyces noursei*	Antifungal for Candidiasis and overgrowth of Intestinal Fungi during excessive antibiotic treatment.
Hamycin	*Streptomyces pimprei*	Antifungal for Thrush
Fumagillin	*Aspergillus fumigatus*	Broad spectrum antibacterial especially against Salmonella and Shigella.
Bacitracin	*Bacillus licheniformis*	Syphilis, Lymphonema or Reticulosis.
Streptomycin	*Streptomyces griseus*	Meningitis, Pneumonia, Tuberculosis and Local Infection. Toxic in some through eighth cranial nerve.
Chloramphenicol Chloromycetin	*Streptomyces venezuelae, S. lavendulae and Now synthetic*	Typhoid, Typhus, Whooping cough, Atypical Pneumonia, Bacterial Urinary Infections.
Tetracyclines/ Aureomycin	*Streptomyces aureofaciens*	Viral pneumonia, Osteomyelitis, Whooping Cough and Eye infections.
Oxytetracycline/ Terramycin	*Chlorotetracycline → Hydrogenation Streptomyces rimosus*	Intestinal and Urinary Infections (Spirochaetes, Rickettsia and Viruses)
Erythromycin	*Streptomyces erythreus (= S. erythraeus)*	Typhoid, Common Pneumonia and Diphtheria, Whooping Cough, etc.
Gentamycin	*Micromonospora purpurea*	Effective against Gram (+) bacteria
Polymixin	*Bacillus polymyxa*	Antifungal

COMPUTER

A computer is an electronic machine which stores, reads and processes data to produce meaningful information as output.

Components of Computer

- **Input Unit** Devices used to give instructions, *e.g.* Keyboard, Mouse, Joystick, Optical character reader, CDs, Bar code reader, Touch screen, Light pen, Scanner, Magnetic Ink Character Recognition (MICR), etc.
- **Central Processing Unit** (CPU) is the device for the manipulation of information inside the computer. CPU is known as the brain of the computer, but commonly called a processor and has the following components
- **Arithmetic Logic Unit** (ALU) performs all logical and arithmatical operations.
- **Control Unit** (CU) instructs, maintains and controls the flow of information.
- **Output Unit** is the device to display the result of processing, e.g. Visual Display Unit, Printer, Monitor, Speaker, Pen Drive, etc.

Memory

Memory holds all the raw and processed data, set of instructions and information inside the CPU.

Primary Memory

Primary Memory stores the data which is currently in use by the computer.

- **RAM** (Random Access Memory) It is a volatile memory. It is a temporary storage.
    - **DRAM** Dynamic Random Access Memory
    - **SRAM** Static Random Access Memory
- **ROM** (Read Only Memory) It is a non-volatile memory where all logical data is stored that cannot be changed.
    - **PROM** Programmable Read Only Memory.
    - **EPROM** Erasable Programmable Read Only Memory.
    - **EEPROM** Electrically Erasable Programmable Read Only Memory.

Secondary Memory

It stores data, program, instruction and information permanently.

Hardware

Any peripheral device which can be seen and touched is hardware. Computer hardware includes input devices, output devices, storage devices and processing devices.

Software

It is a set of instructions that directs the computer to process information. It can be classified as **System Software** and **Application Software**.

Networking

Computer networking relates to the communication between a group of two or more computers linked together. Most common example of networking is Internet, connecting millions of people all over the world together. According to scale or size, computer network can be categorised in three ways

- **Local Area Network** (LAN) Graphical area spread over 1km to 10km or within a same building.
- **Metropolitan Area Network** (MAN) Graphical area spread over a city or town.
- **Wide Area Network** (WAN) Graphical area spread over countries.

Security Threats

- **Worm** It is a self contained program and does not need to be a part of another program to propagate itself.
- **Spam** Spam is an unsolicited message sent over the Internet in the form of e-mails, to a large number of users for the purpose of spreading malware, advertising phishing, etc.
- **Spyware** It is a type of malicious software installed on computers and collects information about users without their knowledge and may send such information to another entity.
- **Malware** A software which is specifically designed to disrupt or damage a computer system. It is a superset of

computer viruses, worms, spyware, trojan horses and other malicious or unwanted software.

- **Virus** A virus is defined as a program or a piece of code that gets loaded onto the computer without users knowledge and replicates itself, e.g. Creeper, Stuxnet, Melissa, Conficker, Code red, SQL Slammer, Nimda (derived from the word 'Admin'), etc.

Antivirus

Antivirus is a software consisting of computer programs that attempt to identify, detect and prevent the malware from the computer.

Some Commonly Used Terms

- **Cache Memory** It is a temporary storage, where frequently accessed data can be stored for rapid access.
- **Registers** These are defined as the special memory units used by the CPU to speed up the rate of accessing information.
- **Operating System** It is a system software, consisting of an integrated set of programs that control computer resources and provides common services for efficient execution of various application software.
- **Compiler** It is a computer program that transforms human readable source code into the Machine readable code at one go.
- **Interpreter** It transforms source code into the machine readable code by converting it line by line.
- **Assembler** It converts assembly language program into machine language program.
- **Modem** (Modulator-Demodulator) An electronic device used to convert computer (digital) electronic signals to communication channel (analog) electronic signals and *vice-versa*.
- **Cloud Computing** is the delivery of on-demand computing resources, everything from applications to data centres, over the Internet, e.g. Google.
- **Dual Core Processor** is the processing technology in which two processors are scheduled together and when one is busy the other takes over.
- **Internet** It is the worldwide, publically accessible system of interconnected computer networks that transmit data by using the Internet protocol.
- **Cryptography** It is a method of storing and transmitting data in a particular coded form so that only those can read and process it, for whom it is intended. It includes encoding and decoding of data.

Super Computers

A super computer can be defined as the most powerful computer in terms of performance and storage capacity. They are highly expensive and are employed for specialised applications such as for weather forecasting, several scientific researches, etc.

Super Computers Developed in India

Name	*Year*	*Mft Company*
Param Ananta	2022	IIT (Gandhinagar)
Param Siddhi	2020	CDAC
Param Shivay	2019	IIT-BHU
Pratyush	2017	IITM (Pune)
Param Kanchenjunga	2016	CDAC & NIT Sikkim
Param Ishan	2016	CDAC & IIT Guwahati
Aaditya	2013	Indian Institute of Tropical Meteorology
PARAM YUVA II	2013	C-DAC, PUNE
SAGA-220	2011	ISRO
ANUPAM-Adhya	2010-11	BARC

Super Computers of the World

Name	*Year*	*Country*	*Operating System*
Frontier	2022	USA	HPE Cray OS
Fugaku	2021	Japan	Custom Linux
Frontera	2019	America	Linux (Cent OS)
IBM Summit	2018	America	IBM
Sunway Taihulight	2016	China	Linux
Tianhe-2	2013	China	Kylin Linux
Titan	2012	America	Linux
Sequoia	2011	America	Linux
K-Computer	2011	Japan	Linux
Mira	2010	America	Linux

Sophia

In October, 2017 Saudi Arabia has provided citizenship to a robot Sophia. This robot can change the facial expressions of the face and can chat with people.

GENERAL KNOWLEDGE

First in the World

First Radio Telescope Satellite launched into Space	HALCA (Japan)
First country to use Glass	Egypt and Mesopotamia
First country to make Map	The Greeks
First Spaceship landed on Mars	Viking-I (July 1976)
World's First Multipurpose River Valley Project	Tennessee River Valley Project (USA)
First Space Shuttle Launched	Columbia (April 1981)
First Rocket to go near the Sun	Helius 'B'
First Country to make written Constitution	The USA
First Country to start Underground Metro Rail	Britain
First Unmanned Mission on the Moon	LUNA-9
First Spacecraft to carry man on the Moon	Apollo - 11
First Country to do Artificial Satellite Experiment	Russia
Country to give Voting Right to Women	New Zealand
First Country to appoint Lokpal	Sweden
First Country to imposed Carbon Tax	New Zealand
First Country to give Rights to Wild Animals	Ecuador

First in the World (Male)

First Asian to Head the International Cricket Council	Jagmohan Dalmiya
First man to climb Mount Everest	Sherpa Tenzing Norgay and Sir Edmund Hillary (29th May, 1953)
First Man to go into Space	Major Yuri Gagarin (USSR) (1961)
First Man to walk into Space	Alexei Leonov (Russia)
First Person to give information about Planets and their motion around the Sun	Nicolous Copernicus
First Man to compile Encyclopaedia	Aspheosis (Athens)
First Person to go on both the Poles (*North and South*)	Ranulph Fiennes
First Man to reach North Pole	Robert Peary
First Man to reach South Pole	Roald Amundsen
First Man to climb on Mt Everest without Oxygen	Phu Dorji Sherpa
First Secretary of United Nation	Trygve Lie (Norway)

First in the World (Female)

First Woman President of a Country	Maria Estela Peron (Argentina)
First Woman in the world to cross the Strait of Gibralter	Arti Pradhan (India)
First Woman Cosmonaut in Space	Valentina Tereshkova (USSR)
First woman Prime Minister	Sirimavo Bandaranaike (Sri Lanka)
First Woman to have a Spacewalk	Svetlana Yevgenyevna Savitskaya
First Woman Vice-President of United States of America	Kamla Harris
First Woman to climb Mount Everest	Junko Tabei (Japan)
First Woman Space Tourist	Mrs. Anousheh Ansari (Irani-American)
First Female Amputee to Climb Mount Everest	Arunima Sinha
First Woman CFO and MD of World Bank	Anshula Kant
First Woman Chief Economist for IMF	Gita Gopinath
First Astronaut to complete historic all female Spacewalk	Christina Koch and Jessica Meir

First Woman appointed as UN Civilian Police Officer	Kiran Bedi
First Woman to lead World Trade Organisation	Ngozi Okonjo

Geographical Discoveries

Superlatives (World)

(The Largest, Biggest, Smallest, Longest, Highest)

Largest Airport (by size)	King Fahd International Airport *(Dammam, Saudi Arabia)*
Highest Airport	Bangda Airport, Tibet *(now in China)*
Tallest Building	Burj Khalifa, Dubai United Arab Emirates (828 m)
Largest Bay	Hudson Bay, Canada
Longest Big-ship Canal	Suez Canal (linking Red Sea and Mediterranean Sea)
Busiest Canal *(Ship)*	Kiel Canal
Longest Epic	The Mahabharata
Largest Diamond	The Cullinan *(South Africa)*
Largest Island	Greenland
Largest Mosque	Masjid al-Haram, Mecca
Largest Delta	Sundarbans, India
Largest Desert	Sahara, Africa
Largest Lake	Caspian Sea
Deepest Lake	Baikal (Siberia)
Highest Lake	Titicaca (*Bolivia*)
Largest Lake *(Fresh water)*	Lake Superior, USA
Largest Coral Formation	The Great Barrier Reef *(Australia)*
Largest Continent	Asia
Smallest Continent	Australia
Largest Country *(in population)*	China
Largest Country *(in area)*	Russia
Longest Dome	World Peace Monument Dome *(Pune)*
Tallest Minar *(Free standing)*	Great Hassan II Mosque, Casablanca, Morocco
Largest City *(in population)*	Tokyo
Highest City	Wen Chuan *(Tibet, China)*
Largest City *(in population)*	Tokyo *(Japan)*
Longest Bridge *(Railway)*	Danyang-Kunshan Grand Bridge *(China)*
Largest Dam *(Concrete)*	Grand Coulee Dam *(USA)*
Highest Dam	Jinping-I Dam, across River Yarlong, China
Highest Straight Dam	Bhakra Dam
Highest Capital City	La Paz (Bolivia)
Highest Asian Desert	Gobi, Mongolia
Largest Democracy	India
Biggest Bell	Great Bell at Moscow
Reptile which changes its colour	Chameleon
Most intelligent Animal	Chimpanzee
Highest Volcano	Ojos del Salado, Andes, Argentina- Chile (6893 m)
Largest Volcano	Mauna Loa *(Hawaii Islands)*
Longest Wall	Great Wall of China
Highest Mountain Peak	Mount Everest *(Nepal)*
Highest Mountain Range	Himalayas
Longest Mountain Range	Andes Central *(South America)*
Biggest Museum	British Museum *(London)*
Highest Waterfall	Salto Angel Falls *(Venezuela)*
Longest Gulf	Gulf of Mexico
Deepest and Biggest Ocean	The Pacific
Largest Peninsula	Arabia
Largest Palace	Imperial Palace *(Gugong)*, Beijing *(China)*
Largest Park	National Park, Greenland
Largest Archipelago	Malay Archipelago

Coldest Place	Verkhoyansk *(Siberia)* Temperature (– 89.2°C).
Driest Place	McMurdo Dry Valleys, Antarctica
Hottest Place	Al-Aziziyah *(Libya, Africa)* 136°F
Largest Platform *(Railway)*	Gorakhpur *(Uttar Pradesh)*
Largest Bridge *(Railway)*	Danyang-Kunshan Grand Bridge *(China)*
Largest Plateau	Tibetan Plateau
Largest River Basin	Amazon Basin
World's Rainiest Spot	Mawsynram *(Meghalaya)*
Largest Gorge	Grand Canyon on the Colorade river, USA
Largest Port	Shanghai *(China)*
Busiest Port	Shanghai *(China)*
Longest Railway	Trans-Siberian Railway
Longest River	Nile (6690 km)
Longest River Dam	Tarbela Dam, Pakistan
Largest Sea-Bird	Albatross
Largest Sea	Philippine Sea

Tallest Statue	Statue of Unity, Gujarat *(India)*
Tallest Tower	Tokyo Skytree *(Japan)*
Longest Swimming Course	English Channel *(between London and Edinburgh)*
Longest Train Nonstop	Flying Scotsman
Longest Tunnel *(Railway)*	Gotthard Base Tunnel
Longest and Largest Canal/Tunnel	Le Rove Tunnel *(South of France)*
Lightest Gas	Hydrogen
Lightest Metal	Lithium
Highest Melting Point	Tungstan, (34100°C)
Hardest Substance	Wurtzite Boron Nitride
Fastest Bird	The Peregrine Falcon
Longest Poisonous Snake	King Cobra
Largest Temple	Angkor Vat *(Cambodia)*
Largest Diamond Mine	Kimberley *(South Africa)*
Tallest Structure	Burj Khalifa *(Dubai)*

Countries with Capitals and Currencies

Country	*Capital*	*Currency*
Afghanistan	Kabul	Afghani
Albania	Tirana	Lek
Algeria	Algiers	Algerian Dinar
Angola	Luanda	Kwanza
Argentina	Buenos Aires	Peso
Australia	Canberra	Australian Dollar
Austria	Vienna	Euro
Bangladesh	Dhaka	Taka
Belarus	Minsk	Ruble
Belgium	Brussels	Euro
Bhutan	Thimphu	Ngultrum
Brazil	Brasilia	Cruzeiro Real
Cambodia	Phnom-Penh	Riel
Canada	Ottawa	Canadian Dollar
Chile	Santiago	Peso
China	Beijing	Yuan, Renminbi

Country	*Capital*	*Currency*
Colombia	Bogota	Colombian Peso
Denmark	Copenhagen	Krone
Egypt	Cairo	Egyptian Pound
France	Paris	Franc, Euro
Germany	Berlin	Euro
Greece	Athens	Euro
Hungary	Budapest	Forint
India	New Delhi	Rupee
Indonesia	Jakarta	Rupiah
Iran	Tehran	Rial
Iraq	Baghdad	Dinar
Ireland	Dublin	Euro
Israel	Jerusalem	Shekel
Italy	Rome	Euro
Japan	Tokyo	Yen
Kazakhstan	Nur-Sultan	Tenge

Country	Capital	Currency
Kenya	Nairobi	Shilling
North Korea	Pyongyang	Won
Kuwait	Kuwait City	Kuwait Dinar
South Korea	Seoul	Won
Libya	Tripoli	Libyan Dinar
Malaysia	Kuala Lumpur	Ringgit
Maldives	Male	Rufiyaa
Mauritius	Port Louis	Rupee
Mongolia	Ulan Bator	Tugrik
Montenegro	Podgorica	Euro
Myanmar	Naypyidaw	Kyat
Namibia	Windhoek	Namibian Dollar
Nepal	Kathmandu	Nepalese Rupee
Netherlands	Amsterdam	Euro
New Zealand	Wellington	New Zealand Dollar
Nigeria	Abuja	Naira
Norway	Oslo	Krone
Pakistan	Islamabad	Rupee
Phillippines	Manila	Peso
Poland	Budapest	Zloty
Portugal	Lisbon	Euro

Country	Capital	Currency
Qatar	Doha	Riyal
Russia	Moscow	Ruble
Saudi Arabia	Riyadh	Riyal
Somalia	Mogadishu	Somali Shilling
Singapore	Singapore	Dollar
South Africa	Pretoria	Rand
Spain	Madrid	Euro
Sri Lanka	Colombo	Sri Lankan Rupee
Sudan	Khartoum	Sudanese Pound
South Sudan	Juba	South Sudanese Pound
Sweden	Stockholm	Krona
Switzerland	Bern	Swiss Franc
Taiwan	Taipei	New Taiwan Dollar
Thailand	Bangkok	Baht
Turkey	Ankara	Lira
Uganda	Kampala	Uganda Shilling
Ukraine	Kiev	Hryvnia
UK	London	Pound Sterling
US	Washington DC	US Dollar
Venezuela	Caracas	Bolivar
Zimbabwe	Harare	US Dollar

Geographical Epithets

Blue Mountains	Nilgiri Hills
Beautiful City	Chandigarh
City of Golden Gate	San Francisco
City of Magnificent Buildings	Washington
City of Palaces	Kolkata
City of Seven Hills	Rome
Cockpit of Europe	Belgium
Continent of Birds	South Africa
City of Smoke	Chicago
Dark Continent	Africa
Forbidden City	Lhasa (Tibet)
Gift of the Nile	Egypt
Granite City	Aberdeen
Holy Land	Palestine
Island Continent	Australia
Island of Cloves	Zanzibar
Isle of Pearls	Bahrain
Key to the Mediterranean	Gibraltar
Land of Golden Fleece	Australia
Land of Maple	Canada
Land of Morning Calm	Korea
Land of the Midnight Sun	Norway
Land of the Rising Sun	Japan
Land of the Thunderbolt	Bhutan
Land of Thousand Lakes	Finland
Land of White Elephant	Thailand
Mistress of Eastern Sea	Sri Lanka
Pearl of the Antilles	Cuba
Pearl of the Pacific	Guayaquil Port of Ecuador
Roof of the World	The Pamirs, Central Asia
Spice Garden of India	Kerala
Sugar Bowl of the World	Cuba

Geographical Discoveries

Discovery	*Discoverer*	*Discovery*	*Discoverer*
America	Christopher Columbus	New Foundland	John Cabot
Sea Route to India *via* Cape of Good Hope	Vasco Da Gama	Hudson Bay	Henry Hudson
Solar System	Copernicus	Circumnavigation of World	Magellan
Planets	Kepler	Mount Everest	Edmund Hillary
South Pole	Roald Amundsen	Brazil	Pedro Alvares Cabral
North Pole	Robert Peary	Tasmania Island	Abel Tasman
China	Marco Polo	Cape of Good Hope	Bartolomeu Dias

Official Books of Major Countries

Blue Book	An official report of the British Government
Green Book	An official publications of Italy and Iran
Grey Book	An official reports of the Governments of Japan and Belgium
Orange Book	An official publications of the Government of Netherlands
White Book	An official publications of China, Germany and Portugal
White Paper	An official paper of the Governments of Britain and India on a particular issue
Yellow Book	An official paper of the Goverment of France

Important Monuments of Some Famous Countries

Monument	*Country*	*Monument*	*Country*
Imperial Palace *(Tokyo)*	Japan	Leaning Tower of Pisa	Italy
Eiffel Tower *(Paris)*	France	Pyramid *(Giza)*	Egypt
Great Wall of China	China	Opera House *(Sydney)*	Australia
Kremlin Palace *(Moscow)*	Russia	Statue of Liberty *(New York)*	USA
Kinder Disk	Denmark	Taj Mahal *(Agra)*	India

The Seven Wonders of the World

Ancient World	*Modern World*	*The 'New' Wonder*
The Colossus of Rhodes	Channel Tunnel	Pyramid at Chichen Itza, Mexico
The Great Pyramid of Giza	CN Tower	Christ Redeemer, Brazil
The Hanging Gardens of Babylon	Empire State Building	The Great Wall, China
The Mausoleum at Halicarnassus	Golden Gate Bridge	Machu Picchu, Peru
The Statue of Zeus at Olympia	Itaipu Dam	Petra, Jordan
The Lighthouse of Alexandria	North Sea Protection works	Roman Colosseum, Italy
The Temple of Artemis at Ephesus	Panama Canal	The Taj Mahal, India

Intelligence/Detective Agencies of the World

Detective Agency	*Country*
Ministry of State Security (MSS)	China
Australian Security and Intelligence Organisation (ASIO)	Australia
KGB/GRU	Russia
National Intelligence Agency	South Africa
MI (Military Intelligence)-5 and 6, Special Branch, Joint Intelligence Organisation	United Kingdom
Inter Services Intelligence *(ISI)*	Pakistan
Research and Analysis Wing *(RAW)*, Intelligence Bureau *(IB)*	India
Central Intelligence Agency (CIA),Federal Bureau of Investigation (FBI)	USA
MOSSAD	Israel
Mukhabarat	Egypt
Naicho	Japan
SAVAK (Sazamane Etelaatva Amniate Kechvar)	Iran
General Security Directorate	Iraq
DGSE (Direction General de la Securite Exterieur)	France

Important Symbols or Signs

Pen	Symbol of culture and civilisation
Lotus	Culture and civilisation
Red Cross	Medical aid and hospital
Red Flag	Revolution; also sign of danger
Black Flag	Symbol of protest
Yellow Flag	Flown on ships or vehicles carrying patients suffering from infectious diseases
Flag flown upside down	Symbol of distress
White Flag	Symbol of truce
Pigeon or Dove	Symbol of peace
A blindfolded woman holding a balanced scale	Symbol of justice
Black strip on face arm	Sign of mourning or protest
One skull on two bones crossing each other diagonally	Sign of danger
Wheel (Chakra)	Symbol of progress
Flag flown at half mast	Symbol of national mourning
Olive Branch	Symbol of peace

Languages Spoken

Language	*Member*	*Language*	*Member*
Mandarin Chinese	955 million	Arabic	295 million
Spanish	405 million	Hindi	260 million
English	360-380 million	Portuguese	215 million

Major Newspapers of the World

Newspaper	*Country*	*Newspaper*	*Country*
The Sydney Morning Herald	Australia	The Hindustan Times	India
The Age	Australia	Mainichi Daily News	Japan
Globe and Mail	Canada	The New Zealand Herald	New Zealand
The Gazette	Canada	The Press	New Zealand
International Herald Tribune	France	The Times	United Kingdom
Die Welt	Germany	The Scotsman	United Kingdom
The Times of India	India	The Guardian	United Kingdom
The Hindu	India	The Herald	United Kingdom
The Tribune	India	The Courier	United Kingdom
The Statesman	India	Washington Post	United States of America

Parliaments of the World

Country Name	*Parliament Name*	*Country Name*	*Parliament Name*
Afghanistan	Shora	Maldives	People's Majlis
Australia	Federal Parliament	Japan	Diet
Bangladesh	Jatiyo Shangsad/ House of the Nation	Nepal	Rashtriya Panchayat
Bhutan	Tshogdu	Pakistan	National Assembly and Senate
Canada	Parliament	Russia	Duma
China	National People's Congress	Spain	Cortes
Egypt	People's Assembly	Sweden	Riksdag
France	National Assembly	South Africa	Parliament
Germany	Bundestag	Mauritius	National Assembly
Britain	Parliament	USA	Congress

Top 5 Largest and Smallest Countries

Largest Country (Area-wise)	*Largest Country (Population-wise)*	*Smallest Country (Area-wise)*	*Smallest Country (Population-wise)*
Russia	China	Vatican City	Vatican City
Canada	India	Monaco	Tuvalu
China	USA	Nauru	Nauru
United States	Indonesia	Tuvalu	Palau
Brazil	Brazil	San Marino	San Marino

Religions of the World

Religion	*Member*	*Percentage*	*Religion*	*Member*	*Percentage*
Christianity	2.4 billion	31.2%	Buddhism	0.5 billion	6.9%
Islam	1.8 billion	24.1%	Sikhism	25 million	0.29%
Hinduism	1.2 billion	15.1%	Jewish	14.5 million	0.23%

National Emblems of Major Countries

Country	*Emblem*	*Country*	*Emblem*
Australia	Kangaroo	*Italy*	White Lily
Bangladesh	Water Lily	*Japan*	Chrysanthemum
Belgium	Lion	*Netherlands*	Lion
Canada	White Lily	*New Zealand*	Southern Cross, Kiwi, Fern
Chile	Candor and Huemul	*Norway*	Lion
France	Lily	*Pakistan*	Crescent
Germany	Corn Flower	*Spain*	Eagle
India	Lioned Capital	*United Kingdom*	Rose
Iran	Rose	*United States of America*	Golden Rod

First in India

Newspaper	*Bengal Gazette (James Hickey)*
Vernacular Daily	*Samachar Darpan (Bengali)*
Hindi Newspaper	*Udant Martand* (Pt. Jugal Kishore Shukla)
Telegraph Line	*Diamond Harbour to Kolkata*
International Telephone Service	*Mumbai to London (1851)*
Silent Movie	*Raja Harish Chandra (Dadasaheb Phalke 1913)*
Talkie Movie	*Alam Ara (Ardeshir Irani-1931)*
Aircraft Carriage Warship	*INS Vikrant*
Satellite	*Aryabhatta (19th April, 1975)*
Satellite dedicated exclusively for Education purposes	*EDUSAT*
Dedicated multi wavelength space observatory	*Astrosat*
Successful indigenous launch vehicle	*SLV-3*
Nuclear Reactor	*Apsara (1956)*
Lunar Mission	*Chandrayaan-I (October, 2008)*
Mars Mission	*Mars Orbiter Mission (5th November, 2013)*
Hydroelectric Project	*Sidrapong (1897)*
Asian Games	*Delhi (1951)*
Census	*1872*
Regular Decadal Census	*1881 Onwards*
Biosphere Reserve	*Nilgiri*
National Park	*Hailey National Park (Jim Corbett), 1936*
First asymmetrical cable stayed bridge	*Signature Bridge (New Delhi)*
E-court	*Ahmedabad*
Court exclusively dedicated to women	*Malda (WB)*
Technology Park	*Technopark, Thiruvananthapuram*
Cloned Animal	*Samrupa*
Rail University	*Vadodara*

First in India (Male)

First Governor-General of India	*William Bentinck (1828)*
First and last Indian Governor-General of Free India	*C Rajagopalachari*
First Commander-in-Chief of Free India	*General KM Kariappa*
First Field Marshal of India	*General SHFJ Manekshaw (1971)*
First Indian to go in Space	*Rakesh Sharma*
First Indian to climb the Mount Everest without Oxygen	*Sherpa Ang Dorje*
First Indian to become the Managing Director of World Bank	*Gautam Kaji*
First Indian Judge in the International Court of Justice	*Dr Nagendra Singh*
First Indian to get Nobel Prize in Physics	*CV Raman (1930)*
First Indian to get Nobel Prize in Literature	*Rabindranath Tagore (1913)*
First Indian to get Nobel Prize in Economics	*Dr Amartya Sen (1998)*
First Indian to get Nobel Prize in Medicines (Physiology)	*Dr Har Govind Khorana (1968)*
First Indian to get Bharat Ratna	*Dr S Radhakrishnan, C Rajgopalachari and Dr CV Raman (1954)*
First Person to be Honoured with the Jnanpith Award	*G Sankara Kurup (Malayalam)*
First Person to get Bharat Ratna (Posthumously)	*Lal Bahadur Shastri*
First Cricketer to get Padma Bhushan	*CK Naidu*
First Indian to get through ICS	*Satyendra Nath Tagore (1869)*
First Indian to swim across the English Channel	*Mihir Sen (1958)*
First Judge of International Court of Justice	*Dr. Nagendra Singh*
First Chief of Defence Staff	*Bipin Rawat*
First Indian Pilot	JRD Tata
First Indian to win Nobel Prize in Economics	Amartya Sen

First in India (Female)

First Indian Female Chairperson of Indian National Congress	*Sarojini Naidu (1925)*
First Woman to climb the Everest	*Bachendri Pal (1984)*
First Woman Cabinet Minister	*Rajkumari Amrit Kaur* (1947)
First Woman Chairman of the UN General Assembly	*Vijaya Laxmi Pandit*
First Woman President of India	*Pratibha Devi Singh Patil*
First Woman Speaker of Lok Sabha	*Meira Kumar (2009)*
First Woman Deputy Chairman of Rajya Sabha	*Margaret Alva (1983-85)*
First Woman Prime Minister of India	*Indira Gandhi*
First Woman to reach Antarctica	*Meher Moos (1977)*
First Woman IAS Officer	*Anna Rajam George (1950)*
First Female Chief Justice	*Leela Seth (1991)*
First Women Defence Minister	*Nirmala* Sitharaman
First Woman to get the Bharat Ratna	*Indira Gandhi*
First Female Nobel Prize Winner	*Mother Teresa (1979)*
First Woman to complete Century in World Cup Cricket	*Thirush Kamini*
First to win Silver in Olympics (Badminton)	PV Sindhu
First Indian Woman to become member of International Olympic Committee	Nita Ambani
First to win Bronze in Olympics (Wrestler)	Sakshi Malik
First Indian Woman Fighter Pilot to fly a fighter jet	Avani Chaturvedi *(2018)*
First Indian Naval Woman Pilot	Shubhangi Swaroop *(2018)*
First Female ICC Match Referee	GS Lakshmi
First Indian Women to go to Space	Kalpana Chawla

Superlatives (India)

(Biggest, Highest, Largest, Longest, Smallest etc)

The longest River	The Ganga (2525 km)
The longest Canal	Indira Gandhi Canal or Rajasthan Canal *(Rajasthan)* (649 km)
The longest Dam	Hirakud Dam *(Odisha)* (26 km)
The longest Sea Beach	Marina Beach *(Chennai)* (13 km)
The highest Lake	Cholamu Lake *(Sikkim)*
The largest Saline Water Lake	Chilka Lake *(Odisha)*
The biggest River Islands	Majuli, Brahmaputra river *(Assam)*
The largest Fresh Water Lake	Wular Lake *(Jammu and Kashmir)*
The highest Dam	Tehri Dam *(Uttarakhand)* *(260 mt)*
The highest Waterfall	Kunchikal Falls *(Karnataka) (455 m, 1493 ft)*
The deepest River Valley	Bhagirathi and Alaknanda
The longest River Bridge	Bhupen Hazarika Setu, Assam (9,150 m)
The biggest Cantilever Bridge	Rabindra Setu or Howrah Bridge *(Kolkata)*
The state with longest Coastline	Gujarat (1600 km)
The longest river without Delta	Narmada
The longest Sea Bridge	Bandra-Worli Sea Link (5.6 km)
The largest Artificial Lake	Dhebar Lake *(Rajasthan)*
The longest River of Southern India	Godavari (1465 km)
The longest Railway Platform	Gorakhpur, Uttar Pradesh (1366.33 m)
The longest National Highway	NH-44 *(Srinagar to Kanyakumari)*
The longest Corridor	Corridor of Ramnathswami Temple at Rameshwaram *(Tamil Nadu)*
The highest Road	Road at Khardungla *(in Leh-Manali Sector)*
The highest Airport	Leh Airport *(Ladakh)*
The largest Desert	Thar *(Rajasthan)*
The largest Delta	Sunderbans *(Paschim Banga)*
The state with maximum Forest Area	Madhya Pradesh (25.14% of its geographical area)
The largest Zoo	Zoological Garden *(Kolkata)*
The biggest Stadium	Yuva Bharti *(Salt Lake)* Stadium, Kolkata
The highest Award	Bharat Ratna
The highest Gallantry Award	Param Vir Chakra
The largest Gurudwara	Golden Temple, Amritsar
The largest Cave Temple	Kailash Temple *(Ellora, Maharashtra)*
The highest Peak	Godwin Austin I, K 2 (8611 m)
The largest Mosque	Jama Masjid *(Delhi)*
The longest Tunnel	Atal tunnel (Himachal Pradesh)
The largest Auditorium	Sri Shanmukhanand Hall *(Mumbai)*
The largest Animal Fair	Sonepur *(Bihar)*
The largest Cave	Amarnath *(Jammu and Kashmir)*
The highest Gate Way	Buland Darwaza, Fatehpur Sikri *(Uttar Pradesh)*
The tallest Statue	'Statue of Unity' Gujarat, India *(182 m)*
The largest Public Sector Bank	State Bank of India
The most Populous City	Mumbai (Maharashtra)
The biggest Church	Saint Cathedral at Old Goa *(Goa)*
The highest Battlefield	Siachen Glacier *(5753 m)*
The longest Road Bridge	Bhupen Hazarika Setu (Assam)

Books and Authors

Author Name	Book Name
Alexandre Dumas	The Three Musketeers
Amartya Sen	*Identity and Violence* : The Illusion of Destiny
Amartya Sen	The Argumentative Indian
Amartya Sen	Development as Freedom
Amitav Ghose	River of Smoke, Sea of Poppies, The Circle of Reason, The Great Derra-ngement: Climate Change and the Unthinkable
Amrita Pritam	Death of a City
Anita Desai	Clear Light of the Day
Aristotle	Politics
Arun Shourie	A Secular Agenda
Arundhati Roy	The Algebra of Infinite Justice
Arundhati Roy	The God of Small Things
Arundhati Roy	Greater Common Good
Ashwaghosha	Budda Charitham
Aung San Suu Kyi	Freedom from Fear
Bankim Chandra Chatterji	Anand Math, Durgeshnandini
Barack Obama	Dreams from My Father, 4 Promised Land
Barrett Lee, Marina Chapman	The Girl with No Name
Benazir Bhutto	Pakistan the Gathering Storm
Javier Moro	The Red Saree
Chandrashekar	Meri Jail Diary
Charles Dickens	David Copperfield
Chetan Bhagat	Revolution 2020, What Young India Wants, Half Girl Friend, One Night at the Call Centre, Making India Awesome, One Indian Girl
Chitra Subramaniam	India is for Sale
Dalai Lama	Freedom in Exile, Ethics for the New Millennium
Dante Alighieri	The Divine Comedy
Dr C Rangarajan	*Indian Economy* : Essays on Money and Finance
Edward Luce	Inspite of the Gods
Eleanor Catton	The Luminaries
EM Forster	A Passage to India
Gen V P Malik	*Kargil* : From Surprise to Victory
Gunter Grass	The Tin Drum
H R Bhardwaj	Law, Lawyers and Judges
Herbert George Wells	Time Machine

Author Name	Book Name
Indira Gandhi	My Truth
Jai Shankar Prasad	Ajatshatru
Jawaharlal Nehru	Discovery of India, Glimpses of World History
Jayaprakash Narayan	Prison Diary
K Natwar Singh	Walking with Lions, Curtain Raisers
Kapil Dev	Straight from the Heart
Karl Marx	Das Kapital
Karl Marx and Fredrik Engels	Communist Manifesto
Khushwant Singh	Train to Pakistan
Kiran Bedi	I Dare, As I See
Kiran Desai	The Inheritance of Loss
Kuldeep Mathur	Too Old to be Bold
LK Advani	A Prisoner's Scrap
Mahatma Gandhi	My Experiments with Truth
Malala Yousafzai	We Are Displaced
Mark Tully	The Heart of India
Mulk Raj Anand	Untouchable
Narendra Modi	Exam Warriors
Pranab Mukherjee	The Coalition Years, The Presidential Years
Premchand	Godan
Ramchandra Guha	Gandhi, Makers of Modern India
RK Narayan	The Guide
Ruskin Bond	A Garland of Memories, Death under the deodars
Sarojini Naidu	Golden Threshold, The Broken Wings
Shashi Tharoor	A Long Era of Darkness, Paradoxical Prime Minister
Sir Richard Burton	The Arabian Nights
Sri Aurobindo Ghosh	Essays on Gita
Stephen Hawkings	A Brief History of Time
Taslima Nasreen	All About Women
Thomas Pynchon	Against the Day
V S Naipaul	*India* : A Wounded Civilisation, Letters Between a Father and Son Half a Life, An Area of Darkness, Magic Seeds
Ved Vyas	Bhagwad Gita
Vikram Chandra	Love and Longing in Bombay
Vikram Seth	An Equal Music
Vimal Kumar	Sachin Cricketer of the Century

Books and Authors

Author Name	*Book Name*
Saurav Ganguly and Gautam Bhattacharya	A Century is Not Enough
Yuvraj Singh	The Test of My Life
Vijay Lokapally	Driven : The Virat Kohli Story
Nand Kishore Acharya	Chilte Hue Apne Ko (2019)
Natwar Singh	One Life is not Enough
P. Chidambaram	A View from Outside
Raghuram Rajan	I Do What I Do
Naveen Chawla	Every Vote Counts
Rajdeep Sardesai	How Modi Won India (2019)
Vasdev Mohi	Cheque book (2019, Saraswati Samman)
RK Narayan	The Guide
Salman Rushdie	Midnight's Children
Vikram Seth	A Suitable Boy
Suketu Mehta	Maximum City
Khushwant Singh	Train to Pakistan
Shashi Tharoor	The Great Indian Novel
Anita Desai	In Custody

International Decades

2010-2020	UN Decade for Desert and Fight against Desertification
2014-2024	UN Decade of Sustainable Energy for All
2015-2024	International Decade for People of African Descent
2016-2025	UN Decade of Action on Nutrition
2018-2028	International Decade for Action "Water for Sustainable Development"
2019-2028	UN Decade of Family Planning
2021-2030	UN Decade of Healthy Ageing
2022-2032	International Decade of Indigenous Language

International Years

2009	International Year of Astronomy
2010	International Year of Biodiversity
2011	International Year of Forests
2012	International Year of Cooperatives
2013	International Year of Water Cooperation
2014	International Year of Family Farming
2015	International Year of Light and Light based Technologies
2016	International Year of Pulses
2017	International Year of Sustainable Tourism for Development
2019	International Year of Indigenous Languages
2020	International Year of Plant Health
2021	International Year for Elimination of Child Labour
2023	International Year of Millets
2024	International Year of Camelids

Important Dates and Days of the Year

January

1 Global Family Day
9 NRI Day
12 National Youth Day (of Swami Vivekanand)
15 Indian Army Day
25 National Tourism Day, Voter's Day
26 Indian Republic Day, International Customs Day
28 Data Protection Day
30 Martyr's Day (Mahatma Gandhi's Martyrdom), World Leprosy Eradication Day

February

4 World Cancer Day
13 World Radio Day
20 World Day of Social Justice
24 Central Excise Day
28 National Science Day

March

8 International Women's Day
15 World Consumer Rights Day,
21 World Forestry Day, International Day for the Elimination of Racial Discrimination
22 World Water Day
23 World Meteorological Day
24 World TB Day

April

4 International Day for Mine Awareness
5 National Maritime Day,
7 World Health Day
18 World Heritage Day
21 Civil Services Day
22 World Earth Day

May

1 International Labour Day (May Day)
3 World Press Freedom Day
8 World Red Cross Day
17 World Telecommunications Day
21 Anti-Terrorism Day

June

5 World Environment Day
7 World Food Safety Day
8 World Oceans Day
12 World Day against Child Labour
21 International Yoga Day

July

1 National Doctor's Day
7 International day of Cooperatives
11 World Population Day
12 International Malala Day

August

6 Hiroshima Day
10 World Bio-Fuel Day
12 International Youth Day
20 Sadbhavna Divas
29 National Sports Day (Dhyanchand's birthday)

September

5 Teachers' Day (Dr Radhakrishnan's Birthday)
14 Hindi Day, World First Aid Day
16 World Ozone Day
21 International Day of Peace
26 International Day for Elimination of Nuclear Weapons
27 World Tourism Day

October

2 International Non-Violence Day,
2 Lal Bahadur Shastri and Mahatma Gandhi's Birthday
3 World Habitat Day
5 World Teacher's Day
8 Indian Air Force Day
11 National Education Day (India)
16 World Food Day
24 United Nations Day
31 National Integrity Day

November

9 National Legal Services Day
14 World Diabetes Day, Children's Day
20 Universal Children's Day (UN)
26 World Environment Protection Day, Samvidhan Diwas

December

1 World AIDS Day
3 International Day of Person with Disabilities
4 Indian Navy Day
7 Armed Forces Flag Day
10 Human Rights Day
16 Vijay Diwas
25 Good Governance Day
25 Good Governance Day
26 Veer Baal Diwas

ABBREVIATIONS

A

ABM Anti Ballistic Missiles
ADB Asian Development Bank
AERE Atomic Energy Research Establishment
AFSPA Armed Forces Special Power Act
AGOC Asian Games Organising Committee
AIDS Acquired Immuno Deficiency Syndrome
AIIMS All India Institute of Medical Sciences
ALH Advanced Light Helicopter
APPLE Ariane Passenger Payload Experiment
AMRUT Atal Mission for Rejuvenation and Urban Transformation
APEC Asia-Pacific Economic Cooperation
ASAT Anti-Satellite Weapon
ASIAN Association of Southeast Asian Nations
ASCII American Standard Code for Information Interchange
ASLV Augmented Satellite Launch Vehicle
ASI Archaeological Survey of India
ATM Automated Teller Machine
ATS Anti-Terrorism Squad
AU African Union
AVES Acute Viral Encephalitic Syndrome

B

BC SBI Banking Codes and Standard Board of India
BARC Bhabha Atomic Research Centre
BBC British Broadcasting Corporation
BCG Bacillus Calmette Guerin (Anti-Tuberculosis Vaccine)
BCTT Banking Cash Transaction Tax
BCCI Board for Control of Cricket in India
BENELUX Belgium, Netherlands, Luxembourg
BIMSTEC Bay of Bengal Initiative for Multisectoral Technical and Economic Cooperation
BIS Bureau of Indian Standards
BMD Ballistic Missile Defence System
BPO Business Process Outsourcing
BRO Border Roads Organisation

C

CAA Citizenship Amendment Act
CABE Central Advisory Board of Education
CAG Comptroller and Auditor General
CAPES Computer-Aided Paperless Examination System
CAZRI Central Arid Zone Research Institute
CBI Central Bureau of Investigation
CECA Comprehensive Economic Cooperation Agreement
CFC Chlorofluoro Carbon
CID Criminal Investigation Department
CISF Central Industrial Security Force
CITES Convention on International Trade in Endangered Species
CNG Compressed Natural Gas
COFEPOSA Conservation of Foreign Exchange and Prevention of Smuggling Act
CPCB Central Pollution Control Board
CPRI Central Power Research Institute
CRR Cash Reserve Ratio
CSIR Council of Scientific and Industrial Research

D

DAVP Directorate of Advertising and Visual Publicity
DDT Dichloro-Diphenyl Trichloro-ethane (disinfectant)
DNA De-oxyribonucleic Acid
DPSA Deep Penetration Strike Aircraft
DPT Diphteria, Pertussis and Tetanus
DRDO Defence Research and Development Organisation
DTH Direct-to-Home (broadcasting)
DVD Digital Versatile Disk

E

ECG Electro Cardiogram
EEG Electro-Encephalography
EET Eastern European Time
ESCAP Economic and Social Commission for Asia and the Pacific
EVM Electronic Voting Machine

F

FDI Foreign Direct Investment
FII Foreign Institutional Investor
FBI Federal Bureau of Investigation
FERA Foreign Exchange Regulations Act
FICCI Federation of Indian Chambers of Commerce and Industry
FDR Fixed Deposit Receipt
FLAG Fibre Optic Link Around the Globe

G

GAIN Global Alliance for Improved Nutrition
GANDHI Green Action for National Dandi Heritage Initiative
GATS General Agreement on Trade in Services
GATT General Agreement on Tariffs and Trade
GEF Global Environment Fund
GMPS Global Mobile Personal Communications System
GNSS Global Navigation Satellite System
GPS Global Positioning System
GSLV Geosynchronous Satellite Launch Vehicle

H

HAC Hindustan Aluminium Corporation
HAL Hindustan Aeronautics Limited
HIV Human Immunodeficiency Virus
HTML Hypertext Markup Language
HTTP Hypetext Transfer Protocol
HYV High Yielding Variety

I

IAAI International Airport Authority of India
IAEA International Atomic Energy Agency
IBRD International Bank for Reconstruction and Development
ICAO International Civil Aviation Organisation
ICAR Indian Council of Agricultural Research
ICMR Indian Council of Medical Research
ICRC International Committee of the Red Cross
IDBI Industrial Development Bank of India
IMA Indian Military Academy
IMO International Maritime Organisation
INMAS Institute of Nuclear Medicines and Allied Sciences
INSAS Indian Small Arms System
INSAT Indian National Satellite
INTERPOL International Police Organisation
IPCC Intergovernmental Panel on Climate Change
IRBM Intermediate Range Ballistic Missile
IRS Indian Remote Sensing Satellite
ISCS Integrated Smart Card System
ISRO Indian Space Research Organisation
ITU International Telecommunication Union

JKL

JNNURM Jawaharlal Nehru National Urban Renewal Mission
LCA Light Combat Aircraft
LOC Line of Control
LOAC Line of Actual Control
LTA Light Transport Aircraft

M

MAT Minimum Alternative Tax
METSAT Meteorological Satellite
MNP Mobile Number Portability
MSS Multimedia Message Service
MODEM Modulator-DEModulator
MRI Magnetic Resonance Imaging
MRTS Mass Rapid Transit System
MSP Minimum Support Price
MTCR Missile Technology Control Regime

N

NAA National Airport Authority
NABARD National Bank for Agriculture and Rural Development
NADA National Anti-Doping Agency
NASA National Aeronautics and Space Administration
NEERI National Environment Engineering Research Institute
NATA Natural Aptitude Test for Architecture
NCEP National Committee on Environmental Planning
NCERT National Council of Educational Research and Training
NeGP National e-governance Plan
NEP National Education Policy
NEPA National Environment Protection Authority
NHDP National Highways Development Project
NHRC National Human Right Commission
NITI Aayog National Institution for Transforming India
NRC National Register of Citizens

O

OCI Overseas Citizenship of India
OAS Organisation of American States
OAU Organisation of African Unity
ODS Ozone Depletion Substances
OIC Organisation of Islamic Countries
OPEC Organisation of the Petroleum Exporting Countries
OSCE Organisation for Security and Cooperation in Europe

P

PURA Providing Urban Amenities in Rural Areas
PATA Pacific Asia Travel Association
POTA Prevention of Terrorism Act
PPE Personal Protective Equipment
PSLV Polar Satellite Launch Vehicle

QR

QIB Qualified Institutional Buyer
QIP Qualified Institutional Placement
RAF Rapid Action Force
RBI Reserve Bank of India
RCC Reinforced Concrete Cement
RDSS Radio Determination Satellite Service
RTGS Real Time Gross Settlement System
RTE Right to Education
RTI Right to Information

S

SAARC South Asian Association for Regional Cooperation
SAFTA South Asian Free Trade Area
SAIL Steel Authority of India Limited
SAPTA SAARC Preferential Trading Agreement
SATNAV SATellite NAVigation
SALT Strategic Arms Limitation Talks
SAVE SAARC Audio Visual Exchange
SCO Shanghai Cooperation Organisation
SEBI Securities and Exchange Board of India
SIDBI Small Industries Development Bank of India
SPIN Software Process Improvement Networks
STARS Satellite Tracking and Ranging Station
START Strategic Arms Reduction Treaty
SWIFT Society for Worldwide Interbank Financial Telecommunications

T

TADA Terrorist and Disruptive Activities (Prevention) Act
TAPS Tarapur Atomic Power Station
TIN Tax Identification Number
TRAI Telecom Regulatory Authority of India
TRIPS Trade Related Intellectual Property Rights
TVOA Tourist Visa on Arival

U

UAV Unmanned Aerial Vehicle
UNCTAD United Nations Conference on Trade and Development
UNDP United Nations Development Programme
UNEP United Nations Environment Programme
UNFPA United Nations Fund for Population Activities
UPS Uninterruptible Power Supply

V

VAT Value Added Tax
VOIP Voice Over Internet Protocol
VPN Virtual Private Network
VSAT Very Small Aperture Terminals

W

WADA World Anti-Doping Agency
WAP Wireless Application Protocol
WAVE Wireless Access for Virtual Enterprise
WFP World Food Programme
WFTU World Federation of Trade Unions
WHO World Health Organisation
WLL Wireless in Local Loop
WWW World Wide Web

XY&Z

XML Extensible Markup Language
YWCA Young Women's Christian Association
ZSI Zoological Survey of India
ZUPO Zimbabwe United People Organisation

AWARDS AND HONOURS

INTERNATIONAL

Nobel Prize

- The most prestigious award in the world. It was set-up in 1900 under the will of **Alfred Bernhard Nobel.**
- The Nobel Prizes are presented annually on 10th December (The death anniversary of the founder).
- It is given in the fields of Peace, Literature, Physics, Chemistry, Physiology or Medicine (from 1901) and Economics (from 1969).

Winners of Nobel Prize from India

Winner	*Field*	*Year*
Abhijit Banerjee	Economics	2019
Kailash Satyarthi	Peace	2014
Venkatraman Ramakrishnan	Chemistry	2009
Amartya Sen	Economics	1998
Subrahmanyan Chandrasekhar	Physics	1983
Mother Teresa	Peace	1979
Hargobind Khorana	Medicine	1968
CV Raman	Physics	1930
Rabindranath Tagore	Literature	1913

Grammy Awards

- It is awarded for the outstanding achievements in the music industry by National Academy for Recording Arts and Sciences, America. It was started in 1959, Indian Origin Pt. Ravi Shankar got this 3 times.

Pulitzer Prize

- Instituted in 1917 and named after US publisher Joseph Pulitzer.
- It is conferred annually in the United States for the accomplishments in journalism, literature and music.

Magsaysay Awards

- Instituted in 1957. Named after Ramon Magsaysay, the former President of Philippines.
- The award is given annually on 31st August, the birth anniversary of Magsaysay, for outstanding contributions in Public service, Community Leadership, Journalism, Literature and Creative Arts and International Understanding.

Man Booker Prize

Instituted in 1968, is the highest literary award of the world, set-up by the Booker Company and the British Pulishers Association along the lines of the Pulitzer Prize of USA.

Right Livelihood Award

- The Right Livelihood Award was established in 1980.
- It is also referred as **'Alternative Nobel Prize'.**
- It is given to persons to honour those "working on practical and exemplary solutions to the most urgent challenges facing the world today."

Oscar Awards

Instituted in 1929, these awards are conferred annually by the Academy of Motion Pictures, Arts and Sciences, USA, in recognition of outstanding contribution in the various fields of film making.

- The Indian films nominated for Oscars are Mother India (1957), Salaam Bombay (1988), Lagaan (2001)
- Bhanu Athaiya was the first Indian to win an Oscar Award in 1982 for costume design in Gandhi Movie.
- AR Rahman won 2 Oscar in 2009 for his work in Slumdog Millionaire.

UN Human Rights Award

Instituted in 1966, this award is given every 5 years for individual contributions to the establishment of human rights.

NATIONAL

Bharat Ratna

- Bharat Ratna is India's highest Civilian Award. It was first awarded in 1954.
- The actual award is designed in the shape of a **peepal** leaf with *Bharat Ratna* inscribed in Devanagri script in the Sun Figure.
- The reverse side of the decoration Satyameva Jayate has been written in Hindi with an inscription of state emblem.
- The emblem, the Sun and the rim are of platinum. The inscriptions are in burnished bronze.

Winners of Bharat Ratna

- Pranab Mukherjee (2019)
- Bhupen Hazarika (2019)
- Nanaji Deshmukh (2019)
- Madan Mohan Malaviya (2015)
- Atal Bihari Vajpayee (2015)
- Sachin Tendulkar (2014)
- CNR Rao (2014)
- Pandit Bhimsen Joshi (2008)
- Lata Dinanath Mangeshkar (2001)
- Ustad Bismillah Khan (2001)
- Prof Amartya Sen (1999)
- Lokpriya Gopinath Bordoloi (1999)
- Loknayak Jayprakash Narayan (1999)
- Pandit Ravi Shankar (1999)
- Chidambaram Subramaniam (1998)
- Madurai Shanmukhavadivu Subbulakshmi (1998)
- Dr Abul Pakir Jainulabdeen Abdul Kalam (1997)
- Aruna Asaf Ali (1997)
- Gulzari Lal Nanda (1997)
- Jehangir Ratanji Dadabhai Tata (1992)
- Maulana Abul Kalam Azad (1992)
- Satyajit Ray (1992)
- Morarji Ranchhodji Desai (1991)
- Rajiv Gandhi (1991)
- Sardar Vallabhbhai Patel (1991)
- Dr Bhimrao Ramji Ambedakr (1990)
- Dr Nelson Rolihlahla Mandela (1990)
- Marudur Gopalan Ramachandran (1988)
- Khan Abdul Ghaffar Khan (1987)
- Acharya Vinoba Bhave (1983)
- Mother Teresa (Agnes Gonxha Bojaxhiu) (1980)
- Kumaraswamy Kamraj (1976)
- Varahagiri Venkata Giri (1975)
- Indira Gandhi (1971)
- Lal Bahadur Shastri (1966)
- Dr Pandurang Vaman Kane (1963)
- Dr Zakir Hussain (1963)
- Dr Rajendra Prasad (1962)
- Dr Bidhan Chandra Roy (1961)
- Purushottam Das Tandon (1961)
- Dr Dhonde Keshav Karve (1958)
- Pt Govind Ballabh Pant (1957)
- Dr Bhagwan Das (1955)
- Jawaharlal Nehru (1955)
- Dr Mokshagundam Vivesvaraya (1955)
- Chakravarti Rajagopalachari (1954)
- Dr Chandrasekhara Venkata Raman (1954)
- Dr Sarvapalli Radhakrishnan (1954)

Republic Day Awards

Padma Awards

Padma Awards, which were instituted in 1954, is announced every year on the occasion of Republic Day. The award is given in three categories–Padma Vibhushan, Padma Bhushan and Padma Shri. The awards fall in line after the Bharat Ratna. These awards are not given to government employees except doctors and scientists.

There are three Padma Awards

- **Padma Vibhushan** is the second highest National Award given for exceptional and distinguished service in any field.
- **Padma Bhushan** is the third highest National Award given for distinguished service in any field.
- **Padma Shri** is the fourth highest award given for distinguished service in any field.

Gallantry Awards

- **Param Vir Chakra** is the highest decoration of valour award. It is the most conspicuous act of bravery or some act of valour or self-sacrifice in the presence of the enemy, whether on land, at sea or in the air. The medal is made of bronze.
- **Mahavir Chakra** is the second highest gallantry award for acts of conspicuous gallantry in the presence of the enemy whether on land, at sea or in the air. The medal is made of standard silver.

- **Vir Chakra** is awarded for acts of gallantry in the presence of enemy, whether on land, at sea or in the air. The medal is made of standard silver.
- **Ashok Chakra** This is awarded for valour, courageous action or sacrifice, away from the battlefield. It is highest military award during peacetime.
- **Kirti Chakra** The decoration is awarded for conspicuous gallantry. It is made of standard silver and is circular in shape. The obverse and the reverse are exactly the same as in Ashoka Chakra.
- **Shaurya Chakra** The decoration is awarded for an act of gallantry during peacetime.

Sports Awards

- **Rajiv Gandhi Khel Ratna** is instituted in 1991-92 with the objective of honouring most outstanding sports- person to enhance their general status. It is the highest award bestowed to a sports person in India. It has been renamed as Major Dhyan Chand Khel Ratna Award, as per an announcement made by Prime Minister Narendra Modi on 6th August, 2021.
- **Arjuna Award** instituted in 1961 by the Government of India to recognise outstanding achievement in National Sports. The award carries a cash prize, a bronze statue of Arjuna and a scroll of honour.
- **Dronacharya Award** instituted in 1985 by the Government of India to recognise excellence in sports coaching. The award carries a cash prize, a bronze statue of Dronacharya and a scroll of honour.
- **Dhyanchand Award** instituted in 2002, carries a cash prize, a plaque and a scroll of honour. This honour is given to those sportspersons who have contributed to sports by their performance and continue to promote sports even after their retirement from active sporting career.

Indian Cinema Awards

Dadasaheb Phalke Award

- Dadasaheb Phalke is known as the Father of Indian Cinema. The highest National Film Award is named after him in 1969.
- This award is given to a film personality for his/her outstanding contribution to the growth and development of Indian cinema. The award comprises of a swarna kamal, a cash prize of ₹ 10,00,000 and a shawl.
- Dhundiraj Govind (Dadasheb) Phalke's silent feature film, **Raja Harishchandra** (1913) was first indigenous feature film of India.
- Ardeshir Irani in 1931, released first full length talkies film **Alam Ara**.

Mrs Devika Rani Roerich was the first person to receive Dadasaheb Phalke Award in 1969.

Other National Awards

Bharatiya Jnanpith Award

- Instituted in 22nd May, 1961, carries a cash prize of ₹ 11 lakh, a citation and a bronze replica of Vagdevi (Saraswati).
- This award is given for the best literary writing by an Indian citizen in a language listed in Eighth Schedule of the Indian Constitution. G. Sankara Kurup received 1st Bharatiya Jnanpith Award.

Gandhi Peace Prize

- Established in 2nd October, 1994, on the occasion of the 125th birthday anniversary of Mahatma Gandhi, carries a cash prize of ₹ 1 crore.
- Indian Government instituted this annual prize to encourage and promote the significance of Gandhian values over the world. Julius Nyerere got first prize.

Indira Gandhi Prize for Peace, Disarmament and Development

- Instituted in 1985, this prestigious award is regarded as 'Nobel' and over the years, it has been awarded to those persons who have done outstanding work for international peace, disarmament and development.

Borlaug Award

- Instituted in 1973, carries a cash prize of ₹ 5 lakh. Instituted to honour outstanding agricultural scientists.

Sahitya Akademi Award

- Awarded for outstanding literary work and carries a cash prize of ₹ 1 lakh.
- Sahitya Academi gives 22 awards for literary works in the languages which has recognised works.
- RK Narayana received first Sahitya Akademi Award.

INDIAN DEFENCE

Indian Army Commands

Command	*HQ Location*	*Command*	*HQ Location*
Central Command	Lucknow	South-Western Command	Jaipur
Eastern Command	Kolkata	Western Command	Chandigarh
Northern Command	Udhampur	Training Command	Shimla
Southern Command	Pune		

Indian Air Force Commands

Command	*HQ Location*	*Command*	*HQ Location*
Central Air Command	Prayagraj	Western Air Command	New Delhi
Eastern Air Command	Shillong	Maintenance Command	Nagpur
Southern Air Command	Thiruvananthapuram	Training Command	Bengaluru
South-Western Air Command	Gandhinagar		

Indian Navy Commands

Command	*HQ Location*
Western Naval Command	Mumbai
Eastern Naval Command	Vishakhapatnam
Southern Naval Command	Kochi

Note *Andaman and Nicobar Command at Port Blair is the only Tri-service Command of Armed Forces.*

Indian Defence Training Institutions

Training Institution	*Place*	*Estd in*
Rashtriya Indian Military College *(RIMC)*	Dehradun	1922
Army Cadet College *(ACC)*	Dehradun	1929
Indian Military Academy *(IMA)*	Dehradun	1932
National Defence Academy *(NDA)*	Khadakwasla, Pune	1941
High Altitude Warfare School *(HAWS)*	Gulmarg	1948
National Defence College *(NDC)*	New Delhi	1960
Officers Training Academy *(OTA)*	Chennai	1963
Counter Insurgency and Jungle Warfare School	Vairengte *(Mizoram)*	1970
College of Defence Management	Secunderabad	1970
College of Combat/Army War College	Mhow *(Madhya Pradesh)*	1971
Army School of Physical Training *(ASPT)*	Pune	1978
Army Air Defence College *(AADC)*	Gopalpur *(Odisha)*	1989
Officers Training Academy	Gaya	2011
Indian National Defence University *(INDU)*	Gurgaon (Haryana)	2013

Ranks of Commissioned Officers

Army	*Air Force*	*Navy*
General	Air Chief Marshal	Admiral
Lt. General	Air Marshal	Vice Admiral
Major General	Air Vice Marshal	Rear Admiral
Brigadier	Air Commodore	Commodore
Colonel	Group Captain	Captain
Lt. Colonel	Wing Commander	Commander
Major	Squadron Leader	Lt Commander
Captain	Flight Lieutenant	Lieutenant
Lieutenant	Flying Officer	Sub-Lieutenant

Missiles and other Weapons

Name	*Class*	*Range*
Agni II	MRBM	2500 km
Agni III	IRBM	3500 km-5500 km
Agni IV or Agni II Prime	IRBM	4000 km
Agni V	ICBM	5000 km-6000 km
Agni VI	ICBM	8000-10000 km
Barak	MRSAM	100 km
Dhanush	SRBM	350 km
Nirbhay	Subsonic Cruise Missile	1000 km
Brahmos	Supersonic Cruise Missile	290 km
Brahmos 2	Hypersonic Cruise Missile	290 km
Prithvi I	SRBM	150 km
Prithvi III	SRBM	350 km
Rudram	Air to Surface Anti-radiation Missile	125 km
Sagarika	SLBM	700 km
Shaurya	TBM	700 km
Astra	Air to Air Missile	80 km-100 km
Nag	Anti-Tank	7 km

Note *Recently, a post, Chief of Defence Staff is created to help improve coordination among the three services of Armed Forces. It is the highest ranking (4-Star Officer) in the Armed Forces and is head of the military staff of Armed Forces and Chief Executive of Department of Military Affairs.*

Paramilitary, Reserve Forces and other Agencies

Indo-Tibetan Border Police (ITBP)	▪ It was established in 1962, after the Chinese attack. ▪ It is basically employed in the Northern borders for monitoring the borders and also to stop smuggling and illegal immigration.
National Security Guards (NSG)	▪ It was established in 1984 to counter the surge of militancy in the country. ▪ It is a highly trained force which deals with the militants effectively.
Central Industrial Security Force (CISF)	▪ It was set-up in 1969 after the recommendations of Justice B Mukherji. Its objective is to monitor the industrial complexes of Central Government.
Assam Rifles	▪ It was established in 1835 and is the oldest paramilitary force in the country. ▪ Its main objective is to keep vigilance of international borders in North East and counter insurgency operations in Arunachal Pradesh, Manipur, Mizoram and Nagaland.
Border Security Force (BSF)	▪ It was established in 1965. ▪ It keeps a vigil over the international borders against the intrusion in the country.

National Cadet Corps (NCC)	▪ It was established in 1948. ▪ Its main objective is to stimulate interest among the youth in the defence of the country in order to build up a reserve manpower to expand armed forces.
Central Reserve Police Force (CRPF)	▪ It was set-up in 1939. ▪ Its main objective is to assist the State / Union Territory Police in maintenance of law and order. ▪ The 88th Battalion of CRPF, known as 'Mahila Battalion' (commissioned on 30th March, 1986) is the world's first paramilitary force comprising entirely of women.
Territorial Army (TA)	▪ It was established in 1948. ▪ It is a voluntary, part-time force (between 18 and 42 years), not of professional soldiers, but civilians who wish to assist in defence of the country.
Home Guard	▪ It was established in 1962, to assist the police in maintaining security, to help defence forces and to help local authorities in case of any eventuality.
Indian Coast Guard	▪ It was set-up in 1978. ▪ Its objective is to protect the maritime and other national interests in the maritime zones of India.
Intelligence Bureau (IB)	▪ It was set-up in 1920. ▪ Its objective is to collect secret information relating to country's security. ▪ It was originally set-up as Central Special Branch (CSB) in 1887 and renamed IB in 1920.
Central Bureau of Investigation (CBI)	▪ It was established in 1963. ▪ Its objective is to investigate cases of misconduct by public servants, cases of cheating, embezzlement and fraud. ▪ CBI is also entrusted with the investigation of international crime cases in collaboration with INTERPOL.
National Crime Records Bureau (NCRB)	▪ It was established in 1986. ▪ Its objective is to collect crime statistics at the national level, information of inter-state and international criminals to help investigation agencies.
Rapid Action Force (RAF)	▪ It was established in 1991. ▪ Under the operational command of CRPF, 10 battalions of the CRPFs have been re-oriented for tackling communal riots in the country.

Nuclear and Space Research Centres in India

Research Centre	*Place*
Indian Rare Earths Limited	Mumbai
Uranium Corporation of India Limited	Jadugoda *(Jharkhand)*
Atomic Energy Commission *(AEC)*	Mumbai
Electronics Corporation of India Limited	Hyderabad
Bhabha Atomic Research Centre *(BARC)*	Trombay *(Mumbai)*
Radio Astronomy Centre	Ootacamund *(Tamil Nadu)*
Tata Institute of Fundamental Research	Mumbai
Saha Institute of Nuclear Physics	Kolkata
Centre of Earth Sciences Studies	Thiruvananthapuram *(Kerala)*
Physical Research Laboratory	Ahmedabad
Space Commission	Bengaluru
Vikram Sarabhai Space Centre	Thiruvananthapuram
Indian Space Research Organisation *(ISRO)*	Bengaluru
Space Application Centre	Ahmedabad
Thumba Equatorial Rocket Launching Station	Thumba *(Kerala)*
Second Satellite Launch Port (Planned)	Thoothukudi (Tamil Nadu)

SPORTS

Olympics

- Olympics games were started in 776 BC on Mount Olympia in the honour of Greek God, 'Zeus'. The modern Olympic Games were started in **Athens**, the capital of Greece on **6th April, 1896** with great efforts made by French nobleman, **Baron Pierre de Coubertin**.
- The Olympic Games are organised after every 4 years. The Olympic Flag is made up of white silk and contains five interwined rings as the Olympic Emblem.
- The five interlaced rings are arranged in 3-2 pattern on a white background, with the blue ring to the extreme left, followed by yellow, black, green and red, in the same order. Blue for Europe, Black for Africa, Red for Americas (North and South America), Yellow for Asia and Green for Oceania (Australia and New Zealand).
- The official Olympic Motto is **Citius, Altius, Fortius**, a Latin phrase meaning **Swifter, Higher, Stronger**. 2024, Summer Olympic will be held in Paris, France.
- In 2024, Olympics is scheduled to be held in Paris (France).

Commonwealth Games

- The first Commonwealth Games were held in 1930 in Hamilton, Canada.
- Since 1930, the games have been conducted every 4 years except for 1942 and 1946 due to World War II.
- The Commonwealth Games Federation (CGF) is the organisation which is responsible for the direction and control of the Commonwealth Games.
- There are currently 53 members in the Commonwealth of Nations.
- The 2018 Commonwealth Games (21st) were held an Gold Coast, Queensland, Australia. Most gold medals were won by Australia. 2022 Commonwealth Games was held in Birmingham, England.
- 23rd Commonwealth Games (2026) will be held in Victoria, Australia.

The Asian Games

- The Asian Games, also called the Asiad, are a multi-sport event held every 4 years among athletes from all over Asia.
- The games are regulated by the Olympic Council of Asia (OCA), under the supervision of the International Olympic Committee (IOC). The first Asian Games were held in 1951 in New Delhi (India). 18th Asian Games of 2018 were held at Jakarta (Indonesia) in which India finished at eighth position. 19th Asian games was held in Hangzhou, China in 2022.
- 20th Asian Games (2026) will be held in Aichi-Nagoya (Japan).

Cricket World Cup

- The first Cricket World Cup was organised in England in 1975. A separate women's Cricket World Cup has been held every 4 years since 1973.

List of Cricket World Cup

1975	*England*	West Indies beat Australia
1979	*England*	West Indies beat England
1983	*England*	India beat West Indies
1987	*India*	Australia beat England
1992	*Australia*	Pakistan beat England
1996	*Pakistan*	Sri Lanka beat Australia
1999	*England*	Australia beat Pakistan
2003	*South Africa*	Australia beat India
2007	*West Indies*	Australia beat Sri Lanka
2011	*India*	India beat Sri Lanka
2015	*Australia and New Zealand*	Australia beat New Zealand
2019	*England*	England beat New Zealand
2023	*India*	Scheduled

T-20 Cricket World Cup

2007	*South Africa*	India beat Pakistan
2009	*England*	Pakistan beat Sri Lanka
2010	*West Indies*	England beat Australia
2012	*Sri Lanka*	West Indies beat Sri Lanka
2014	*Bangladesh*	Sri Lanka beat India
2016	*India*	West Indies beat England
2021	*India*	Australia won against New Zealand
2022	*Australia*	England won against Pakistan

Hockey World Cup

The first Hockey World Cup was organised in Barcelona (Spain) in 1971. Women's Hockey World Cup has been held since 1974. The 13th Men's Hockey World Cup held in the Netherlands (Hague) in 2014. The 14th Men's Hockey World Cup was held in Bhubaneswar India in 2018. Belgium won this championship beating Netherlands. The 15th Men's Hockey World Cup is Scheduled to be held in 2023 at **Bhubaneswar** and **Rourkela**.

Football World Cup

- The Football World Cup is organised by FIFA (Federation of International Football Association). The World Cup is called 'Jules Rimet Cup' named after the name of FIFA President Jules Rimet. The first Football World Cup was organised in Uruguay in 1930.
- In 1942 and 1946, the Football World Cup was not played due to World War II.
- The 20th FIFA World Cup held in Brazil in which Germany became the champion by defeating Argentina 1-0 in the final.
- Brazil is the only nation to have participated in every World Cup so far. The 2018 Football World Cup was held at Russia. France won this Championship beating Croatia. 2022 Football World Cup was held in **Qatar**. Argentina won this championship beating France.
- 2026 FIFA World Cup is scheduled to be held at Canada, Mexico.

United Nations Organisation (UNO)

- The United Nations (UN) is a world organisation formed in 24th October, 1945. It came into existence after World War II, when the leaders of the world, including American President Roosevelt and British Prime Minister Churchill, decided to create a world organisation that would help to ensure peace.
- The original membership of 51 nations has grown to 193 members. The 193rd member being the newly created South Sudan. The United Nations Headquarters is in New York City. The UN also has offices in Nairobi (Kenya), Geneva (Switzerland) and Vienna (Austria).
- **The General Assembly** is the main place for discussions and policy making in the United Nations.
- **The Security Council** has primary responsibility for the maintenance of international peace and security. The Security Council is made up of 15 members.
- There are five permanent members of the Secutiry Council-China, France, Russia, United Kingdom and USA and 10 non-permanent members elected for 2 years terms starting on 1st January.

Non-Permanent Members of UNSC

Country	*Term Ends*
Estonia	2021
India	2022
Ireland	2022
Kenya	2022
Mexico	2022
Niger	2021
Norway	2022
Saint Vincent and the Grenadines	2021
Tunisia	2021
Vietnam	2021

- Economic and Social Council is the principal body for coordination, policy review, policy dialogue and recommendations on economic, social and environmental issues. The secretariat comprises the Secretary-General and other staff who carry out day-to-day work of the U.N.
- **The International Court of Justice** (ICJ), located in the Hague, Netherlands, is the primary judicial organ of the United Nations, established in 1945 by the United Nations Charter, the Court began work in 1946, as the successor to the Permanent Court of International Justice.

- Trygve Lie of Norway (1946-52) was the first Secretary-General of the UN.
- **Antonio Guterres** is the new Secretary- General of UN. He succeed Ban ki-Moon.

Some Important UN Agencies

Name	*Estd in*	*Headquarter*	*Purpose*
International Telecommunication Union (ITU)	1865	Geneva	Sets international regulations for radio telegraph, telephone and space radio communications.
International Labour Organisation (ILO)	1919	Geneva	To improve conditions and living standards of workers.
International Monetary Fund (IMF)	1945	Washington DC	Promotes international monetary cooperation.
United Nations International Children's Emergency Fund (UNICEF)	1945	New York	To promote children's welfare all over the world.
Food and Agricultural Organisation (FAO)	1945	Rome	To improve living conditions of rural population.
United Nations Educational, Scientific and Cultural Organisation (UNESCO)	1946	Paris	To promote collaboration among nations through education, science and culture.
World Health Organisation (WHO)	1948	Geneva	Attainment of highest possible level of health by all people.
International Atomic Energy Agency (IAEA)	1957	Vienna	To promote peaceful uses of atomic energy.
International Development Association (IDA)	1960	Washington DC	An affiliate of the World Bank, aims to help under-developed countries raise living standards.
United Nations Development Programme (UNDP)	1965	New York	Helps developing countries increase the wealth producing capabilities of their natural and human resources.
United Nations Environmental Programme (UNEP)	1972	Nairobi (Kenya)	Promotes international cooperation in human environment.
World Trade Organisation (WTO)	1995	Geneva	Setting rules for world trade to reduce tariffs.
United Nations Office on Drugs and Crime (UNODC)	1997	Vienna (Kenya)	To preventillict trafficking and abuse of drug, crime prevention.
UN Women	2010	New York City (USA)	To enable member states to achieve gen den equality and women empowerment.
World Food Programme	1961	Rome	To eradicate hunger and malnutrition.
Organisation for Economic Cooperation and Development (OECD)	1961	Paris (France)	To stimulate economic progress and world trade.

Other International Organisations and Groups

Name	*Estd*	*Headquarter*	*Objective*
The Commonwealth	1926	London	*It was originally known as 'The British Commonwealth of Nations'. It is an association of sovereign and independent states which formally made up the British empire.*
Asia Pacific Economic Cooperation (APEC)	1989	Singapore	*To promote trade and investment in the Pacific basin.*
Asian Development Bank (ADB)	1966	Manila	*To promote regional economic cooperation.*
Association of South-East Asian Nations (ASEAN)	1967	Jakarta	*Regional, economic, social and cultural cooperation among the non-communist countries of South-East Asia.*
Commonwealth of Independent States (CIS)	1991	Minsk (Belarus)	*To coordinate inter-common wealth relations and to provide a mechanism for the orderly dissolution of the USSR.*
Group of 7 (G-7)	1975	—	*To promote cooperation among major non-communist economic powers.*
Group of 15 (G-15)	1989	Geneva (Switzerland)	*To promote economic cooperation among developing nations.*
International Olympic Committee *(IOC)*	1894	Lausanne (Switzerland)	*To promote the olympic ideals and administer olympic games.*
International Organisation for Standardisation *(ISO)*	1947	Geneva (Switzerland)	*To promote the development of international standards.*
Non-Aligned Movement *(NAM)*	1961	—	*Political cooperation and separate itself from both USA and USSR (in the cold-war era).*
European Union	1993	Brussels (Belgium)	*To create a united Europe in which member countries would have such strong economic and political bonds that war would cease to be a recurring fact.*
North Atlantic Treaty Organisation *(NATO)*	1949	Brussels (Belgium)	*Mutual defence and cooperation.*
Organisation of Petroleum Exporting Countries *(OPEC)*	1960	Vienna (Austria)	*Attempts to set world prices by controlling oil production and also pursues member interest in trade and development.*
South Asian Association for Regional Cooperation (SAARC)	1985	Kathmandu (Nepal)	*To promote economic, social and cultural cooperation.*
Amnesty International (AI)	1961	London (UK)	*To keep a watch over human rights violation worldwide. Got Nobel Prize in 1977 for Peace.*
World Wildlife Fund *(WWF)* for Nature	1961	Gland, *(Switzerland)*	*To save the wildlife from extinction.*
Sanghai Cooperation Organisation (Previously Sanghai Five)	1996	Beijing (China)	Strengthen relation and cooperation among members in diverse fields like Security Economic, culture etc.
Gulf Cooperation Council	1981	Riyadh (Saudi Arabia)	Cooperation among states bordering Persian Gulf on located near the Arabian Peninsula.
Bay of Bengal Initiative for Multi-sectoral Technical and Economic Cooperation (BIMSTEC)	1997	Dhaka (Bangladesh)	Multi-sectoral cooperation among members of Bay of Bengal region.

www.ingramcontent.com/pod-product-compliance
Ingram Content Group UK Ltd.
Pitfield, Milton Keynes, MK11 3LW, UK
UKHW021659190726
13853UKWH00001B/353

9 789357 013789